Acclaim for

Penelope Leach's

CHILDREN FIRST

BOOKS BY PENELOPE LEACH

*Children First: What Our Society Must Do—And Is
Not Doing—For Our Children Today*
(1994)

Your Baby & Child: From Birth to Age Five
(1979, 1989)

The First Six Months: Getting Together with Your Baby
(1987)

Your Growing Child: From Babyhood Through Adolescence
(1984)

Babyhood: Infant Development from Birth to Two Years
(1974, 1983)

Penelope Leach

CHILDREN FIRST

Penelope Leach, author of *Your Baby & Child*, *Your Growing Child*, *Babyhood*, and *The First Six Months*, was educated at Cambridge University and the London School of Economics, where she received her Ph.D in psychology and lectured on psychology and child development. A Fellow of the British Psychological Society and Chair of the Child Development Society, she works in various capacities for parents' organizations and sits on the Commission on Social Justice. Her program "Your Baby & Child" is broadcast on Lifetime Television. Penelope Leach is married to an environmental policy analyst, and they have two children.

CHILDREN FIRST

*What society must do — and
is not doing — for children today*

—◆◇◆—

Penelope Leach

VINTAGE BOOKS

A DIVISION OF RANDOM HOUSE, INC.

NEW YORK

This book is dedicated to four women:

My mother, Elisabeth Ayrton, who got me started;
my friend and colleague Anne Hurry, who kept me, and it, going;
my daughter, friend, colleague and creative critic, Melissa Leach;
and Katherine Hourigan, to whom I owe much more than
"friend and editor" suggests.

First Vintage Books Edition, February 1995

Copyright © 1994 by Penelope Leach

All rights reserved under International and Pan-American Copyright
Conventions. Published in the United States by Vintage Books,
a division of Random House, Inc., New York, and simultaneously
in Canada by Random House of Canada Limited, Toronto.
Originally published in hardcover by Alfred A. Knopf, Inc.,
New York, 1994.

Chapter 5, "Growing Up Takes Time," was excerpted in *Child* magazine.

The Library of Congress has cataloged the Knopf edition as follows:
Leach, Penelope.
Children first: what our society must do—and is not
doing—for our children today / Penelope Leach. – 1st ed.
p. cm.
Includes bibliographical references and index.
ISBN 0-679-42133-5
1. Child rearing. 2. Child care. 3. Parenting. I. Title.
HQ769.L3265 1994   93-35476   CIP
Vintage ISBN: 0-679-75466-0

Manufactured in the United States of America
10 9 8 7

CONTENTS

ACKNOWLEDGMENTS

During the five years I have spent amassing material for this book, hundreds of people whose names do not appear in the notes have helped me with their experiences and their ideas. I would like to take this opportunity to thank them all.

A book of this kind relies on so many sources of research and opinion that the notes can only refer readers to a small selection. I gratefully acknowledge my debt to all the rest.

Friends and colleagues have given most generously of their time in discussion and in reading and commenting on drafts of the manuscript. In particular I should like to thank James Fairhead, Judy Gardner, Rachel Hodgkin, Anne Hurry, Melissa Leach and Peter Newell; each had expert input, all were endlessly patient.

Finally, I am immeasurably grateful to Katherine Hourigan and Gerald Leach for their unfailing enthusiasm for what I was trying to do. She has edited everything I have ever written, and nursed and steered this project in particular from the moment I thought of it; he has put up with months of abstraction and hours of talk as well as keeping my software sorted out and my statistics untangled.

Despite all this help, responsibility for the facts selected and the opinions expressed throughout the book is mine alone.

Penelope Leach
1993

INTRODUCTION

Are today's kids spoiled rotten or are selfish parents giving them a rotten time? Choose your answer with your newspaper or talk show, your politician or your cab driver. On my last transatlantic trip I rode to Heathrow with a driver who told me: "Today's parents aren't fit to have kids. They think about nothing but their pockets and pleasures—out to work, off to the bar; poor kids aren't brought up: they have to drag themselves up . . .". But it was the other story on the ride in from Kennedy: "Kids today don't know when they're well off. When I was a boy I worked for what I got and then it wasn't much, I'm telling you. Now kids from decent homes where parents work to buy them everything just think they're entitled to do as they like . . . beating up teachers, raping, robbing."

Today's parents . . . Kids today . . . When I was a boy . . . Social debate always relies on statements about past times and distant places to throw the present into high relief, but most such statements should start with "Once upon a time," as in "Once upon a time there was a golden age of the family . . . a proper balance between rights and responsibilities . . . majority agreement on decent social values." Many people certainly believe that things are worse than they have ever been, but many people in each successive generation always do, and our generation is rendered especially susceptible by mass communications.

A torrent of media messages reflects, and may also create, societies that are fascinated by their boundless potential for horror and horrified by themselves. Fiction and faction, commentary and news seem to compete to make us think about the unthinkable, and to find new limits to challenge us as our tolerance rises. Rape has become a subject everyone can discuss, so now we must face male rape, mass rape and the rape of children. Everybody has been forced to accept that many children are abused in "ordinary families," but there is still shock value in child abuse by bishops and priests, by satanists and porno rings and in the institutions we set up to care for children who are "at risk." And if we are near to having faced the limits of horror with children as victims, there is still mileage in children as aggressors and more still if *their* victims are children, too. Rape by a twelve-year-old is certain of headlines, while the recent death of a British two-year-old allegedly at the hands of two ten-year-olds received more coverage than all the 100-odd murders of toddlers at the hands of adults in the same year put together. We are being shown children and young people from every kind of background—yours and mine as well as his and hers—not just failing in schools but terrorizing them; not just flouting teachers but injuring them; not just getting into mischief but joyriding, burglarizing, destroying, out of control.

These are real pictures of real happenings but they may nevertheless distort reality as a zoom lens distorts a landscape—highlighting selected detail and contrast and distracting us from a context that is less dramatic but at least as deserving of our concern. It is that context of ordinary, everyday lives and experiences that this book explores, through the widest possible lens.

My lens has not always had such a wide angle. I spent most of ten years in child development research and most of another ten passing on the findings to parents and using them myself in bringing up our own two children. I believed that "good parenting"—the kind that meets the needs of both children and parents—was not something that could be authoritatively generalized, but something that had to keep evolving out of the constantly changing interaction between growing children and adults who felt sufficiently supported and self-confident to respond to them. I believed that the more people knew about children in general, the more fascinating they would find their own child in particular—and I believed that while finding a child fascinating is no substitute for loving her, it could be a most useful support at 4 a.m. when there was not much love around.

I still believe all that, but the last ten years have forced me to widen my focus. I know that most individual parents do everything they can to facilitate the health and happiness, growth and development of their babies; to deliver socialized and sociable children into society's formal education system and to support them through it and out into adult life. But everything parents can do is clearly not enough. Whatever the real scale and scope of horrors perpetrated on or by children, there are not hundreds, not thousands, but millions more who are being failed by Western society, and are failing it. We leave parents the responsibility for children's well-being and happiness, but do we also empower them to ensure it?

This book argues that our society is inimical to children and has therefore devalued parents to such an extent that individual good parenting is not only exceedingly difficult but, ultimately, insufficient. Dissemination of information concerning child development remains valuable to individuals, but parent education alone cannot create a better future for children, nor parent bashing explain their grim present. When a company is ailing, the board often tries to blame the training, performance and wage demands of its work force, but shareholders know that its success or failure depends on adequate capital investment and good management. All of us are shareholders in society's children and it is time we widened the focus of our attention from what is happening at the bottom, in individual families, to what is happening at the top in society as a whole.

Looking to the top means looking to policy-makers and opinion-makers in government, civil service and social institutions, in the media and the professions, in financial markets and in industry. That does not mean looking to people *other* than parents and children, though. Top people were all children first and most of them became parents later, but to meet the demands of the job they were encouraged to leave all that at home with their jeans and sneakers, and put on indifference with their business suits. The charge of indifference to children will offend many of them, as will the suggestion that Western children are having a lousy time. I regret that offense because I am sure that on a personal level most people *are* concerned for children, and that almost all those who are actively parenting are doing their utmost to give their own children a good life. But the offense has to be given and gotten through, because it is only when we get to the far side of the personal that we can start to see what may have gone wrong and rethink what might be right.

On a personal level, the birth of a healthy child is as much cause for celebration in Western societies as it is all over the world, and for the same reasons. Children's survival depends on adults, so the survival of the human race depends, as it always has depended, on women and men wanting and caring about them. We do not have children for their own sakes but for ourselves. Parents of both sexes from many cultures sum up their reasons for wanting them in words that best translate as "for pleasure and for fun." Childbirth and health are not solely individual concerns, though. The newborn baby, focusing the universal blue gaze that spans time and place, culture and race, and is simply human, sees nothing of substance beyond her mother's face. But her parents or parent figures will only be the foreground of her life-style and chances. What parents do—and what they can do—depends on what their society allows, approves or arranges.

Compared with other times and places, newborns and their parents in post-industrial Western societies are fortunate. They are heirs to a legacy of scientific attention to childbirth and related "women's matters" that goes back to the nineteenth century and has given us an awesome and increasing control over the production of babies. Parents can opt for quality rather than quantity. We can prevent conception without limiting sexual activity and assist it with a range of techniques from simple artificial insemination to sophisticated in vitro fertilization. We can practice quality control on the conceptus, using diagnostic techniques *in utero* and abortion—or even corrective surgery—when fetal development does not meet our norms. We can intervene to ensure women's survival through perilous labors and employ intensive care and pediatric surgical techniques to save babies who would not be viable in any other place or time. Safely born to women whose physical and mental health has not been debilitated by early and repeated childbearing or the fear of it, and to men who are not overburdened with mouths to feed and bury, or the dread of being so, Western babies get the world's best start.

A good start is only a start, though. Focused on the beginning of life, Western societies see later needs far less clearly. The frontiers of medical science and associated technology have been pushed forward without a matching commitment to social science and human relations. We know much more about the reproductive biology and genetics of parenthood than we know about the social, emotional and psychological impacts of parenting and we devote far greater research resources to producing physically healthy babies than to rearing emotionally stable children. Indeed, while family planning, artificial baby foods and a host of childcare aids have dramatically reduced the burdens of traditional mothering roles, those roles themselves have been invalidated and have not been replaced with a workable restructuring of gender roles and relationships. What is needed now is something that cannot be produced by further scientific advance or a new technical fix: a reappraisal of the importance of parenting and fresh approaches to the continuing care and education of children in, and for, changing societies.

We need to remind ourselves that human children require intensive, personalized and long-lasting care. Babies have to be fed, warmed and protected, and we are good at that, but if physical care is all they are given, many fail to thrive and some die. Affectionate interaction with a few familiar people is not merely enjoyable; it is a necessity for good health and development. Yet we ration it. The ending of infancy alters the necessary commitment of parents or their surrogates but does not end it. Children under seven still need constant adult protection. In middle childhood, survival and life skills, along with morals and manners, go on being learned over at least five more years of close apprenticeship to adults. Even then, on the edge of puberty, it takes people at least five further years of physical growth and intellectual and social maturation to refine those skills so that adolescents can begin to function as adults within the value system of their particular culture. However much they may delegate to other caregivers and to educational institutions, parents and parent figures are crucial to every phase of this long human childhood, not least because it is individual parents who most passionately want to meet the needs of their own children, and passion is part of what is needed.

In these final years of the twentieth century, Western states are well placed to help and facilitate parents through their governments and institutions and through their opinion-makers and media, but they do so far less than they could. We enjoy the greatest wealth and productivity and the most advanced health care, broadly based education and widespread communications the world has ever known. That means that we have room for choice and maneuver, and it means we have information to guide us in using it, too. Accumulated research evidence suggests that child-friendly choices would not only make things better for today's children and their parents, but also for yesterday's and to-morrow's, improving the least desirable aspects of modern Western life for everybody. How long are we going to go on ignoring all that evidence while moaning about "today's parents" and "kids today," yearning nostalgically for an undefined past time when every rainbow had "family values" in its pot of gold?

If the powers-that-be are ever to recognize the need to make choices for children, and face the results of their own failure to make those choices to date, they will first have to relinquish the moral high ground of their assumption that today's children "have never had it so good." Of course children in post-industrial Western societies are better off, in our terms, than the children who worked with their parents on the cotton plantations and in the mills of nineteenth-century America and Britain, or those who work in the sweatshops of contemporary cities in countries that are industrializing now. Of course our children's world is privileged beyond the dreams of millions in the villages of developing nations. And of course we can see our treatment of children as humane and respectful if we compare it with the treatment of children swept around Eastern Europe in an orgy of "ethnic cleansing" or shot as vermin in the streets of Brazil. But hindsight, and value judgments that tell us life is better for most children here and now than somewhere else or at another time, are cop-outs. The moral imperative for any society, surely, is to do the best it can in response to its own unique conditions; doing better than other societies that are less well-placed is no good cause for complacency. The comparisons that matter, and the ones that anger me, are between how things are for our children and how they could be. When we make those comparisons the moral high ground crumbles beneath us, because our society could do so much better for children than it does.

Which modern Western trends are inimical to children?
How do they distort policy and practice in areas of known parental and child need?
How, practically, could we do better?

Those are the three broad questions addressed in turn by the three parts of this book.

PART ONE

Parents and Society

— 1 —

People, Profits and Parenting

Whether they live in Manchester, Milwaukee or Milan, most people want to be self-respecting, solvent citizens and good parents and find it exceedingly difficult to be both at the same time. There is conflict between these two parts of most adult aspiration at every level: from the particular everyday experience of individuals striving for a balance between working and caring, through the social institutions that isolate rather than integrate the public and personal aspects of life, to an overall "social ethos" of individualism and competition. That ethos is inhospitable to all personal caring roles because caring always demands a sharing, even a subsuming, of self. It is especially inhospitable to parenting because children's minute-by-minute physical and emotional dependency may be as great as that of even the most dependent adults—the acutely sick, the frail aged—and lasts much longer.

Social attitudes and institutions reflect that individualism and reinforce the conflict. Individual endeavor and achievement, personal fulfillment and self-esteem, social recognition and rewards are all focused on work that is both conceptually and actually separated from interpersonal aspects of living and sometimes so salient to individuals that it serves as a replacement for those aspects. Work is paid for with money, of course, but money that is valued for itself as well as for what it buys. Nobody can ever have enough money—more would always be preferable—so working for a living, in the sense of choosing or aspiring to a life-style and then working to support it, turns into working for money—and more money. Once social status and self-image are not merely associated with but built through the accumulation of wealth itself, personal and pecuniary motives for work become inextricably entangled, unpaid activities degraded, and satisfaction in the actual processes of daily work, or in anything it produces other than money, a rare privilege. Rarest privilege of all—as parents particularly know— is the time and energy to enjoy what work and money buy: to have fun with the children, use the longed-for products, visit the saved-for vacation home. It is difficult to take time when more work would make more money. Time is money. Most employed people must seek extra hours, and negotiations for shorter working weeks are often intended to ensure increases in overtime rather than leisure time. Even the seriously wealthy are usually as rushed as they are rich.

For our societies, money is a god, the marketplace is its temple and mass communications—from TV advertising to motivational speakers—ensure that its creed is an inescapable driving force not just in corporate lives but in the lives of every one of us.

With societies' attention, energy and excitement focused on the marketplace, areas of human endeavor that cannot be directly bought with money and sold for profit tend to be regarded as peripheral. It may be thought worthy to work at personal relationships (as parents work to relate to their children and each other), but it will usually be considered more interesting to work at professional ones (as daycare workers or marriage counselors)—and get paid for doing so.

We still pay lip service to the pursuit of knowledge and excellence for their own sake but they earn little credit unless they are marketable. Forty years ago C. P. Snow castigated Britain for allowing arts and sciences to diverge into what he called "two cultures." Now the conflict is not only between arts and sciences but also between the pure and applied forms of each. Funding for pure science is rare unless an eventual application is expected; the accepted tonic for an ailing engineering institute is an industrial sandwich for its students; fine art and literature departments shrink while commercial art and media studies flourish. It works the other way around, too: if somebody recognizes or creates commercial possibilities, the most improbable areas may suddenly become intensely exciting. Religion, for example, became big business in the United States because somebody saw the commercial possibilities of televising it. The spread of Fundamentalism we live with today was almost incidental. Even public concern for anticommercial issues, such as protection of the environment or the sexual abuse of children, can be exploited to produce handsome profits from "environment-friendly" toilet paper or "anatomically correct" dolls.

It sometimes seems that nothing is generally interesting that cannot be bought and sold; that "anything goes" (and must be allowed to go) if it sells; that almost anything—object, fact, idea or ideology—will sell if enough capital and associated power and influence are put behind the effort, and that if the prospective profit is large enough, they will be.

Just as activities that cannot be bought and sold are peripheral to post-industrial societies, so the people who do the least buying and selling are marginalized. Whole segments of populations are sidelined, including all those whom industry classifies as elderly when they cross an arbitrary age line. As soon as people retire (or are retired) from the marketplace, Western societies become unable to use the skills for which they paid last year, the leisure they have imposed this year, or the likely concomitants of age itself, such as experience, which increase year by year. Almost overnight the elderly become social appellants rather than participants, and generally rather unsuccessful ones. Only in trader terms can it be seen as "necessary" to expend substantial parts of health budgets on hi-tech heart and transplant surgery to keep a few workers (and many highly paid surgeons and medical technicians) in business and "impossibly expensive" to provide the simple podiatry that would keep millions of chair-bound elderly people comfortably mobile. Again, though, it works both ways: if "social service" can be made profitable, it will be provided. The United States has a long tradition of private health insurance as well as an aging population. Adjustment of the social security contributions paid throughout their working lives has given senior citizens commercial potential, and the American market in retirement homes and golf courses, elder care, and out-of-season cruises is booming. Perhaps that unglamorous podiatry will also be forthcoming when it dawns on somebody that the old spend better when they can walk.

Children are a special case. Like the very old, the very young do not earn and therefore play little direct part in the marketplace. Indeed children are doubly unproductive because their maintenance and education cost money they cannot earn for themselves, and their care absorbs adult time that could otherwise be spent producing it. But because children are the producer-consumer units of tomorrow rather than yesterday, no economy can disregard them. The prospect of a shortage of children, or of adequately qualified young people, within aging populations is a nightmare for economists. Although the return on any investment in children is very slow, all Western societies do invest heavily in quantity and quality control over the production of babies—thus freeing women to work—and in the education that prepares children and young people for work. The net cost is not as high as it seems because an enormous seller's market in children's goods—nursery equipment, baby clothing and diapers, toys, CDs, designer clothing, sports equipment—has been created as a powerful incentive to *parents* to earn and spend. Investment on children themselves goes little further though. During the eighties the United States spent less than 5 percent of the federal budget on programs supporting families with children, compared with 24 percent spent on people over sixty-five years old. In Canada, by 1990, government per capita expenditure on the elderly was 2.7 times as great as its expenditure on the young. Outside the Nordic nations, where children's care is regarded as a joint responsibility of parents and the state, Western governments leave responsibility for children to their natural families as a matter of individualist, laissez-faire principle—and economics.

Responsibility for children brings parents considerable rights over them; indeed many social institutions reflect a view of children as parents' personal possessions rather than as members of society in their own right. But that does not mean that parents have the right to rear their children entirely as they please or the right to help and facilitation in rearing them in socially approved ways. Parenting is set about with prescriptive and proscriptive laws and regulations concerning children's safety and well-being, but it is not cushioned by an equivalent set of privileges. Doing it well brings people no special personal or institutional recognition but doing it badly brings personal criticism, institutional intervention and the final legal sanction of losing their parental rights—losing their children.

Society insists that parents must care for their own while competing in the marketplace with individuals who are currently childless, but it does not even try to ensure that they compete on a level playing field.

Western Families

There is nothing unusual in children being seen as primarily family business—they have been and are so in most times and places—but there is much that is unusual about our families and children's position in them. Children have always been an integral part of marriage and family, but it is only in the recent West that family has come to be seen as an institution that is *created* by marriage or by any first birth, and is primarily for and about children.

No concept of family is acceptable worldwide, but a more widely accepted concept than our own is a top-down model in which "family" radiates from the most senior, grandparent generation (or from dead ancestors) and is not primarily concerned with children and childish matters but with adults and adult needs. Marriages often enlarge and enrich family networks, of course, and may be contracted to do so, but in most of the world current marriages do not *create* families and the children born to them come in at the very bottom of an existing family hierarchy.

Being born into the bottom of top-down family hierarchies does not make children less important to their parents than the Western children who make parents into families, but they do tend to be important in importantly different ways. The chances are that they will be not only wanted but also *needed:* needed to validate marriage settlements and inheritance arrangements; needed to work and to help adults work; needed within the complex exchanges of favors and patronage that extend families' political influence and economic scope; needed to broaden kinship ties through their own betrothals and marriages, and needed, perhaps above all, to support parents and other relatives in old age. Being needed may not be an unmixed blessing, of course: socioeconomic usefulness can mean child labor, even wage slavery; lack of education; arranged and personally unwanted marriage. But being a necessary part of the adult world, and knowing that they are, may also give children a kind of respect and self-respect that few Western children enjoy: respect as present participants in, and future heirs to, adult affairs, in families that are not primarily concerned with the children *as* children but as apprentice people—families that do not exist *for* them but that will continue to exist because of them.

However much individuals in modern Western societies may want a child—and most men as well as women want at least one very much indeed—they certainly do'not *need* children for any practical purpose and, practically speaking, would almost always be better off without any. Furthermore, although children are usually their parents' heirs, only the few destined for "family businesses" are brought up with a sense of apprenticeship to an adult world they will grow into and then take over. Most Western children are encouraged to grow out of, rather than into, their families of origin—to see themselves as separate and autonomous individuals rather than as links in a continuing family chain. As soon as they reach some marker of maturity—such as the end of compulsory schooling or higher education—they are expected to leave home and prove themselves in the workplace, divorced from roots and older generations. Family does not become central again to most young adults' lives unless or until they "start a family" of their own.

The accepted definition of "starting a family" is having a first baby. The intention to start a family still involves marriage much more often than not and few couples who marry for the first time intend to remain childless. The oft-quoted figure of more than a third of Western births to people who are not currently married includes many second or later-born babies and therefore tells us more about families in flux than families in the making. Irrespective of marriage or intention, though, the peculiarly Western concept of a "nuclear family" is so closely tied to children that a woman and her baby are referred to by that term even if the father is not around, acknowledged or known, and even if there is nothing for the two of them to be the nucleus *of*.

Nuclear families are still idealized as children and their mothers and fathers at the center of "extended family" networks of grandparents, aunts, uncles and cousins. In reality, though, few of today's families match that image. Although longer lives mean more living grandparents, smaller families mean more limited networks, and changing patterns of marriage, divorce and remarriage mean different kinds. The numbers of children per couple have been shrinking in most countries over several generations, so that today's one- or two-child nuclear family may have few relations by blood or marriage. Additionally, children who do start life as part of a neat nucleus and network may not remain so. In 1990, the number of divorces granted for every 1,000 people was 5.1 in the United States, 3.2 in the United Kingdom, 2.6 in Canada, 2.4 in Sweden, 1.6 in France and 0.2 in Italy. Over the whole post-industrial West fewer than two thirds of parents who are legally married when their first child is born remain together until their youngest child leaves school. Once-nuclear families may re-form, once or several times, involving and excluding not only various parent figures and perhaps half- or step-siblings, but also their relations. If a man comes to live with a divorced woman who has two children, does his mother become their grandmother? Can he, himself, be their stepfather if there is no marriage? If so, how long must he be in residence before he graduates into that role from being the mother's lover? And if there is a marriage, does he, the stepfather, remain part of the children's family if their mother divorces him?

Modern Western families no longer fit the conventional nuclear family mold but nostalgic attempts are still being made to confine or interpret them within it. Nostalgia seems misplaced since it is only the mold that is being abandoned, not families themselves. Nostalgia can even be destructive because it distracts us from objective consideration of the range of relationships that may constitute families and meet people's needs. Rising divorce rates are discussed in terms of "broken homes" and "single parents"; the role of soaring remarriage rates and informal partnerships in mending some of those homes and hearts is scarcely considered.

Kinship alone clearly cannot define modern Western families. The concept of household adds a useful dimension (and facilitates the collection of census data and taxes) but it still does not accurately reflect complex reality because people can feel part of a family without living together—and vice versa. Where children—or other individuals requiring hour-by-hour hands-on care—are concerned, though, the shared household concept is particularly important because people who are available to give that care have special salience irrespective of other aspects of the relationship between them. A father who lives in Australia remains precious to his toddler in Vancouver, but mother's new partner who holds the household steady and plays ball may be even more precious in a different way. Grandparents may hold a special position in relation to children by virtue of their blood and irrespective of their role, but the role played by some unrelated caregivers makes them "part of the family" in every other meaningful sense.

Childcare in Nuclear Families

The needs of children and other dependent individuals for personal care used to be (and in many parts of the world still are) met within diverse, extended family groups, clans and communities and shared, in diverse degrees and ways, among various individuals, as best suited to their resources, wishes and other commitments. Each time and place, culture and subculture is different, but most have more in common with each other than the post-industrial West has with any of them in this respect. Only here and now is responsibility for the daily care and long-term upbringing of children left entirely to parents—often lone parents—without any viable support system.

The lack of support networks for parents is not entirely due to the small size and fragmentation of families, to which it is commonly ascribed. Geographical mobility is an important factor. Even where exceptionally large families exist and have extensive kin networks intact, they are often too geographically dispersed to be useful to each other on a day-to-day basis. According to the Census Bureau, over 90 percent of American households relocated between 1960 and 1989, and almost half of all American individuals moved from one home to another between 1986 and 1990. A recent British survey showed that most children had moved at least four times before they reached their sixteenth birthday. As political and economic barriers between Western European countries come down, mobility is increasing. Most important of all, though, is the pull of paid employment and the push of poverty. Every nation still has rural areas, or urban concentrations of ethnic minorities or recent immigrants, in which related groups of people do still live closely together, but even in those, the adults of both generations tend to be similarly committed, or aspiring, to the marketplace, so that the presence of a grandmother, aunt or sister just down the street offers parents no guarantee of sharing in their caring. Whatever their individual circumstances, Western parents can seldom take support networks for granted, nor are we searching for new ways to ensure them, because it suits the individualistic ethos of post-industrial societies to regard the whole business of "starting a family" as parents' alone.

Meeting children's dependency needs without the support of a wider circle limits parents' freedom of individual action and therefore their ability to live by that ethos. The very process of having a child therefore conflicts with some social values even while it confirms others. According to those values, for example, sexual partnerships are the central relationships of adult life and children extend and cement them. Very often, though, the advent of a child blows sexual partnerships apart like a social bomb. Illusions of ungendered equality are shattered by the different feelings parenthood arouses in each partner. Sex—so heavily relied upon to keep partnerships glued together—may lose some of its power and mutuality. Careers—especially women's careers—falter and may fail, and finances and life-styles fall out of equilibrium.

The material standards of living many of us enjoy and most of us aspire to are higher than they have ever been, but so is their cost. People who can earn enough can achieve a good life but only those who can keep earning more and more can hold on to it, because however fast money or credit accumulates, luxuries are transformed into necessities even faster. Both getting there and keeping up are far more difficult for parents than for others. In many Western countries having even one child cuts by two thirds the lifetime income a woman can expect to earn, whether she takes time out of work to care for that child herself or money out of her wage or salary to pay someone else to do so. And childcare is not the whole story. Whether they are partnered or lone, parents also have to meet both the direct costs of feeding, clothing and maintaining a child and the indirect costs—such as different housing— that a parenting life-style demands. And to all that must be added the accumulated costs of missed earning opportunities caused by competing demands for their attention and their time. The composite costs of raising a child have been estimated at between $200,000 and $265,000 in the United States and between £50,000 and £80,000 in the United Kingdom. Detailed budgets, published in 1993, show that it cost an average of around £3000 per year to keep a child in Britain at just above poverty level. The cost of a child—even a wanted child—is often so high that parenthood is as much a sacrifice as a pleasure and children more speculation than investment.

Home and Work

Direct competition between time for economically productive work and time for personal caring is a notable aspect of post-industrial Western societies. Women as well as men work everywhere, of course, and always have done—indeed it is only in the modern West that questions about their right and duty to do so have even been asked. In pre-industrial times and places, however, women combine work with the care of children—and other dependent individuals—conducting both from a home base and within a female network. Industrialization always creates jobs for women (and children) that are separated from home, but it does not initially lessen the economic importance of home production or reduce the numbers of people who contribute to and rely upon it. In much of modern urban Africa, for example, women's gardens remain a vital source of food, and three-generation families, extended by obligations more complex than direct blood relationships, remain common.

The organization of post-industrial Western families and livelihoods is very different because virtually *all* productive work has moved out to the marketplace, causing almost all adults to follow it there. People do still produce things at home—jam or bread, vegetables or clothes, watercolors or photographs—but they do so more for the creative satisfaction of the process than because the products are wealth or needed artifacts. Jam, sweaters and celluloid sunsets are all available more cheaply from the specialization and mass production of the marketplace, so many traditional women's skills have become hobbies rather than "real work" and for most people there is nothing economically productive to do at home.

Homes are still important, of course; people make them as best they can wherever they find themselves. The decorated shacks in shantytowns in the developing world and the careful arrangements of cardboard boxes under London bridges and in New York doorways are poignant reminders of the human need to nest. More privileged homes even *create* a kind of "work." Elaborated as wealth rises, they reflect material success in increasingly sophisticated gadgetry and creative decoration, and require maintenance rituals of weekend lawn mowing and car washing. But although these kinds of elaboration and maintenance, and a wide range of home-based hobbies, may bring important personal satisfaction, they take money rather than making it, and since society's value system is based on the creation of wealth, such activities are peripheral to it.

For most people it is workplaces rather than homes that are the nerve centers of personally fulfilling and socially recognized activity and the site of salient relationships beyond their nuclear families. Even where homes are packed together in a horizontal sprawl of suburban streets or a vertical slab of apartments, community structure and a sense of communal purpose are rare. Homes are essentially private, individual spaces, sealed from neighborly intrusion by closed doors, fortified against criminal invasion by locks and bars and functioning as little more than a place for rest and relaxation after work, and a meal and clean clothes before it—unless, of course, they contain children. If there are young children at home somebody has to be there with them all the time. Failing any other reason for being at home, she or he is likely to be there because of and *for* those children and isolated from other adults.

Bringing up a child is a uniquely creative activity with satisfaction to be derived from both the process and the product, but that does not mean that many people can build a satisfactory life-style entirely around a baby. Some women do make a personally satisfying way of life out of mothering in an unusually rich home environment, perhaps in neighborhoods and villages that do still function as communities and stay alive on weekdays. There are some women for whom the good life of the moment is filled with the minutiae of childish lives, whose hackles do not rise at the thought of being financially supported by a partner in parenthood and who can do the chores and get the evening meal because they are at home, without feeling typecast in a retrograde role. There are some men who seek a mutual balance between working and caring and like to cook anyway. But those women, and especially those men, are a minority. Varying combinations of financial and other needs make most mothers feel that unbroken childcare would drive them stir-crazy, and ensure that most fathers do not consider it for themselves or even share it with their partners in any way that interferes with their work. Most Western children get equal parenting the way Alice got jam in Wonderland: yesterday and tomorrow, but never today.

We should not be surprised. One adult can fulfill all of a baby's needs for companionship and stimulation, but one baby cannot fulfill the far more complex needs of an adult—nor is it her role to do so. Caring for one or two children in a modern home is certainly not easy or stress-free, but without other productive work that can be done at the same time, and other adults around with whom to do it, neither is it often sufficiently satisfying or stimulating for long.

There are still many people who feel that it should be sufficient. Dad going out to earn money while mom stays home with the kids and bakes apple pie is still widely regarded as basic to "family values," and "full-time, exclusive motherhood" is often assumed to be an integral part of women's traditional role. That assumption is as careless as it is unfortunate. While it is certainly true that in the West—as elsewhere— there are long traditions of division of labor between the genders, and that "women's work" has been structured and rewarded differently from men's in almost every time and place, the idea that women should do *no* work other than care for children (and that the most privileged, who did not even do their own caring, should do no work at all) is not part of anybody's tradition, having a short history and a political provenance. Industrialization took millions of women into the paid labor market and although pregnancy took many of them out again, it seldom ended their economic contribution. Even in the early years of the twentieth century many mothers in most countries undertook a wide range of (ill)-paid outwork and all fulfilled with their unpaid labor the vast range of functions that make up modern service sectors.

The first proponents of motherhood as something akin to a paid profession were Nazi leaders, intent on breeding babies for the German Fatherland. After the Second World War full-time motherhood was idealized by politicians in most countries of the Western Alliance. The vital jobs women had filled throughout the war years were needed for returning soldiers, and there was money to be saved by closing down the nurseries and after-school clubs that had cared for their children while they did them. All involved nations, even those that had escaped the horrors of bombing or invasion, were war-traumatized. The United States, for example, was disrupted by fifteen million civilians moving around in search of work, as well as by having five million "war widows." Propaganda for stay-at-home mothering had wide appeal. Soldiers supported it, of course, and so did many humanitarian professionals who, appalled by the tragedies of bereaved and evacuated children and refugees, saw mother care as a cure-all. And although many women resented their summary ejection from the labor force, the politicians did have some female support, because after the long separation from husbands and sons suffered by one sixth of North American families and almost every family in the European theater of war, many mothers were desperate to re-establish and expand their families. None of these people knew, or could have known, what shape life in the new West would take, but by the end of the fifties it was already becoming clear that the cookies-and-milk image of motherhood was a maladaptation to a post-war world run by men. Two generations of the women's movement have still not expunged that image altogether but they have changed the world. Today, despite some signs of a return to stay-at-home mothering—dubbed "the new familism" in the United States—the woman who sees herself as "only a mother," even if she lives at a high material standard and mothers with excitement and devotion, is likely to feel herself stranded in a backwater, missing the mainstream current that is rushing everybody else to the real focus of aspiration and achievement and social acknowledgment of both: the workplace. She needs to stay but she also needs to go; she needs to be not "only" but also a mother. . . .

Working and Caring

The geographical location of work relative to home is crucial to lifestyle. Industrialization concentrates employment, bringing people off the land, thronging to cities faster than services and infrastructures can expand to accommodate them. Post-industrial societies usually reverse that trend, leaving work in the cities and moving homes to the suburbs, and then leapfrogging work over both city and suburbs to relocate in outer-suburban or previously rural areas. Different planning policies interact with geographical features to produce different results—London, for example, is affected by the United Kingdom's long-established green-belt policy; New York, by the fact that Manhattan is an island—but whatever the specific differences between places, the physical separation of home from workplace is one important generality. Traveling to work, commuting, is everywhere taken for granted, its basic wastefulness and inhumanity accepted without question and only its local conditions and costs much discussed. Millions of Western commuters make longer journeys every working day than anyone would make occasionally to have a meal with friends, and many do it daily in conditions of crowding and claustrophobia, dirt and dismay that they would not tolerate or be expected to tolerate once a year to reach a vacation destination. They pay dearly to do it, in time and in money, and the world's environment pays dearly for it too. That hour, or two or even three, of acute discomfort that separates the worlds of home and work is useful to neither. It is limbo time. Those wasted hours make it impossible for individuals to move quickly and flexibly between home and work even if a fax machine at one end spews out a vital contract or a child at the other end is throwing up. And they add time away from home to working days that, despite official statistics, are often longer now than twenty years ago.

It is not only commuting that makes official statistics concerning working hours questionable; their interpretation also needs to take account of the nature of most employment and the behavior of many employed people. Calculations suggest that average weekly working hours are falling in most Western countries. Even in Britain, where much longer hours are worked than in the rest of the EEC, they are said to have fallen from 42 to 40 during the last decade. But those figures are based on manufacturing, which is in decline. In the growing service sector, the average "full week" is estimated at 48 hours, and is growing. Men in the United Kingdom spend about 4 more hours each week in offices than men in other EEC countries such as Germany, but not more than men in the United States. There, a recent survey suggests that the average working week for everybody jumped from 41 hours in 1973 to 47 hours in 1989; that entrepreneurs in small businesses average 57 hours, professionals 52.2 hours, and those with incomes over $50,000 per year 52.4 hours. On both sides of the Atlantic the recession has increased what London's city bankers call "American masochism—putting yourself through a pointless and unproductive period of work at the end of the day to prove to your superiors that you are prepared to undertake tasks which you do not want or have to do."

Even when leisure time is offered, many British and American workers dare not take it. Normal paid vacation periods are far longer in the EEC than in the United States, and in countries such as France and Germany, with an entitlement of five to six weeks, there is a strong tradition of family summer vacations away from home. In the United Kingdom, though, the entitlement is seldom more than three weeks, and about 30 percent of people fail to use it all. In the United States the average entitlement is only sixteen days, and some American firms frown effectively on anyone taking more than a single week's vacation at a time. As Zelda West-Meade of the marriage guidance organization Relate put it: "Leisure time is what people crave but they are too worried to take it. I have been speaking to people recently whose companies issue lay-off notices on days off or vacations. . . ."

Not all paid work is physically separated from personhood, of course. There are people who do combine productive activities with personal caring, free-lancing from home or living on the job. Those who do it often prefer it, but those who have never tried it seldom want to. Perhaps working at home is still redolent of cottage industry and outwork in the Great Depression, when women and children labored for a pittance to turn entrepreneurs' raw materials into artifacts and fortunes. Or perhaps mixing work into home spoils the professionalism of the one and the personal haven of the other. Certainly many people currently feel that the social desirability of going to work is matched by the desirability of being able to get away from it. Attitudes towards working at home may soon be changed by market forces. The capital and travel costs of office space and commuting are soaring, while the costs of communications technology—computer terminals, fax machines and so forth—are coming down and more and more business is conducted over the telephone and paid for by credit card. These trends are making it increasingly feasible and economical for large businesses to equip employees to work from home. Many mail-order operatives already function in this way and people in less casual occupations are beginning to do so. British Telecommunications' information inquiries, for example, are answered almost entirely by women in their own homes, and there are more than five million American white-collar workers who "telecommute," with plans for many more from companies such as Bankers Trust and American Express. It may be that the bridges individuals need between home and work will eventually be built by industry, not for their benefit but for its own. In the meantime, though, the work that adults take into their homes is mostly *extra* to their working day outside it.

New bridges that cross the gulf the other way so as to take children into the workplace seem less likely. Workplace nurseries sound promising but seldom prove to be so. High capital costs usually mean that daycare facilities are housed in less expensive nearby premises rather than in workplaces themselves, so parents must subject their children to commuter travel but still be apart from them all day. Even if children are tolerated or welcomed in them, most work environments are too dangerous or too boring for children to be safe, happy or participant for long. So most parents who are at work are not just physically away from home, but in a world that is quite separate from their children's, being people those children do not know and leading lives they can neither understand nor share.

Not every parent is in paid work at all, of course. With national unemployment rates between 5 and 10 percent in most countries, and areas and groups for which that figure is far higher, little more than half the women with children under school age in many of these countries—America and Canada, Britain and Belgium, for example—are employed in a way that gets them into national statistics. Some of those women (and a handful of men) choose to stay out of the marketplace because they believe that their children need more of their time than they could otherwise give, but most are kept out by lack of available work and above all by lack of work that can be combined with parenting. "Full employment," meaning the established male model of forty-odd hours in each of forty-nine weeks of every year between the end of full-time education and the beginning of retirement, remains part of the ethos of Western countries even while they struggle for economic recovery and hope for a consequent expansion of their labor markets. Some respected economic commentators are beginning to suggest that full employment of that kind may be a permanently unrealistic aspiration— that more various and variable working patterns, incorporating personal and parenting responsibilities for both sexes, and voluntary options as well as recurrent retraining, may be the models of the future. Right now, though, such arguments are seldom reflected in policy or personal experience. Everyone is expected to work full-time hours throughout their "working lives" and almost everyone wants to do so. Despite the fears and suspicions of those who must balance welfare budgets, freeloading on welfare payments is generally rare and unemployment abhorred. Voluntary work, although often respected in itself, is not regarded as a valid alternative. As for parenthood, mothers, and fathers, who are employed often worry about the limited time they can spend with their children but seldom get social support in acting to increase it. Indeed, the individual who contemplates refusing the only available job because of its long commute or turning down the promotion that will mean less time at home will usually be assured that life without that raise or prospect, or on one salary, one wage or one parent's social security payments, "would not be fair to the children." Poverty and deprivation are always relative to expectations so those arguments are as powerful when Nintendos or Nikes are in question as school trips or jeans. In societies where money measures all that is desirable, nobody can afford not to earn. Not many of the women who are at home full-time with children are there because they reject the separation of caring and working; they are there because they cannot arrange it. They are trapped.

Like most effective traps this one is deceptively simple. Babies and young children have to be cared for by committed adults in suitable environments for twenty-four hours of every day. Society expects all able-bodied citizens of working age to earn the money they need and the satisfaction they crave at specialized all-day jobs in special, distant and unsuitable places. People cannot be in two places at once; ergo one person cannot be simultaneously a solvent, self-respecting citizen and an actively caring parent.

The Post-Industrial Children's World

Once infancy is over, mothers everywhere share their children's care with other people. It is not the need for children to be cared for by someone other than the mother that is peculiar to modern Western societies but the special features of shared care in their context.

In most parts of the world young infants go where mothers go attached to their bodies, and mobile children are partially cared for by several people simultaneously, while all those people also work. Groups of women who are working together may pool the care of all their children. When they undertake physically taxing or potentially danger-ous tasks, hands-on charge of children may be delegated to one elderly woman as her suitably lighter share of the work and when a woman works on her own or with her husband, an older child may be expected to keep younger ones safely occupied instead of helping with the adult task. As groups of children roam the compound, village, shantytown or city streets, all are usually supervised and reminded of their responsi-bility for younger companions by the adult relatives of any of them. There are always women—often but not necessarily including the mother—available to every child, but only rarely and briefly will one adult be involved with one child to the exclusion of all other activities.

In the post-industrial West, however, children tend to be cared for entirely by one person and as the sole task of the moment. If mother is there at all she will often be there *for* the child and giving him most of her attention. But the corollary is that she will often *not* be there but working elsewhere, and when she absents herself the child is not left in the care of a residual and ongoing group of which she is usually part, but in the charge of another adult, who is specially called upon to take charge of him, at home or elsewhere. Children's care may sometimes be "paid for" within an ongoing relationship and exchange of favors, but it is more likely to be paid for with money. So children who can seldom be cared for *while* mothers work, and therefore often cannot be cared for by mothers *because* they must work, are cared for by others *as* work.

Separation of parents' work from children's care means that children have lost their taken-for-granted presence in, and apprenticeship to, what adults see as the most important aspect of their lives. Instead of spending much of childhood watching, "helping" and emulating a range of adult people doing adult things, Western children spend it in special environments designed to keep them out of harm's and adults' way: children's worlds, staffed by people—mostly women—for whom childcare or education is paid work and therefore valued more highly than the personal care of parents.

Children still "live" at home, of course—only in Britain or North America is it sometimes counted a privilege to send seven-year-olds to boarding schools or residential summer camps—but even at home they get little opportunity to share or contribute to adult concerns. Many of the routine chores assigned to children in other cultures and centuries, such as the care of animals and younger children or the fetching and carrying of fuel, water and messages, are irrelevant to Western households, and the chores that have replaced them mostly involve the use of gadgetry that is considered too delicate or dangerous for children to use.

Most Westerners take it for granted that children benefit from being excluded from adult work. Unlimited playtime in the first years, followed by a careful mix of play with formal education and the hybrid we call sport, is widely accepted as the prerequisite of a "good childhood." As a matter of policy, the years of freedom from formal work—and therefore, in a sense, of childhood itself—have been extended at least into mid-adolescence, and going to school is no longer a privilege, as it is in most other parts of the world. Children are legally required to attend school and parents are obliged not only to allow them to do so but to see to it that they do. Even outside school hours the amount and type of paid work young people may undertake is stringently limited in most countries.

Such a complete separation of children from the work that structures and absorbs so much of adult life may be a mixed blessing both for children themselves and for society. Play and education are indeed crucial to the development and self-fulfillment of individuals, but it is towards adulthood that children develop and into adult society that they must eventually be integrated. Children accomplish that by using parents or parent figures as models. Exclusion from important parts of adult lives and purposes renders those models incomplete.

Few parents are in a position to offer their children a more complete version of themselves. Most have only the small and interim part of their lives called "leisure time" available to share, and integrating children comfortably even into that is not easy because full-time work needs balancing with rest and personal space. Childless people can come home to do their own things after the day's work, go out on Saturday nights and sleep late on Sunday mornings; parents cannot. Children's needs for company and conversation, supper and supervision, expeditions, entertainment and endless cleaning up often seem like extra and unfairly stressful demands rather than an integral part of ordinary daily life.

The Post-Industrial Parents' World

Insofar as parents' stressful dilemmas are recognized at all, the socially approved mechanisms for coping with them do not aim for greater integration of children but for increasing separation from them: separation of personal and domestic commitments from work commitments and therefore of children's lives from adults' lives; separation of all the Janes and Jakes from their moms and dads so that mom and dad can pursue their public lives as if they were childless. Employers and colleagues often seem to view other people's children as an acceptable, even admirable hobby, like a sailboat or a garden. But those children do not feel like hobbies to their parents. Children cannot be laid up or left fallow until parents have time for them, nor can all thought of them be put aside at will. Even when acceptable and affordable daycare seems to resolve practical difficulties, emotional tensions remain. Many parents—especially mothers—live like trapeze artists: always striving to maintain a balance between opposing obligations, always anticipating the trivial slip—chicken pox, an evening conference—that will spell disaster. Most stressful of all, perhaps, is the perpetual feeling of inadequacy that comes from never having quite enough time or single-mindedness to give to work or home. Whether a woman gives today's priority to children or to work, she may face tomorrow with unresolved feelings of guilt and regret.

For many mothers, compartmentalization is the daily experience of peeling off a clinging baby and attaching her to someone else; covering the beseeching silence of a small child with bright chatter about the gift he will get on her return tonight; swapping mother hat for working-woman hat on the way to join commuting colleagues and making that "I'll be late—again" call without letting anyone see how much she minds how much they mind. But the focused, private pain of physical separation is only part of it. There is a broader, vaguer unease that many parents share but rarely voice: a sense of loss, even foreboding, arising from leaving much of their children's socialization, education and acculturation to paid labor and the values of the marketplace. Post-industrial societies increasingly consider it normal for the children parents have for love to spend most of their waking hours with people whose job is to care for them for money. As members of those societies, most parents also consider it normal and strive to arrange it. But parents still worry about the relative strength of their own and other influences and wonder whether their children are going to turn out as they wish.

Parents remain the primary influence on their children even when they are not their primary caregivers. But the less time parents and children spend together, and the fewer thoughts and activities they share, the more powerful secondary influences are likely to be. Growing, changing, developing children cannot be left on ice when parents are not around, so time, and space in minds and hearts, get filled by other people. Unless those are trusted delegates—members of the family de jure if not de facto—parents may fear that transmission of their own values will be overwhelmed by the sheer volume of competing messages.

Messages from an adult world whose values are centered in the marketplace and disseminated by powerful media trouble even those parents who are confident of enough time with their children. Many, surely most, parents still wish their children to absorb traditional values such as honesty in word and deed, and respect for other people's rights and property. In order to absorb particular values at home, children need to model themselves on parents who live by them, or are seen to try. But in order to participate fully in the adult world beyond home, parents need more complex and flexible values that allow them to accept yesterday's government lie as today's political joke, enjoy the entertainment media's overnight transformations of criminal into antihero and license into liberty, be prepared to take a fresh look at junk when opinion-makers call it art and put their children to bed with were-bears instead of traditional teddies. In market- and media-led societies it is so difficult to decide what *is* right or wrong, good or bad, smart or wicked, that most people tend to avoid such questions, regarding the words themselves as old-fashioned, moralistic and judgmental, and those words, in their turn, as almost abusive. So teaching moral values to children involves yet another kind of compartmentalization between the roles of person and parent.

Because moral values have the most direct application to children's behavior, they are the kind that are of most obvious concern to many parents. But moral values do not stand alone; they fit into contexts of cultural values that set the tone, taste and texture of whole societies. Western cultural recipes are rich with age and diversity, but will today's children inherit, enlarge and pass on the full cookbook or only an edited version of microwaved fast-foods and monosodium glutamate soups? If culture is what people make today using their inheritance from yesterday, it cannot be lost. But if we do not ensure that our children inherit everything, it could be impoverished. Mass production and communications should make it easier to ensure that full inheritance for every child. In idealistic theory the best of literature and learning and of the visual and performing arts, together with information and controversy about everything in the world, can be available to, and potentially added to, by everyone. But is "the best" increasingly available? This decade opened with children on both sides of the Atlantic talking excitedly of Leonardo, Donatello, Michelangelo and Raphael. Has every child been shown what those names stood for in Western culture before a man with money on his mind attached them to Ninja Turtles and swept them from the sublime to the sewers? Does every adult know? Will each who knows tell? There is no reason why minority interests should ever be forced on people *in place of* what a majority find comfortable and profitable, but every new child is a reason why they should always be offered *as well*. Children cannot know what is inside our art galleries and libraries if we do not take them, any more than they can know what is in our conscience if we do not tell them.

And if we do not take and tell them in childhood, many will not go or listen in adolescence and then they will lose their proper freedom to look back over a broad cultural canvas and choose what to take with them into adulthood and forward into the upbringing of their own children.

Childcare Choices

Western societies pride themselves on their individual freedoms. Within wide legal limits, people can bring their children up in any way they choose, bypass most social institutions and adopt and pass on to their children life-styles and values that are different from those of most citizens—if they can afford to. All parenting carries a high price and the more personal parenting is, the more it is likely to cost in time and effort, if not in cash. Choice is conditional, then, rather than free.

Parents who seek to replace the mass children's culture of the place where they live with the interests, activities and values of their culture of origin or chosen subculture, for example, know that the only effective technique is displacement. Simply depriving children of the life-style that is normal among their peers, or debunking the values they see all around them, does not work. The children have to be offered extra experiences and exposed to additional values. Exactly the same applies to parents who want to modify the impact of certain aspects of children's culture. Many Western parents complain that children read too little because they watch TV too much. If that is true, so is the reverse: children watch TV because they do not read. It is that reverse that parents must use if they want to alter, rather than merely moan about, TV culture. Make children passionate about books, by filling the house with them and constantly reading to yourself as well as to them, and however interested they may be in *Bubsy* and the soaps, time pressures will ensure a shift in the balance between the two. In exactly the same way, an exclusive diet of fast food is far more likely to be modified by a shared enthusiasm for cooking, or for eating Italian food, than by lectures on a healthy diet. It sounds easy, but of course it is not. Mass children's culture, indeed the whole special children's world of care, education and entertainment, is not only what is easily available to children; it is also what is easily available to parents for their children. Tailor-made additions take extra time and most of them take money too.

The more time and effort parents give to their children, the less time and commitment they can give to the world of work and the less money they will have. Giving extra time and effort to children may make people feel like better parents—they may even be recognized as exceptionally devoted—but if it also makes them less solvent citizens they can expect little social recognition of their sacrifice, let alone compensation or practical help. As far as society is concerned, "good enough" parenting is good enough; beyond that, making more money matters more.

As the personal parenting all children need and most parents want to give becomes increasingly uneconomic, it is being presented as decreasingly desirable. Lies, half-truths and truths left untold are combining to convince people that women's sense of symbiosis with young babies arises from their needs, not their infants'; that parents' dreams of close companionship with growing children are unrealistic; that their desire to be the prime influence on their offspring's development is atavistic arrogance. Parents are being told that the care compromises which circumstances force upon them are actually better for their children, that "quality time" is enough of their time and the rest should go to the linked achievement of "self-fulfillment" and the salary check. The subtext must be that parents are not very important to children or that children are not very important to society.

Children are a large part of many people's present and the whole of everybody's future. The richest societies, the most democratic governments and the most complex social institutions the world has ever known have evolved a kind of parenting that puts people-who-are-parents at serious disadvantage compared with all other adults yet fails to meet many children's acknowledged needs. It cannot be good enough because they can do better.

Looking Forward

We can do better for children via their parents. If we do, we shall also do better for all adults who are parents. And if we do *that,* the whole of society will benefit because most people are, have been or will be parents and everyone was once a child with parents.

There are better choices for children available to us. We are not making them because we are not seeing them. We are not seeing them because we are not looking. A fresh focus on children's known needs opens up a range of different approaches to old problems:

The women's movement has dismantled many barriers that protected men's powerful public lives, but gender equality is still defined as sameness and the model for it is still a male one. Focus on pregnancy, and the nonsense of that is thrown into sharp relief. Men's and women's experiences of becoming parents are not the same nor do infants ever experience parents as ungendered. Focus on infants' early needs, and the importance of celebrating both femaleness and maleness becomes clear. Babies need mothers and fathers.

Infants cannot have mothers or fathers around them all the time. Current debate about daycare is wide-ranging but it is more about finding solutions to daily cares that dog parents than about finding kinds of care that meet children's needs. A child-centered agenda produces a very different debate.

Adult society is highly competitive but children's development is a process, not a race. Children mature faster if parents let them take their own time; farther if parents broaden and share their experiences rather than pushing them down an achievement track.

Society relies on childhood socialization to produce good citizens but keeps child-apprentices in a separate world from the adults they need to emulate. Instead of learning to do as adults do, children are expected to do as adults say. Discipline that is achieved by the exercise of power can never be as effective as self-discipline achieved through influence.

Childhood is long because human children have so much to learn and we have extended it because our educational aspirations are so high. But although we know a great deal about how, what and when children learn, educational institutions scarcely reflect that knowledge. Early-years educcation is distorted by preparation for school; schools are not child-centered and the demands made on teachers range from unrealistic to dishonest.

New choices for children and parents would cost money. Can Western nations afford them alongside huge national debts and trade imbalances, mass unemployment and increasing expenditure on welfare that still does not stem the inexorable rise in poverty? The clearer it becomes that present socio-economic policies are neither successful nor self-sustaining, the more obvious the answer becomes: they cannot afford not to.

Giving social and economic priority to children's well-being, development and education could deal with the worst ravages of poverty and underprivilege now, prevent waste of reparative resources and productive potential in the next generation, and ultimately shape self-sustaining societies.

Recognizing children as young citizens, and paying as much attention to their rights and opportunities as to adults', would bring parents' rights and responsibilities into balance.

Putting children at the center of society would re-value parenting and open up new solutions to conflicts between working and caring.

New choices exist. We can choose to do as we like. If we choose well perhaps we can even like what we do.

PART TWO

---◆---

Children and Parents

— 2 —

Mother, Father or Parent?

Last year in New York I gave a talk that referred to "mothers" and "fathers" and was taken to task by a journalist for being politically incorrect. These terms, she explained, are unacceptably sexist and elitist. I was not altogether surprised—there is real difficulty here—or unrepentant: I had not intended to challenge, let alone to distress. But I was, and I remain, stymied. Mother and father are biological terms; as such they clearly differentiate both genders and genes but equally clearly they imply no value judgments. Biology is often sexual but never sexist; it is naturally selective but never elitist. The political incorrectness—and cruel stupidity—of sexual and genetic discrimination is not in the rootstock of the human species but grafted onto it by human behavior.

The individualist social ethic of Western societies makes everyone responsible for his or her own success or failure but promises each an equal chance. Many individuals frown on differential opportunities resulting from accidents of blood and birth, and take an egalitarian view of natural justice. But sympathetic though such attitudes may be, they are neither generally shared, even in the West, nor problem-free. The more determined we become to rid ourselves of discriminatory attitudes and practices, the more we are inclined to reject the gene and gender differences that provoke them, as if those differences were themselves reprehensible. Differences between mother and father, and between parent or other, *are* in the rootstock of our species. If we try to get rid of them in our anxiety to be rid of what people have grafted onto them, we risk throwing out the babies along with the dirty bath water. We must try to understand where our biological and social heritages meet.

My journalist friend's prime objection to use of the terms mother and father was that it was sexist to differentiate between two parents on the grounds of their gender. The shared area within which women and men operate interchangeably as parents has expanded enormously in this last decade; I hope it will expand much further. But however far modern parenting encroaches on old established maternal and paternal roles, it can never completely overlay the separate gendered spaces women and men occupy in their children's lives. Mommy and daddy are each an individual person and gender is an integral part of individuality. We can, and must, prune out stereotypes about who can nurse croup, create and embroider a bedtime ritual or a quilt, play particular games or model particular behaviors. We should, above all, dig out the old idea that no man can take full care of a child and that every woman can. But whatever fathers and mothers *do* with their children, those children will always remain aware of differences in the ways they do it, and parts of those differences will always be associated with gender.

As well as seeming sexist, though, the terms mother and father seemed elitist to this journalist, because they differentiated between "natural" parents and other parent figures or caregivers. In the course of childhood, more and more children experience life in different households where a succession of adults function as family. A parental divorce followed by even one lover per parent and one new spouse each makes five combinations of parent and parent figure, and each new combination may bring the child new grandparent, aunt or uncle figures, as well as quasi-adult step- or half-siblings. Adoption, not only of infants within cultures but of older children and across cultures, further complicates family, while egg and sperm donation and various forms of surrogacy are beginning to complicate it even further. Although we still regard it as normal for children to grow up with both their natural parents, only a minority do so. The whole concept of Western family has to expand and loosen so as to legitimize, and optimize, the varied experiences of the majority. Some countries, such as Britain, are recognizing that in legislation that also ensures that parental responsibility *for* a child always outweighs parental rights over him or her. However, while everyone should realize that a blood relationship with a child is neither a necessary nor sufficient condition for mothering or fathering him or her, nobody should believe that taking a mothering or fathering role makes him or her into a child's parent. Roles and relationships are not inseparable, either way around. Foster parents and stepparents are substitutes—mother and father *figures*—vital sometimes, and in some ways preferable, but never the same. Even adults who adopt infants and are the only parents they have ever known are still replacements for the parents they had but never knew. People will always want to know about their origins.

Differences between mothers, fathers and others are biological facts. We cannot escape them and we do not have to fear them because the evils of sexism and elitism are not inherent in the facts themselves but in their traditional social implications. Many of those social expectations need changing, but that cannot be accomplished by pretending that gender and gene differences do not exist, by ignoring them, or keeping quiet about them. On the contrary, acknowledgment and enjoyment of basic biological differences are a more likely basis on which to graft a new social order of rich and respected diversity.

Such acknowledgment will not be easy to achieve because recognition of the uniqueness of mothering and therefore of fathering seems to threaten the most vulnerable, that is, female, half of the population. Many women believe that within establishments that are still overwhelmingly male, any assertion of sex differences is inevitably interpreted as an admission of female weakness. Many mothers believe that if they openly acknowledge differences between their own and their partners' parenting relationships and roles, they risk handing men a gift-wrapped justification for reasserting their economic dominance, and freeing themselves of domestic duties at home and of women colleagues at work. As long as both sexes battle for position in a male game plan, that risk will remain real. Many individual women will seek to avoid it by keeping their heads down while hanging on to whatever position they have achieved, and some will believe that they are winning. But the position of all women will remain precarious until they insist that societies alter the game.

The rules are up to us. Women are a group by virtue of biology but it is not biological gender differences but accidents of history that have produced inequity and then characterized the struggle for women's rights as a struggle to be less (stereotypically) female—or even more male—rather than as a struggle to have femaleness validated. Wherever and whenever women's movements have begun, most of the personal, political and economic power has been in male hands so that the fastest escape routes from traditionally female roles have been traditionally male ones. In its early years, parts of the North American and European women's movement therefore concentrated on playing men at their own game and were extraordinarily successful. Female membership of the squad is accepted everywhere and although there are still dismally few women in the top teams of most nations, there *are* female prime ministers (if not presidents or popes); the title Chairman is largely abandoned and terms like doctor and lawyer (though not yet nurse or secretary) are becoming ungendered. As long as Western individuals remain childless and look to the work world for focus and fulfillment, gender differences can usually co-exist, often reach comfortable irrelevance and sometimes achieve real complementarity. Is it enough? Will "progress" for women continue towards genuine gender equality or is everybody still playing a game whose rules will always leave most women inequitably vulnerable to failure despite the successes of some?

Most people do not remain childless forever and for women playing under male rules, babies are a severe embarrassment. Planted by men who can (and often do) then walk away, unheeding, unknowing or unable to cope, babies-in-prospect visibly disadvantage women relative to men, while babies-in-arms require kinds of care so incompatible with male models of work and so redolent of traditional housewifery that many women find themselves out of the game altogether. Choosing to remain childless, or at least to delay and limit their childbearing, keeps some females playing and gives an illusion of equal opportunities. But such choices are dependent on contraception and abortion, and therefore vulnerable to interference by church or state, to human and technical error and to economic and health concerns. And even when they are freely made, such choices about children are never truly equitable because carrying, delivering and nurturing a baby is an integral part of most women's self-fulfillment and cannot be of men's.

That is the crux of the gender difference. As long as it is assumed that society will continue to be organized by men, according to a distinctively male model to which every individual aspires, it will remain too dangerous a differentiation for women to acknowledge. But is it not that assumption itself that needs rethinking?

Looking at the painful confusions that ignoring biologically based differences is creating for women and men when they come to produce the next generation, it seems that the route that ignores gender differences instead of honoring them may have taken us closer to sexual equality but be incapable of taking us all the way. Now that women have proved their ability to play by men's rules, perhaps we should turn our attention to raising the status of a female league so that men can similarly demonstrate their ability to play by women's rules and we can evolve new games of egalitarian diversity.

The business of having babies begins to differentiate between males and females as soon as they stop being babies themselves. During the first year of life, all infants see their mothers or mother substitutes as their principal source of gratification and as tremendously powerful figures with whom they identify. Part of the mother's power is vested in her ability to bear and to nurture babies, and both sexes seek to emulate and share it. During the second year boys, as well as girls, often stick pillows up their sweaters in pretend pregnancy and act out tender nurturance and tough discipline with dolls or soft toys. That core identification with mother and her femaleness will be crucial to every child's eventual capacity for caring parenthood but even as it forms, the development of girls and boys begins to diverge under the biological demands of gender. That first identification is across-gender for boys, same-gender for girls. Female identification continues for the little girl. Her eventual identification with her father as "other" will add to rather than disrupt it, and her eventual ability to bear children, like her mother, is the culmination of a continuity. The little boy's course is more complicated because his cross-gender identification with his mother will never culminate in fulfillment of that infantile desire for maternity but must give way to same-gender identification with his father. It is out of the conflict between these two, and his particular integration of them both within himself, that a boy's gender identity and potential for nurturant fatherhood grows.

Those two opposites can be integrated within individuals in many different ways, but however various male identities may be, they all depend on boys' relinquishing—or rather sublimating into phallic concerns—their desire to be just like their mothers and to carry, deliver and nurse children. Every boy "forgets" those infantile wishes, of course, but the more they are repressed rather than resolved, the more their unconscious operation will affect his maturation, life-style choices and sexual relationships. Pregnancy ushers in the supreme test of what Bell has called "the paradox of masculinity." If a man's integration is less than adequate, he may be overwhelmed with envy of his partner's childbearing capacities, unable to accept the reality of his exclusion from maternity, and therefore unable to accept the creativity implicit in his consequent difference as a parent who will be a father rather than a mother. Some men indulge those unconscious wishes by competing with their pregnant partners; some flee both wishes and women, absenting themselves emotionally, physically or both. In contrast, men whose male identification sits comfortably on that first female one may share their partners' excitement about coming children, find it easy to sympathize with the discomforts pregnancy brings them, yet find that they themselves are energized by it and unusually creative or productive within their separate areas of work or play.

Like infantile wishes to have a baby, an adult desire for children is common to both sexes. By this time, though, the complexities of identification in the intervening years have often produced important gender differences. For both sexes there is tremendous narcissistic satisfaction in reproduction—a sense of omnipotence and self-completion. But if men have struggled to achieve a male self-image, that may be reflected in a greater desire to produce a baby of the same sex as themselves, and a greater tendency to welcome that baby's "masculine" behaviors and characteristics (and be made anxious by "feminine" ones) and to seek to realize unfulfilled ambitions through their sons. If women have struggled against their female identification, perhaps seeking to be the sons their fathers would have preferred, they may find the physiological demands of pregnancy very hard to bear. Both sexes reopen and replay aspects of their own infancy and infantile relationships through their own babies, but it seems more often to be men than women who see their children as linking them to the future as well as the past, assuring them of immortality, or at least a continuing lineage.

Interacting with all those developmental and psychological differences are the overwhelming physical differences between becoming a father and becoming a mother which although they are obvious are usually underrated. The crucial importance to women of the effects of pregnancy, birth and breast-feeding is generally acknowledged, but the equal importance to men of being unaffected is not. It is not only that men have to accept their partners' primacy in the production of their joint children, it is also that no physical experience will ever tell them whether they have fathered a child or not. A man must accept a woman's word that a child is part of him as well as her. Women, whose own sexual relationships have been so dominated by the possibility of an individual impregnating them, give little thought to the effect on their partners of the possibility that someone else might do so. A man is a biological father if he believes that he is. Many women, as well as men, find that idea uncomfortable, preferring to believe that there is some subtle recognition between men and their offspring: that somehow or other most would recognize the cuckoo in their nest. But while men who do believe themselves to be fathers are quick to find confirming similarities between themselves or their forebears and their babies, only those who already doubt their paternity commonly note disruptive dissimilarities.

Clearly, then, the obvious biological differences between females and males do not only ensure that their adult experience of parenthood is different, but that they arrive there by divergent developmental paths. Gender is only one, but an important, ingredient in the mix that makes every individual unique. Modern Western societies try to stir every possible variety of adult sexuality into one equalitarian pot, but gender differences, confusions and anxieties are still thrown into sharp relief by having a baby.

Biological facts are only facts; like other scientific facts, their significance in human affairs depends on the selective social use people make of them. "Traditional" expectations of mothers and fathers used to emphasize a divergence between the sexes that was real, but by no means as great, and certainly not necessarily as significant, as their allocated roles implied. It is true that every little girl wishes to have and to nurture a baby "just like Mommy," but that does not mean that every big girl *should* do so or that maternity must be every adult female's primary fulfillment. It is true that every little boy shares that wish and has to give it up for a realistic identification with his father, but that does not mean that men *should not* remain in touch with that identification with femaleness—that paternity is only safe within a macho context.

Those "traditional" gender roles used to underpin accepted social structures, but the structures have changed so that they do so no longer. Modern Western societies are concerned to acknowledge complexity and offer choice in what adults do with their infantile wishes and drives, and with their infants. Stereotyped sex roles are rightly seen as social straitjackets. But our determination to be rid of them, and the resulting modern expectations of mothers and fathers, may offer a liberty that is only illusory. Instead of acknowledging valid differences between mothers and fathers, but minimizing their social significance so that individuals are free both to be themselves and to mix and mingle in any way that feels comfortable to them, we seek to deny the differences themselves. It is a desire for asexual sameness that makes the terms "mother" and "father" seem offensive and the term "parent" preferable. The notion of asexuality is as poor a fit with scientific facts and personal feelings as the old sexual stereotypes, and such a notion can never be truly *anti*sexist. Instead of promoting the mutual respect between men and women which is a precondition for ending sexism, it is producing considerable confusion concerning parental roles, responsibilities and rights.

Most Western countries now idealize mutual parenting, starting with men "sharing" their partners' pregnancy. Attempts to make that more than social participation in a biological event easily trespass on women's rights. There are moves, for example, to give men equal rights over fetuses with the women they impregnate. But babies do not just grow inside their mothers' bodies—as we tell young children—they grow out of and as part of those bodies. Women and men shed ova and sperm without a thought, but once a particular ovum is fertilized and implanted, it is part of her and not of him. A man cannot lay claim to the conceptus of one particular sperm unless a woman will grant him a lease on the body of which she is the freeholder. A man who must stand by while a fetus he wanted grown into his baby is aborted may evoke sympathy, but surely not realistic support. Biology dictates that he cannot have a child unless his sexual partner wants it too. Social attitudes suggest that she should take his wishes into account in reaching her decision, but any legal measures to compel her to do so would breach widely accepted ideas of human rights. For a woman, though, the situation is reversed. Biology enables her to have a child if she wants one, irrespective of the father's wishes—or even knowledge—and there is less and less social pressure against her going it alone. It would be just as unthinkable to forbid women to have babies if they want to as to force them to do so if they do not. But a woman's biologically based rights over her own body—and therefore over the fetus that grows from it—carry social responsibility to the third person in the equation, the baby. The fact that she *can* have a child without reference to his father does not necessarily give her an inalienable right to do so because from the baby's point of view a father and a mother provide different and complementary aspects of parenting. If a child must grow up without a father or father figure, he can do so. But while extra mothering will help, it cannot make up for lack of fathering, any more than extra calories from carbohydrates can complete a diet that is lacking proteins from milk or meat or nuts. So why is it socially reprehensible for a man to leave a baby fatherless, but courageous, even admirable, for a woman to have a baby whom she knows will be so?

If a partnership is intact when a child is conceived, mutual parenting is assumed to be achievable because folklore still has it that a baby brings a couple together. The statistical picture is different. However successfully they have lived together as a childless couple, the birth of a first child puts relationships between women and men under tremendous stress and, with hindsight, is often seen as the beginning of their ending. Becoming mothers disadvantages women in adult individual-fulfillment stakes because giving birth expands their experience of individuality to encompass the baby and makes it impossible to seek self-fulfillment that is separate from fulfillment of his perceived needs and wishes. The psychic symbiosis that binds women and their infants after the physical separation of birth is incomprehensible, and therefore worrying and unwelcome, to most men. It seems to mock their attempts to share parenting, and it is almost impossible for women to explain to them. One couple tried very hard to understand each other when, four weeks after their baby's birth, the woman found herself unable to leave him to go to a planned party, and her husband found himself disappointed and hurt:

*Did she feel anxious about the sitter? No. She knew the baby
would be safe with this particular woman.*

*Was she, perhaps, being overanxious about the baby? No; she
was confident that he was fine and flourishing.*

*Did she not want to go to the party: perhaps she was too tired
and using the baby as an excuse? No. If it were not for the
baby (or if it would be comfortable for the baby to go with
her) it was an occasion she would enjoy.*

*Then surely she was being unnecessarily self-sacrificing? No, she
was not being self-sacrificing at all. She was not refusing
to leave the baby for his sake but for her own. She felt so
interlocked with the baby that just knowing that he would
be happier if she was there when he woke meant that she
would be happier to be there.*

At that point conversation between these parents foundered. The
woman was not taking her stand for the baby or for herself but for a
temporarily two-part self that was both her and him. She did not de-
serve—and was not asking for—congratulations on being unselfish,
but neither did she merit the charges of selfishness eventually leveled at
her by her disappointed partner.

That woman, implicitly charged with betraying her sexual relationship by putting her maternal relationship first, is a paradigm for millions of mothers who wonder if they betray their sex when they put
children ahead of what they perceive as feminist ideals. But to betray
their sex, women have to behave in a way that makes females seem less
than males. Being a mother is not less than male but uniquely, splen-
didly female and therefore something men cannot be, and find it difficult to understand.

If that was accepted, men and women might mutually respect the
feelings babies evoke in each other and find their differences interesting
rather than damaging. But the romantic social ideal of full participation
in every aspect of the baby business is taken to mean not only that the
experience should be shared but that it should be identically experienced. It cannot be, of course. All experiences are unique to individuals.
No two people experience anything in exactly the same way, and least
of all this experience of parenthood which is so salient to both partners

yet so different for each of them. Insofar as we tell men that they should share their partners' experiences around childbirth, rather than sharing the event within the context of their own experiences, we commit them to try to do the impossible. Meeting insurmountable external and internal obstacles, it is no wonder that many men are left feeling ineffectual and guilty.

Many fathers now attend their babies' births, but for every one who understands that the real point of being there is to ease his partner through the labor and delivery and welcome their baby, there is another who feels inadequate because she is in pain and he is not. Fathers are supposed to bond with their newborns just like mothers, but no two *mothers* do that in the same way, so why should a mother and father? Most mothers get more opportunity than most fathers, though. An hour or two after the delivery, many fathers are supposed to have done the bonding bit and get back to work. If lack of several months of paid leave for all new mothers is a scandal, lack of even a few *days* for all new fathers makes nonsense of equal participation. By the time that baby is ensconced in his home at the grand old age of forty-eight hours, father has already lost out to mother in recognition of his needs and expertise in meeting them. He may never catch up.

The daily absences at work of a man in a full-time job are long on the time scale of a brand-new person who changes and grows from minute to minute and whose memories are still fleeting. There is no way that a working father can be as aware of a baby's needs, moods and feelings as a mother who is sharing their ebb and flow. Even a father who can stay close may still be aware that the biological mother has a unique head start into a relationship with their newborn. But that is a head start into *mothering*. If he can be there to start into his own fathering from the beginning, he has the best possible chance both of building a relationship with his baby and experiencing its separate validity. If he cannot be there during the first days he may feel that he has no relationship of his own with the baby, no personal validity as a parent, and therefore feel compelled to compete with his partner for a share of hers. Competition, uncomfortable for both parents, creates a vicious circle for the father who inevitably loses. Practical childcare skills—like keeping a baby's flopping head in line with his body while he is lifted, or changing a really well-used diaper without also having to change everybody's clothes—can be quickly learned by almost anyone over about ten years old. But practice makes for dexterity and dexterity makes for a calm baby. If a father can spend little time with the baby until the first weekend comes up, and then expects to undertake an equal share in physical caring, he is likely to find that the mother is already "better" with their child than he is and may interpret the baby's greater calm with her as greater "love" for her.

The baby loves no one yet; nor is competence in physical care a sine qua non for parenting. If both parents are content for the father to assist his partner in those, and other, aspects of her mothering, while making his own unique and autonomous relationship with the baby through cuddling, talk and play, all may be well. But if he relies on being given part of that mothering relationship, all may be very unwell indeed. The baby needs nursing in the night. Father cannot nurse his son but he can fetch him—if only he can wake to his cries. He begs his partner not to leap up herself but to wake him instead. He would really like to make this contribution to the newborn nights and he is puzzled when she thanks him politely but leaves him asleep. Would she not like to stay in bed? Does she not trust him to get his own baby up? Why is she shutting him out? There is nothing the mother would like more than to stay in bed and asleep, but as long as the baby needs to be fed, his greeting to the adult who rescues him from hungry discomfort is part of her reward for feeding him. It is not that she does not trust her partner but that the baby's cries and her responses are the opening sequence in a night-feeding dance the two of them share. To lie there, awake and waiting instead of responding, would spoil the rhythm of their small-hours pas de deux.

The fact that it is a biological impossibility for mothers and fathers to be interchangeably parents to babies who are being breast-fed does little to convince people that parents are not interchangeable but much to predispose them towards bottle feeding. Nothing demonstrates more clearly the compulsion to make fathers and mothers the same than a willingness to change babies' feeding from breast to bottle in order to include it in shared parenting. Such a choice is more than a confused distortion of biological reality; it is a contradiction of it and, from babies' point of view, measurably wrong. There are appropriate reasons for avoiding, and for ending, breast-feeding, but this surely cannot be one of them. Women tend to say "at least he can do his share now" but, in the event, they seldom yield their place in the early weeks, even though they have yielded their breasts. Men put it somewhat differently: "at least I get to feed him." From the baby's point of view, nursing is better; but then from the baby's point of view a mother and a father is better than two helpings of a mixture.

That mixture, uncomfortable and confusing for many individual parents, is not always the positive force in partnerships that it is intended to be, either. Many fathers who try to share parenting with women who are still playing a duo with their newborns find themselves pushed towards the practical chores, like laundry, about which babies know nothing and care less, or allowed to handle their babies only on sufferance and with prior permission—"she's crying again, shall I pick her up?" And, sadly, many women who are sharing because they think they ought, rather than because they really feel ready, think little of their partners' efforts. It sometimes seems that however hard they try (and many try very hard indeed), men cannot do enough or do it "right." At a gathering of two thousand new parents, a woman who talked as if her scaffolder husband worked overtime for fun rather than for baby equipment, and another who angrily attacked hers for putting a blue sweater with their two-month-old son's yellow pants "when there was a matching one right there in the drawer" both evoked cheers from the other women. The few men present acknowledged "male failings" with sheepish grins. "Equal parenting" was not making for happy togetherness. But despite damage to their dignity and hurt to their feelings, many fathers keep on trying to be mothers because the only alternative they can see is lonely exclusion. Watching and listening to his baby and his partner gazing and purring at each other, small hard head nuzzling large soft breast, small feet digging at soft belly, a man can see that the baby needs his mother and that the mother needs her baby. What he cannot see is who needs him. They both need him, but not as a competitor with the woman who is mothering, nor with the baby who is being mothered; they need him in the uniquely male role of father.

The baby who belongs to both parents needs to wake up to independent life through his mother and to get a firm hold on that life through her nursing, her hormone-driven vigilance and the next stage of an attachment that is already nine months old. The mother is the person who is uniquely equipped to meet these first infant needs but that does not mean that the father has no role; he is crucially important in making it emotionally safe—as well as practically possible—for her to do so. He does not have to feel or behave as she does. Mothers who are devoting their whole selves to their new babies almost always know that their partners feel differently, even if they are not being economically and socially pressured to behave differently. What both she and his baby need him to do is to acknowledge, accept and approve of *her* feelings and behavior, privately and publicly, welcoming the efforts she makes for the baby because those efforts ensure that their mutual child is well cared for. If a woman is struggling to establish breast-feeding, her partner's support is crucial. However tired or tearful she may be, premature suggestions that she give up and use a bottle may disrupt not only the baby's feeding but the mother's relationship with his father. On the other hand, a mother who comes to feel that it is time to turn to formula will find intolerable any suggestion from the father that she should go on trying to nurse, for the baby's sake. She is the one with the sore nipples. Basic biology separates them as it did during the birth.

Whatever is going on within the micro-world of parents and baby, the male needs to be there to facilitate the female's mothering and to shield her, if necessary, against "advice" or pressure from the outside world. The role demands such sensitivity that some experienced fathers wryly remark that there is no way to get it right. Trivial gestures, in either direction, can assume disproportionate importance. Wedging an extra pillow under the arm that holds the nursling and is beginning to ache can convey a man's supportive determination to care for his partner so that she can care for their joint child. Asking "Haven't you ironed my blue shirt?" can seriously undermine the fragile new threesome. When they were two equal people, both earning money at outside work, they both ironed or they paid for laundry service. Now that she is at home—and sometimes irons baby things—does he assume that she will iron his? It may be entirely reasonable that she should do so: divisions of labor often are; she may even have done so already. But any assumption that today's mothering throws their partnership all the way back to the marriage roles of yesteryear demeans her new role, and any implication that she should take care of the man who is supposed to be her adult partner, as she takes care of the baby of them both, is unfortunate.

Many men find it difficult not to ask for a share in the care women give to their babies. Parenthood is for adults but none of us is ever grown up all the way through; there is a part of everyone that remains childishly needy, dependent and egocentric. Deep down, we all need our mothers and fathers. It is easier for most women to function on a grown-up level with their infants than it is for most men, though, because of the psychological impact of pregnancy and birth and the hormonal messages that hum between brain and breast. For a woman, having a baby is a culmination of adult sexuality but for her partner, the signs of that female sexual maturity—those milk-filled breasts, for instance—may not trigger a matching awareness of himself as sexual mate and father of a joint family, but may instead catapult him back to long-buried memories of his own mother and his own infancy. No man is all-male either, any more than any woman is all-female: envy of the ability to have babies is still somewhere inside him and few men are so secure in their sexuality that a baby at the partner-mother's breast cannot seem a competitor and the mother love he receives something that has been taken from him rather than something he has outgrown and replaced. The man who can nevertheless avoid making conflicting emotional demands on the woman-who-is-mothering renders both her and the child real service. If he is impatient of the baby's bedtime ritual because he wants his partner's full attention to the latest office gossip, he will shake her confidence: however resentful she may sometimes feel of the baby's demands, the slightest hint of criticism from anyone else will feel like criticism of part of herself and of her mothering. If he lies in bed at 2 a.m. waiting for his nursing partner to turn back into his lover, he will tear her in two. She needs to be loved so that she can pour love out on the baby, but it may (or may not) be months before she wants to make love. It is not just because she is tired or sore (though parents who have always tried to ignore gender differences in their sexual relationship may find such practical explanations the most acceptable) but because, for her, and for now, lovemaking has fulfilled its function and produced the baby who is a sexual fulfillment.

Having a baby—especially a first baby—is a cataclysmic change and the first days are seldom easy for anyone, including the child. These particular troubles are not halved by being shared, though, if the sharing is a pretense. The days might pass more easily, and lead into more satisfactory parenting and partnership, if women and men expected them to be different for each of them and knew that it was appropriate for them to be so. If a man believes that it is important for newborns and mothers to form single units for a while, it will be easier for him to foresee, contain and disperse his jealousy: on a conscious level at least, he will want his to be a unit because he wants what is best for his child. If he can calmly see his partner and his new baby as a unit, he will also see that their relationship with each other does not threaten his with either of them. He is not a parent being kept from his baby by his partner, or a lover being ousted by his child. He is a man fulfilling the exclusively male role of father. The self-negation these early days may involve is a positive part of that role, not a sign of being without one. It does not last for long, either. Although it is important for women to be able to cocoon themselves with their babies for a while, it is just as important for them to emerge. It is because men are seldom as totally engulfed in the quicksand of new-baby love that women can usually trust their partners to remain on firm ground and give them a hand out when they, and the babies, are ready. Infants cannot have too much continuous closeness with their mothers and need caregivers who serve as substitutes whenever mothers are not available. But while closeness with fathers is just as desirable, substitutes during daily absences are not as necessary. As long as mothering (by somebody) is constant, fathers' comings and goings, into relatedness and out to adult affairs, offer an important balancing discontinuity and the recurring treat of somebody who is *not* always available, who is *not* that mothering person and is *not* like her. Father is bigger (maybe), gruffer (certainly), different to feel and smell (always); because he is different, everything he does is different and he may do different things, too. It is his difference—his maleness—that makes him wonderful to a baby who is feeling on top, and may make him too much for one who is not. Fathers really do not have to feel hurt if babies they have been playing with all afternoon cry for their mothers as they tire towards bedtime. That is part of what mothers are for. As the first year draws on, fathers lure their offspring from that enclosing, rightly dependent relationship with the female parent or parent figure and out towards autonomy, with glimpses of a big world and its exciting challenges, with clarification of their dawning sense of sexual identity and with confederacy in their vital small rebellions. Mothers or caregivers really do not have to feel hurt if the toddlers they have cared for and companioned all day abandon them the moment fathers come home. That is part of what fathers are for.

What if mother and father both come and go to adult affairs, leaving a caregiver in the mothering role; will the natural mother lose her "motherly" interaction with the baby and seem to him like another "father"? Not unless she left the baby so early and so completely that she never established herself as his primary attachment. Extra mothering is just that—*extra*—and babies are happy to receive and reciprocate it.

What if it is father who spends most of his time caring for the baby and mother who comes and goes: is that confusing for the baby? Not unless parents change their identities, including their sexual identification, as well as changing what they do. As far as we know, a baby can flourish with any balance between mother care and father care. The minutiae of his behavior will usually reflect the amount of time he spends with each parent and his expectations of them, but nothing suggests that he becomes confused as to who they are. The toddler who spends all day with his father will probably go to him when he wants a bottle, rather than to the often-absent mother. But that does not mean that he thinks Daddy is Mommy: it is not *children* who have rigid ideas about what fathers and mothers do.

Many people dislike the idea that mothers and fathers are "for" different things because such gender differentiations seem to threaten ideals of sexual equality and joint parenting. The differences are real but they do not really threaten those ideals because they have to do with who people are rather than with what they do; with sexual identity rather than social roles or stereotypes. Differences between women and men in parenting are not just inevitable; they are positively desirable. Acceptance of them makes for self-awareness and self-awareness facilitates the sensitive awareness of others that is a necessary precursor of respect.

Mutual respect between mothers and fathers whose differences are accepted is the key to sexual equality in parenting as it is to ending sexism as a whole. Respectful recognition of gender differences implies no gender limits to what individuals of either sex may do and no value judgments on what they choose to do. The more certain a woman and a man can be of the core identity and difference that makes them mother and father, the more ungendered space they will discover in which they can function interchangeably as parents and the less defensive and confused they will feel about its limits. Of course a man can take full daily care of his child. Any suggestion that he cannot is as insultingly absurd as the suggestion that his partner cannot run a corporation. He will do it better though, and feel better about doing it, if he relates to his child as a caring father rather than as a pseudo-mother, just as his partner will fill her seat in the boardroom more comfortably and more creatively as herself than as a pseudo-male. Parents can interpret and fulfill their roles as they wish. When we truly believe that, we shall stop talking, even admiringly, of "role reversal" because we shall know that fathers and mothers, men and women, are not reversible and do not need to be because they are freely different, always equal, people.

— 3 —

Getting Started

Everybody loves babies in theory; since it is assumed that their mothers will do the loving in practice, everybody can afford to celebrate another person's pregnancy.

Low birthrates make pregnant women rare enough to be interesting; interesting enough to get a lot of attention from partners and professionals, families and friends, colleagues and strangers, who, amazingly, vacate seats and volunteer supportive arms, advice and reminiscence. For many women, even for those accustomed to seniority over male colleagues, pregnancy is a first experience of inarguable female superiority combined with permission to trade on long-abandoned "female weakness" and actually let men open doors and carry bags. And it may also be the first time that a woman, even in her thirties, feels accepted as an equal—or at least a novitiate—by her own mother: truly "grown-up," at last. As the weeks pass, the bulge expands and prenatal care and classes gather urgency, it becomes clear that, courtesy of that potential baby, the woman has, for the moment at least, recognized personal importance. It is not just that most expectant fathers will try to catch the earlier train home; many colleagues will make it possible for them to do so. It is not just that medical personnel will provide professional care; many of them will personalize it—consult with "mother" about her body, even talk about her feelings.

Birth and Bonding

Most of this lovely fuss, though, is in preparation for the birth rather than for the baby. An unfortunate and unintended effect of education for birth is a tendency for it to be seen as the climax of a woman's pregnancy rather than as the first beginning of a new person. A pregnant woman is someone who is "going to have a baby" rather than someone who—in biblical but descriptive style—is "with child." Once the brief drama of delivery is over and the baby declared healthy, most of that care and concern will melt away, leaving the woman, whose old life and identity is an unraveled tangle in the infant's innocent fists, to find a way of reknitting it to accommodate them both. No wonder a sense of anxious anticlimax and global depression is common. Males, especially medical males, like to refer to all postnatal depression as "hormonal"—part of the myth of menstrual moon-madness men use to excuse themselves the effort of understanding why women weep. Of course there is much hormonal activity in the bodies of newly delivered women. But in more child-oriented societies "baby blues" are so rare that the very concept is hard to communicate as this puzzled West African response shows: "Has this unhappy woman you tell me of not got her child?"

Well maybe yes, but also maybe no. She no longer has him inside her body, but she may, or may not, have taken him inside her on an emotional level so that she feels that he is part of her and she of him. That is the real meaning of the overworked word "bonding." Once it is complete the mother will scarcely be able to distinguish the infant's needs from her own because her prime need will be to meet his and she will suffer when he suffers and find her own pleasure channeled through him: "Love me, love my baby." But until that bond is built, the delivered baby is an outsider who may even be experienced as an intruder into the mother's personal space, her life, her sexual partnership.

Mothers and midwives have always known that bonding may happen in a flash of welcoming recognition at the moment of delivery: "Hello, baby, I didn't know it was *you*." But they also know that the bonds between mother and baby more usually evolve over hours or days and may not develop their full strength until the baby's first smiles transform one-way responsibility into something that suddenly feels like reciprocated love. Clearly, then, mothers and newly delivered babies need time to be close and get to know each other.

They will be unusually fortunate to get it, though. Post-industrial societies are too busy and interventionist to stand by while babies learn to smile and mothers to love. That individual and indeterminate process has not only been labeled, it has been tidied up—defined and refined into a half-hour delivery-room drama with medical professionals getting top billing. If all is well with both mother and infant they will probably deliver him straight into the cradle of the soft slack belly that tightly housed him moments before, and help him to the breast as his suckling reflexes surface. If no other imminent delivery is scheduled for the room, they may even leave baby and parents undisturbed for twenty minutes. But that is it. Now it is action stations again until the baby, washed and weighed, is in clothes and a crib instead of his mother's arms and she has a cup of tea to hold instead of him. According to recent Swedish research, the sucking reflexes of many such babies have almost disappeared by the next time they are in contact with their mothers. Immediately after delivery each pair needs open-ended time together and undisturbed. It will often be at least an hour before the infant relaxes comfortably in the mother's arms and suckles with satisfaction.

Any contact between mother and newborn is better than none, but writing it into delivery room rules is not a recipe for instant bonding and the more importance we place on them and it, the more women feel they have failed if they find themselves underwhelmed by that first meeting or if it is delayed. And there are millions of such women. Good preparation for birth has diminished the number of American women who are anesthetized or woozy with Demerol in the last minutes of vaginal deliveries, but obstetricians' fears of litigation, or even perhaps pleasure in profits, also means that one in four of them is delivered by Caesarean section. Increasing use of epidural anesthesia in the United Kingdom means that more women complete their labors alert and pain-free, but it also means that more babies have to be helped out with forceps and therefore removed immediately for precautionary medical care. And even when a birth is entirely "normal," according to the definitions used by medical personnel, the experience and their own "performance" often fail to measure up to the high expectations of women who have worked for "natural childbirth." What an indictment of Western birthing that a woman can feel that she has failed in the delivery room even though she has achieved the very purpose of being there: a healthy baby.

Birth educators strive to help women comprehend and cooperate with the birth process, trusting in their own bodies to produce their own babies But it is difficult for mothers—or fathers—to exercise choice or exert control over the conduct of labor because an infant's survival is too high a stake to gamble against the medical establishment. A woman may long to deliver her baby in her own home, helped only by people she has chosen and only as much as she wants. But assure her that the hospital is the safest place for her child, paint her some scenarios of needless stillbirths, and you effectively remove her choice. Faced with more and more high-tech intervention in labor, either parent may long to say, "Don't just do something, stand there," but how dare she or he refuse the monitor that *might* show that the baby is in trouble or the operative intervention that might get him or her out of it?

Although a few post-industrial countries, such as Belgium and the Netherlands, have a continuing tradition of home births conducted by community midwives, and vocal minorities campaign for similar arrangements in other countries, hospital birth is the Western norm, and that does not only mean that women lose control of their deliveries but also that they are likely to be separated from their newborns. Many hospital administrators would hotly deny this: they pride themselves on their "rooming-in" arrangements. But rooming in only means that mother and baby share a room: they will seldom be allowed, let alone encouraged, to share a bed, and infants are often removed altogether so that their mothers "can get some rest." On a recent visit to a British maternity hospital, I saw on one chart, under the heading "special remarks," a message in large red letters: "All nursing care at the bedside please; this mother does not wish baby removed." On a recent visit to an American maternity floor, I saw three newborn boys lying in a row on a counter in the nursing area, howling and bleeding. They had been taken from their mothers for circumcision and none had been returned fifteen minutes later.

Hospitals are expensive. Women are pressured to give birth in them but are seldom encouraged, or even allowed, to stay for the "lying-in period" most societies take for granted. If a baby needs continuing medical care he may even get it instead of (rather than as well as) his mother's, because she is expected to leave without him. We know that such separations are crassly counterproductive: that they make newly delivered women feel as if their babies belonged to the hospital rather than to themselves; make them feel dependent on hospital staff to meet their babies' needs rather than confident of recognizing and meeting those needs themselves; make them feel that their new nonpregnant role is hospital visitor rather than mother. Because we know all that, we make tiny concessions. Most hospitals now "allow" those mother-visitors onto pediatric intensive-care floors and even "let" them touch their own babies through isolette portholes. But we still accept the basic separations because we do not really believe that all that mothering stuff is important enough to be allowed to interfere with hospital hype and hygiene.

Women do not need—and perhaps are better without—the compulsory bed rest that used to follow childbirth in the West, or the ritual seclusion imposed upon them in many societies. But post-industrial societies have banished those traditions in favor of nothing rather than something better. Within two or three days of birth many women are at home and mostly alone with their babies. In the United Kingdom and the Netherlands, a midwife spends a few minutes a day with every newly delivered mother during the first week or two, and British families enjoy the unique services of Health Visitors after that. Other European countries provide a few vital visits from health professionals, and American firms such as MotherCare Services, Inc., are working for third-party insurance reimbursement of a range of postpartum services, but unless female relations come to stay with them at this time few women can rely on any continuous help or company. Most have to be grateful for casseroles from kindly neighbors and the slender, impersonal lifeline of the telephone. New mothers need rest to speed their physical recovery; birth may be as natural as running, but it is as exhausting as a marathon and stitches hurt a great deal more than blisters. New mothers need respite from their previous responsibilities while they adapt to their new ones. Above all, if new mothers are to pour out nurturance and care on their infants, they need nurturance and care poured in to themselves. There is a clear correlation in human affairs between loving and being loved, feeling loving and feeling loved.

Fathers are supposed to fill the vacuum left by those traditions of female postnatal care, but like many other convenient suppositions about modern marriage this one is more romantic than realistic. Up to a third of newly delivered mothers in post-industrial societies have no resident male partner. Because social education is often still sexist, by no means all men who are in residence when their partners give birth are competent to relieve them of household responsibility or give them the peculiarly personal nurturance they need. That leaves a lot of men who could do everything that needs doing, and would like to do so, but still not many who can actually be there. Most Western nations now expect fathers to participate in the birth drama, but very few expect or even allow them to remain central to the life drama of the following days. Refusal to finance, even seriously to contemplate, paid paternity leave makes nonsense of claims to support equal parenthood and leaves millions of women desperately trying to get "back to normal" as they might after surgery, distancing themselves from the new factor in their lives: their babies.

Getting back to normal means different things to different people. To new fathers it too often means swapping the emotionally supercharged atmosphere of a postpartum home for the reassuring sameness of the workplace where, once a few celebratory drinks have been bought, fatherhood makes little difference to life. Fatherhood still makes a difference at night and on weekends, of course, but surely those competent women will soon "get over it" and get home life back to normal as well? Those women have nowhere to escape to. They cannot get back to the normality of their pre-pregnancy lives: those have been over for months—certainly since they lost sight of their toes over their bulges. They cannot get back into pregnancy, however blissful some parts of that time may have been. In truth, they cannot get *back* to normal at all, because birth shakes up lives as children shake kaleidoscopes, leaving the patterns of the past in pieces. Newly delivered women can only get *on* to normal—on to a time when instead of being new and feeling strange, motherhood becomes accustomed and feels comfortable so that a fresh personal pattern can form out of fragments of the past, present and future.

Forming those new patterns takes time, and the woman who is trying to have things as they used to be cannot give that time. Babies cry and their crying is a tyranny demanding action at any moment of the day or night. Almost any action halts it—feeding, holding, rocking—but for how long? Will the baby settle now? Is it worth starting a meal, a bath, a book or a conversation, or will he cry again? Even more time may be spent waiting for crying than coping with it, but either way time goes by with nothing to show for it but undone chores, unbrushed hair and incomprehensible exhaustion. Where is the efficient woman who ran an office and a spotless home, talked sense and nonsense, made dinner and love? Where is the expected supermom who fits one little baby into her life without a ripple? Nobody tells her that the efficient woman is busy growing into somebody's mother; that the infant somebody is the best she could have to show for her time; that supermom is a media myth or that ripples make life interesting. What they tell her, or let her feel, is that her survival as a respected individual (and certainly as a married one!) depends on getting the baby organized into a predictable and sensible routine that leaves time for other concerns—fast.

Premature attempts to organize and routinize new babies are intended to diminish the acute stresses of early parenthood but actually increase them. The erratic and inconsistent neonatal behaviors that drive parents crazy will change, and only can *be* changed, when the infant's physiology has matured and steadied so that he is a settled baby rather than a newborn. The more generously his needs are met in the meanwhile the sooner that will be, and the generosity pays a long-term dividend too. Newborn babies want nothing that they do not need and therefore do not know how to demand anything more than they need; what they ask for they *do* need. Having their needs met, readily and kindly throughout the first days and weeks, teaches them that this new world and its caring adults are benevolent and can be trusted; that trust is the basis of confidence in other people and in self, from infancy to death. Basic trust nourishes self-esteem, nurtures a sense of cooperation with others, and guards both when, later on, wants that are not needs must be refused. Even six weeks' total indulgence of a baby's needs will still be paying off when he is six months, six or even sixteen years old. Denied that investment of tender time, denied what they need when and as they need it, newborns suffer and make their parents suffer. Our refusal to recognize and prioritize these earliest human needs creates a vicious circle of infant difficulty and parental withdrawal.

Breast-Feeding

Obfuscation about babies' real needs starts with the most basic need: food. The perfect food for human babies is the milk they stimulate for their own personal use by suckling their mothers' breasts. Post-industrial Western societies cannot pretend not to know this because, while they have led the world in producing alternatives, they have also taken the lead in confirming that it is so. In the last twenty years medical evidence that has been unimpeachable for generations has been reinforced with increasing knowledge of newborn physiology, the biochemistry of the milk itself and the dynamics of the nursing process. Breast milk is not only a perfectly balanced and universally enjoyed food that costs almost nothing, is produced in direct response to the demands of individual consumers and adapts itself to their maturity and needs, it is also a medicine: preventive, sometimes curative and always protective. Most of our babies do not get it though; they get bottles of expensive manufactured milks instead.

Commercial production of artificial foods for human infants started in the nineteenth century, long before the special properties of breast milk were known. Dairies, providing butter and cream to growing cities, found themselves with surplus whey. Turning that waste product into a substitute for human milk was a brilliant commercial idea and it did fill a real need. Wet nursing was rare; whole cow's milk was expensive and difficult to obtain or store. Babies who could not be suckled by their mothers were often fed on bread-and-water slops, and they did far better on this new breast milk substitute.

Having something to sell that a few people really need is a necessary but not a sufficient condition for commercial success. Formula manufacturers achieved and held on to a mass market because they were easily able to make millions of people want their product, whether they also needed it or not. As long as a baby is being nursed, his mother is committed to being with him almost night and day. As soon as there are socio-economic pressures on that togetherness, and women expect and are expected to work (or play) away from their infants, bottle feeding begins to seem advantageous. As long as a baby is fed only at the breast, men—whether as fathers, doctors or scientists—can have little influence over the feeding pair or what is fed. Bottle feeding offers male pedagogues and partners some control, even as it offers women a chance to escape male control by parenting more as men do, rather than mothering as only women can. The baby-formula industry quickly achieved marketing success, and once powerful commercial interests were vested in it, it was unstoppable. Those commercial forces continue to divert whole societies from breast to bottle, even now that the value of breast-feeding is scientifically proven. Health professionals know that breast is best for babies, yet few of them convey that unequivocally, in word and deed. Mothers—and fathers—want their babies to have the best, yet few of them make offering it unreservedly a priority. The bottle feeding story is a paradigm for many other aspects of our childcare.

Breast-feeding has powerful advocates outside the marketplace. Medical Davids even sometimes attack commercial Goliaths. They have forced them, for example, via the World Health Organization, to limit their advertising claims and acknowledge that a mother's choice for her baby is not just between Nestlé and Gerber but between herself and any of them. But Goliath can afford to lose ground to La Leche among some college-educated Western mothers; these are mere skirmishes; the artificial infant-feed lobby has already won in the West. Breast-feeding is not the ordinary, taken-for-granted way for a baby to be fed but at best an open choice. When women make prenatal hospital appointments, they are asked whether they intend to breast-feed. They are asked again when their babies are born, and even after they have nursed their infants on the delivery table, there are always bottles at the ready "just in case," and rarely a confident assumption that everything the baby needs will be available from those breasts. Western women have lost the tradition of breast-feeding, and in the eyes of society they have almost lost the right as well. In most countries it is not acceptable to show a breast-feeding pair on prime-time TV unless "the subject matter is anthropological." In a 1990 British survey 96 percent of those questioned believed that breast milk was best for infants, but nearly half disapproved of breast-feeding in public places and an astonishing 16 percent disapproved of breast-feeding at home in front of family or friends. A choice? A sacrifice? A secret vice? The percentage of babies put to the breast immediately after delivery varies from country to country but over the whole Western world, fewer than a quarter are fully breast-fed for as much as six weeks. And no wonder.

The formula manufacturers' real fight is now in the developing world, where they are making fortunes out of persuading parents that bottle feeding epitomizes modernity—and frees mothers to work for desperately needed money in growing cash economies. The related deaths of millions of babies and the long-term ecological folly of their whole business are not marketing problems.

Why have Western women allowed a range of expensive manufactured foods, requiring careful storage, preparation and serving, to replace what they, and only they, can produce themselves? The basic answer is that there has been a long slow erosion of confidence in the importance of their mothering role and of pride in their unique ability to fulfill it. For some women, indeed, the very fact that breast-feeding is an exclusively female function seems to put it beyond the pale of aspiration. Males undertake all the really important functions in society so nothing that males do not, by definition, ever do can be worthwhile. Females' lack of confidence in the importance of their gender-specific roles affects every aspect of mothering, but breast-feeding is especially vulnerable to it.

Everyone knows that breast-feeding is a demand-and-supply system but not everyone thinks through what that implies. By nursing, the baby stimulates his mother's brain to produce the hormone oxytocin, which initiates the let-down reflex to release milk already made, and the hormone *prolactin,* which stimulates the breasts to produce more. The baby is literally in control of the production and supply of his own food. This means that a woman's "success" in breast-feeding depends on her doing the one thing society as a whole (and therefore, very probably, her partner, her mother and her friends) disapproves of mothers doing: letting the baby control the feeding process and therefore her time. If a baby is allowed to nurse whenever he feels inclined, and for as long as he likes, he will ensure exactly the right amount of milk for himself today, when he weighs eight pounds, and in six months' time, when he weighs seventeen pounds. Mothers not only do not need to exercise control over their babies' suckling, they ruin the process if they do. But, as a society, we want infants to be controlled by adults and expect mothers to confine them to a tiny time slot in busy adult lives babies cannot share. So we teach mothers that they cannot be expected to be at a baby's beck and call, and we issue grim warnings against "spoiling" to any who show signs of letting their infants lead.

A new baby's physiology demands that he "graze" rather than taking discrete feedings. In the womb he was fed by direct transfusion from the mother's bloodstream into his own. The business of filling his stomach with food, slowly digesting it and then feeding again is outside his experience. He will quickly discover the pleasure of sucking and the comfort of a full belly, but his stomach is so minute that it empties in a few minutes, so while he does not want much milk at a time, he may want some whenever he is awake. He probably will not get it though. Nonstop nursing is impossible—or at least exhausting—for a mother with nobody to care for her and with other demands on her time and energy. Furthermore she will probably take it for granted that the longer the interval between feedings and therefore the more closely the infant's pattern approximates to adult schedules and to sleeping through the night, the better she is doing. There are many mothers who pride themselves on feeding "on demand," and would never keep a baby waiting while he screamed with hunger, but even they almost always defer feeding with distraction and pacifiers, "giving in" only when the baby's requests for milk have turned into distressed demands. Demand feeding is seen as an infant-centered ideal, but it is not. The very word "demand" suggests the battle, basic to many other battles, that Western babies must wage to get their needs fulfilled.

New babies need free-feeding. In cultures where they are constantly carried by their mothers they are not just offered the breast at the first whimper but often at the first lip-smacking, fist-sucking signs of hunger and sometimes before that. What does it matter if an infant gets a suck he does not need or is offered one he does not want? His mother's breasts are there for him and he can use them as he wishes. In the West, though, such an approach is anathema to many parents and heresy to most of their advisers, and there are many pseudo-scientific myths relating infant indigestion to "overfeeding" that stress the importance of controlling babies' intakes. In most countries, parents are taught that once a baby is experienced at nursing, he should never be fed within two (sometimes three) hours of the last feeding, however hard he cries, because "he cannot be hungry that soon."

From the baby's point of view—and therefore from his parents'— that is cruelly bad advice and lacks any real physiological foundation. Part of the perfection of breast milk is that babies cannot take too much of it: as long as no other food is being given, overfeeding is impossible because there is no such thing as overeating. Babies grow so fast that they need a huge number of calories relative to their body weight. Since their immature livers cannot cope with concentrated high-calorie foods, but only with milk which is dilute and therefore bulky, taking in enough food does indeed stress their brand-new food-processing systems so that digestive discomfort in the early weeks is common. But spacing out feedings makes digestive discomfort more rather than less likely, because the less often a baby sucks, the more milk he must take on each occasion in order to get those calories. A baby who is fed according to a schedule may be perpetually uncomfortable because he alternates between feeling stuffed and starving. The baby who is allowed to take exactly as much milk as he wants, as often as he wants it, has the best chance of being comfortable, most of the time.

Nobody can tell how much milk a nursing baby has taken at a time. A desire to know, and therefore be able to control, the size of his "meals" is often an important part of parental preferences for bottle feeding. But that does not mean that adult regulation of breast-fed babies' intakes is limited to scheduling their feedings. Most mothers are also told to limit the time their babies spend at each breast on pain of painful nipples. Factually, sore nipples have nothing whatsoever to do with the time infants spend sucking, everything to do with their position and grip. But the threat is a powerful sanction. Many a new mother suckles her baby while watching a clock instead of his face. If she does as she is told, her nipples may or may not become painful. Either way, fearful clock-watching much increases the likelihood that her baby will soon be getting fed from a bottle.

Breast milk is a dynamic substance: it does not only adjust its quantity and composition in accordance with the baby's weight and maturity, it also adjusts itself within each feeding. The "fore milk" is thirst-quenchingly dilute; the "hind milk" much richer in calories and nutrients. Limit the baby to three minutes at each breast and he may get two servings of soup and no main course. Nothing could more effectively sabotage breast-feeding. The baby will very soon be hungry again—thus confirming his mother's doubts about being able to satisfy him—and if she resists his frequent demands and tries to impose space between his feedings he may actually fail to get enough calories for adequate weight gain so that she (and her advisers) have objective evidence that she has insufficient milk. The bottle is waiting. The formula milk is intended to "supplement" the mother's, but its introduction is a self-fulfilling prophecy of the imminent end of nursing. By partially satisfying the infant, that bottle will reduce the frequency and vigor of his suckling so that he does not stimulate the breasts to increase their milk production to keep pace with his growth. Over days or weeks, that mother's milk supply really will become inadequate.

No reputable and thinking obstetrician, pediatrician, midwife or postnatal adviser in the Western world would argue that this sketch is inaccurate or that it contains anything that is new to them. Such health professionals are held in high esteem by parents, and parents want the best for their babies, so why do all those who advise new mothers not straightforwardly recommend ad-lib, infant-controlled breast-feeding?

Health professionals, like everyone else, are children of their culture. We tend to assume that while medical people and scientific facts can influence social behavior, those people and facts are themselves outside social influences. Of course they are not. How could they be? Western professionals have grown up and been educated in societies that do not take breast-feeding for granted, so despite their special medical knowledge of its advantages most of them do not take it for granted either. Furthermore, the most influential doctors in most Western countries are still men. However convinced an advocate of breast-feeding a male may be, he is unlikely to be as convincing to most women as a comparably qualified female, especially one who has actually nursed a child of her own. Most doctors do encourage women to consider breast-feeding and do intend to be supportive to those mothers who are doing it, but the bottles are there and few of them can resist giving a little advice on choosing a formula "just in case."

Other social factors put extra pressure on health professionals. The great multinational formula manufacturing and marketing companies are inextricably entangled with the medical profession; owners of many hospitals and nursing homes; principal donors of research grants, honors and gifts; sponsors of important conferences, research studies and information packs; advertisers, on a vast scale, in health publications and television programs that would otherwise be uneconomic. In the area of infant care at least, the medical professions would have to be substantially reorganized if those companies suddenly ceased to make—and spend—money. That does not mean that individual doctors cynically recommend to patients products they consider inappropriate. But it does mean that particular names are associated with some of the most positive aspects of their professional practice, and the products are everywhere. Once the use of any commercially produced milk seems appropriate, why not the one whose name is on that expensive piece of medical equipment and that interesting report—the one whose samples are included in the generous hospital "gift packs" new parents enjoy? The gift bags donated by the sponsoring baby-formula company to pregnant women at a recent British conference weighed ten pounds and were worth fifty dollars each.

Ask why a new mother has been recommended a particular artificial baby food and the health professional will produce excellent reasons to do with its quality, its convenience, its value for money. But ask why *any* food other than breast milk has been recommended and the reply will probably be sympathetic but circular and superficial like this Canadian pediatrician's: "Oh that. Well she did try nursing in the hospital, which I do encourage, but I knew she wouldn't go on—not many do, you know; most of them have to get back to work pretty soon anyway—and the last thing I want to do is make her feel guilty about it. She didn't have enough milk and the baby cried a lot. She'll get more rest now and her husband can do some night feedings. I don't think one does any good being cranky about breast-feeding. I tell my patients, 'It's your body, your baby, your choice.'"

It sounds good: responsible, respectful to women. But is it? No mother can make an informed choice without the full facts about her body, her baby and their interaction in nursing. It is not responsible to withhold those from her, and it is certainly not respectful to assume that she does not want or cannot use them. It is not mothers who do not breast-feed who should feel guilty, but societies which play down those facts because they are inconvenient or unprofitable.

Breast-feeding does not only give babies the best food; it also assures them of their mothers' time. This is what Western societies—and therefore many professionals and parents—begrudge them. Breast *milk* would be universally recommended if it could be separated from breast-*feeding*, and there is already a booming market in breast pumps designed to make it easy for individual mothers to produce milk in one place to be fed to their babies from bottles in another. The health consultant of a large group of companies in California has her employers so convinced of the importance of breast milk that they provide special rooms and breaks for what they call "nursing mothers." These rooms do not have *babies* in them though; they have electric breast pumps, sterile jars and refrigerators. In contrast, a new Norwegian law gives breast-feeding mothers not machinery but *time:* an hour a day off— two hours in the public sector—until the baby is nine months old and for longer if a doctor's note confirms that breast-feeding continues. At the moment, most women who milk themselves do so only for their own babies, but some hospitals already ask mothers to pump surplus milk and donate it to "milk banks" for the tube-or-bottle feeding of premature or sick infants. How long will it be before commercial interests move in to make money out of today's lifesaving generosity? How long before somebody finds a way to market sterilized human milk for bottle feeding so that some mothers can earn a bit while they are at home with their babies and others can give their babies breast milk without having to lactate at all, let alone be there to nurse?

Sleeping and Crying

Being there is the real issue, of course. In post-industrial Western societies, time earns money and money buys the goods that make a good life. Parents want the best possible life for their babies and will go into debt to provide what the vested interests of commerce tell them will contribute to it. The more they want to buy (for their babies), the more money they have to earn and the less they can be there (for their babies). Most nursery equipment, furniture, gadgets and first toys are designed to keep babies safe and content without adult attention. And most of the infant-care "problems" that Western parents accept as inevitable—and cope with by purchasing more and more sophisticated gadgets—are largely caused by lack of ongoing adult attention—by attempts to save time by caring for babies in brief, intensive bursts of activity and being free of them in between.

Parents know that most young babies sleep for sixteen to twenty hours of each twenty-four—many hours during which adult attention is surely not required. They purchase a range of elaborate infant beds—small and larger, stationary and portable, indoor and outdoor—in which babies can be safe and warm, and assume that they will sleep in them. They do, but not much. New babies do not do their sleeping in sound stretches of several hours. At the beginning of life there is a high ratio of "light" to "deep" sleep and a very rapid cycling between the two. Babies doze and wake, doze and sleep, wake and sleep, wake and doze again; if they do settle in for a couple of hours it is as likely to be by day as by night. There is no way to make babies go to sleep or make them stay asleep, but that does not stop parents from trying. Most waste a fantastic amount of time and energy in putting babies to bed, going and getting them up again and then having yet another try at "getting him down." In many households an infant's sleeping hours are a yardstick both of his virtue and his parents' efficiency. Good and well-handled babies sleep a lot, especially at night. Why are we so desperate for our babies to sleep? The answer seems so obvious that the question is seldom asked: only when babies are asleep can we be sure of uninterrupted time to do other things (including sleeping ourselves). That answer is not self-evident everywhere though. There are cultures in which mothers do not divide their time between paying total attention to their new babies and ignoring them while they attend to other things. Instead, they do everything they want to do, including sleep, with those babies close, or attached to their bodies. Constantly aware of and available to those babies, they still remain part of adult life. If a new baby is fastened to his mother in a carrying cloth, his sleep offers her no extra freedom nor does his waking interrupt her. Such mothers seldom know how much their infants sleep and as long as the babies are healthy, they do not care.

When a new baby is not getting what he needs, he cries; he has no alternative means of communication. He cries when he wants to suck ten minutes after his mother put him down; he stops when she picks him up and changes his diaper; cries again when he finds himself back in his crib still unfed. He cries when he surfaces from a doze; stops when he is picked up and walked or rocked; cries again when he is settled for sleep he does not want. Even if that baby is never left unattended *while* he cries, trying to get developmentally appropriate responses from parents who are physically apart from him and trying to stick to inappropriate routines means that he has to *start* crying often, and cry hard to be heard.

Pediatricians used to say that crying was insignificant (though they did not say to whom) or even that babies needed to cry to "exercise their lungs." Now, most of them acknowledge that crying always means uncomfortable tension of some kind and is in itself stressful. But though few of today's professionals therefore recommend that very young babies be left to cry alone, even fewer take the next logical step and recommend that most crying be prevented by not leaving them alone. Parents buy intercoms to ensure that they hear that crying from their busy distance, womb-sound recordings to fool babies into thinking their mothers are close by, swaddling wrappers to make them feel cuddled, pacifiers to stand in for nipples, infant seats and hammocks to give infants a change of position, clockwork swings or rockers to make them feel they are being walked, musical mobiles and light shows to make them feel their solitude is sociable ... Really wealthy North American parents can now buy a complete "sleeping environment" for their infant with all these and more built into a single crib large enough to last for perhaps six months. Maybe such luxury makes for less infant crying; maybe it only makes parents feel that they have done the very best they can possibly do to keep their baby happy. Either way that baby would cry even less if he had a real person in responsive contact with him almost all the time.

Everybody knows that unless they are hungry or in pain, babies seldom cry while they are being held. Everybody also knows that unless they are hungry or in pain, crying babies almost always stop when they are picked up. It is hardly surprising, then, that babies who are carried most of the time, sucking when they want and sleeping when consciousness deserts them, hardly cry at all. Adults do not need to set aside special time for cuddling, walking and rocking them because the babies are getting all that all the time. Wakeful babies do not suffer from boredom or overstimulation, either, because unlike our newborns, they are not left alone for long periods and then bombarded with playthings. If they are awake enough to be interested, mother's patterned clothing, her jewelry and hair are available for closeup study, and a world full of color and movement is all around. When people note bright eyes peeping out of a carrying cloth they pause to smile and chat. But when a baby has had enough, he closes his eyes and turns his face into his mother's body and nobody bothers him. The infant is in control of his own input.

In the post-industrial West, where people are more privileged than anywhere else in the world, newborn babies are denied the privilege of using their mothers' bodies as a way station between womb and world. Every mother wants her baby to have the best and will deprive herself to buy it, but she dare not *give* him herself, the freebie that is best of all, because she fears that she might then be tied to the infant, by his needs and her own feelings, more closely and for longer than she can manage or society will permit. Is it fair to let her baby get used to being with her almost all the time *now,* when she will be out at work almost all the time *then?* Is it kind to let him expect to nurse when he is going to have to take bottles? Is it right to pick him up every time he cries instead of teaching him to fit in to other people's lives? And how will she ever get back to her busy life if she does?

If two-week-old babies were two-year-olds those questions would be thought-provoking, but newborns are not toddlers; they are not even settled into babyhood. They are not getting used to "indulgence" but to being outside the womb; they are not building "unrealistic expectations" but a (hopefully realistic) sense of being cared for and of coping. From the baby's point of view, being physically close to his mother at the beginning of his life makes later separation from her more manageable, rather than less, and every postnatal day in which she meets his needs quickly and completely, gets to know him as more of a person and helps him to know her, gives him pleasure and takes pleasure in him adds to a savings account of confidence and calm. Even six weeks of laissez-faire will give him a good start into his new life as a settled baby.

From the mother's point of view, being close to her brand-new baby and responsive to his needs makes for the easiest possible start into the new version of her life that includes him. For a while her life may seem to consist entirely of mothering, but however submerged in her baby she allows herself to be during the first weeks after his birth, he will not dominate her life forever: he will not drown her. Babies grow; their needs change and they become increasingly able to meet some of them through other people and for themselves. Mothers get used to mothering; other aspects of life cannot be ignored forever and there are other people—partners, older children, colleagues, friends—who rightly reassert claims to their attention. Horizons do re-expand.

Fear of being drowned by a baby's neediness, or of drowning in the sea of postpartum feelings, makes for a miserable start to mothering because rationing the attention newborns get does not make them manage with less; it makes them hungry for more. The babies who cry the longest are those who are picked up only when it is clear that nothing else will *stop* the crying. The babies who start crying most often are the ones who are expected to spend the most time alone in cribs.

Society suggests that mothers withhold themselves, stay separate, stay in control. Those social attitudes and recommended practices commit many parents to postpartum weeks of unnecessary stress and exhaustion, depression and despair. It's tough having a new baby. It's probably tough *being* a new baby. Even people who do not think new babies merit priority in themselves must come to terms with the connection between those two statements if they care about parents, because anything mothers can do to make the transition from life inside them to life outside them easy on their babies makes those babies easier on themselves, now and forever.

— 4 —

Daycare: Dreams and Nightmares

Babies and small children have to be cared for every minute of every twenty-four hours. There has to be somebody to feed each baby when she is hungry, cuddle her when she cries, cover her ears when it thunders and show her the rainbow. Somebody must laugh at first jokes, applaud first steps, read stories and steer her between the rock and the hard place of toddlerhood so that she can emerge unscathed into socialized childhood and the new joys of "my friends" and "my teacher." And even then, somebody must be there to welcome her home and then launch her again on each fresh leap into life.

Who is going to do that? Most mothers-to-be answer "me, of course" (fathers are more likely to say "us"), but there is no "of course" about it. As more and more Western parents find themselves unable to afford to spend time with children that could otherwise earn money to spend on them, pressure for more daycare mounts. A daycare debate is raging from the White House to Wall Street, from the European Commission to national parliaments, from multinational corporation boardrooms to Main Street firms, and in political parties, unions and women's organizations at every level. But that debate is about big issues like the economy, the labor market and women's votes; it is not about the small people whose care *is* the issue. Starting from the premise that lack of daycare is depriving economies of needed workers and women of needed work, it is assumed that enough daycare to keep children who are not old enough for school safely out of the way during the working week is vital to national, local and family economies. The agenda for debate is simply this: how can daycare be made available, acceptable and affordable to all (and who should pay)?

Childcare: A Bigger Agenda for a Different Debate

Postwar changes in families, communities, indeed whole societies, have eroded traditional Western childcare patterns based on an earning male married to a dependent female who nurtured their joint children within a context of extended family support. Settled new patterns have not yet evolved in their place and, because children cannot be left uncared-for while a radical rethink goes on, Western policy-makers have turned to daycare without first asking the crucial question: how can children's needs best be met within modern socio-economic circumstances?

Daycare is neither an answer to that unasked question about children's needs, nor a new design for family living within which their fulfillment can be assumed. On the contrary, daycare as it is used today and proposed for tomorrow papers over some of the cracks in the old pattern and this defers radical reform. A new design would certainly include some kinds and degrees of daycare to replace, both for children and parents, some of the companionship, support and social education once offered by siblings, relatives and neighbors, but that does not mean that daycare is the right starting point or ultimate aspiration.

Daycare frees mothers to earn—and thus lessens their economic dependency on partners and states—but that does not mean that it gives women-who-are-mothers real equality of opportunity in the marketplace, either with men or with nonmothering women. Their children, and their feelings for their children, still exist; paying for daycare takes most of their earnings; finding time for loving them limits their availability for advancement and never having enough time for anything puts the mother/worker at the top of the stress table.

Daycare does not give women-who-are-mothers equality at home, either, even when they are in a marriage or partnership. Women do almost all the work of household and childcare whether they work outside their homes or not. Women who return to an outside job after a period at home do indeed shoulder a double burden: few can assume that once they are committed to the same outside working hours as their husbands, those men will feel committed to the same hours of work at home as themselves. Recent American analyses suggest that for every extra hour wives work outside the home, husbands work an extra three minutes within it, and that housework directly associated with children's presence at home takes up an extra 5.5 hours a week of women's time, but only 1.25 hour of men's. Furthermore, while higher-earning couples purchase more help with housecleaning and catering than couples with lower incomes, it is almost entirely women's earnings which pay for that help. Gender roles and inequities are even more sharply delineated in some other countries. A recent Italian survey, for example, showed that when mothers added 40 hours of paid work to their working week at home their partners added twelve minutes a week on household and childcare tasks to their working week outside. Those mothers spent 51.5 hours in "family work" when they had no other job and still spent 31.7 hours if they were also fully employed. The woman who must regularly work a week of 70-plus hours for 40 hours' pay is neither equal to, nor equaled by, anyone.

And what *about* their children? While they are babies or young toddlers, even the very best daycare seldom gives them anything they positively need, and being in daycare, all day and every day, often deprives them of what they need from mothers. Daycare only comes into its own as first choice *for children themselves* towards the end of the toddler period when it begins to fulfill developmental needs for companionship and education from others.

Agenda Item One: What Do Parents Want?

As long as parents are expected to carry the main responsibility for their children's care, childcare planning and practice should be based upon their views and wishes. The current daycare debate does not reflect the way things are in most families and it assumes, rather than asks, how parents would like them to be.

In the Western world as a whole, more children under five (and an even larger majority of children under three) are cared for by mothers (and some fathers) at home than in any form of daycare. Children who are not home-and-parent-based are still usually cared for by relatives. A 1992 survey of six thousand (mainly middle-class) American parents showed that in 53 percent of families with a child under five, one parent stayed at home; 17 percent used daycare; 10 percent had children cared for in a relative's or neighbor's home; 8 percent had an in-home care-giver and 12 percent used a combination of these options. Data from the National Longitudinal Survey shows that only 14 percent of moth-ers stayed out of the labor market until their children reached kinder-garten age, but 40 percent stayed home throughout the first year and only 15 percent put children into group care before they were four years old. A 1993 report from Population Trends and Public Policy shows that American fathers now care for 20 percent of preschool children during hours when their mothers are at work, compared with other relatives who care for 24 percent, daycare mothers who care for 23 percent and childcare centers and preschool programs which care for 24 percent.

While it is clear in most countries that more mothers would go out to work if they had access to acceptable and affordable daycare, it is equally clear that many still would not, especially while their children are infants. In the United States in 1991, 58 percent of women were part of the officially recorded labor force while they had a child below school age (six years). The comparable figure for the United Kingdom (where children start school a year earlier) was around 40 percent. Daycare is scarce in both countries—notably so in the United Kingdom, whose provision compared so badly with most other European na-tions—and it is widely assumed that this scarcity keeps millions of mothers at home unwillingly. But how many millions and for how long? In other countries substantial numbers of women who do have access both to daycare and to jobs are voluntarily forgoing the financial and other benefits of outside work during their children's first years. The Netherlands, for example, has a lower rate of female unemployment and more daycare than Britain, yet it has fewer "working mothers." Denmark has almost universal publicly funded daycare and something approaching genuine equality of opportunity for mothers and fathers in the workplace, but only just over 70 percent of women are in paid employment before their children reach school age.

Whatever the availability of jobs and daycare, few women have a "free" choice about going out to work when their children are very young. Choosing to stay at home to care for children always makes people poorer. Many women are too poor to have any real choice: if they can find any work and any way of having their children cared for while they do it, they must. Some, especially in the United States and the United Kingdom, with their high unemployment levels and low minimum wages, remain poor whatever they choose. So while it is certainly true that more daycare provision would increase the number of mothers in the workplace, it is also true that more financial help with the costs of being a parent would reduce that number, no matter how much affordable daycare was available.

Wherever extensive surveys have been carried out among mothers who are seeking or using daycare in order to go out to work, the results show that many would prefer to remain at home during their children's first years if they could afford to do so. In Britain, for example, a 1990 report by Social Community Planning Research showed that 64 percent of the exclusively female sample thought that women should be at home with children until they reached school age, while in a 1993 Gallup poll, two thirds of mothers said that only economic necessity prevented them from staying at home. In surveys published in 1989 and 1992, almost 80 percent of American women said that they wished it were possible for them to care full-time at home for their very young children. Of course we cannot assume that every woman who expresses such a sentiment would act upon it if she got the chance. In the politically inconceivable event of being offered financial support for personal childcare, some of those women would doubtless find the provision inadequate, life at home intolerable and the lure of careers and companionship irresistible. But what if a period of home-based, child-centered life was not only affordable but companionable, if deferred or interrupted careers were guaranteed and, perhaps above all, if such arrangements existed not for a special category of women called "mothers" but for a special category of people called "parents"? In North America or the United Kingdom such a question would probably be dismissed as unanswerably unrealistic, but it is not unrealistic in Scandinavia. In Sweden, parents have a genuine choice between universally available quality daycare and unmatched financial and social support for personal parenting by either sex. About 70 percent of women and about 30 percent of men care for babies at home for the first eighteen months. According to a national poll sponsored by the Swedish government in 1987, more than 80 percent would regard it as ideal to care for those children at home for twice that period, until they reach the age of three.

Clearly, then, the assumption that universally available, acceptable, affordable daycare would fulfill most parents' ideals is premature and may well be unjustified. So where does that assumption come from?

Agenda Item Two: Sources of Pressure Towards Universal Daycare

Many mothers, especially in North America and the United Kingdom, see only one parenting choice: between staying home and being broke in a boring backwater, or finding daycare and joining the rich regatta of mainstream work before it leaves them "out of it" forever. Of course only those with financial resources that assure them of a home to stay in, and the personal resources to value themselves as people and therefore be confident of their value to their children, will choose to stay at home. And that means that most are going to see leaving their children in daycare as the best option—if only there were enough daycare . . .

That is the way the people in gray suits with computers for minds want women to choose. Their blinkered bias, conscious and unconscious, fuels the assumption that "everybody (or certainly anybody who is ever going to *be* anybody) uses daycare."

Presentations of official statistics often overstate the overall need for daycare and almost invariably ignore the ages of the children who will receive it. In Canada, for example, a 1987 Labour Force Survey by Statistics Canada stated that 60 percent of women with children below school age were in the labor force and 40 percent were not. It was therefore estimated that 60 percent of Canadian families required daycare centers. Attention to the detailed realities of the survey subjects' lives produced a different picture. Of those 60 percent of mothers, 6 percent were currently unemployed—often on maternity leave—and 17 percent were working part-time, often in the evenings or on weekends, and sharing the care of babies with partners or relations. Of the remaining 37 percent of "full-time working mothers," between 5 and 10 percent were running small businesses or caring for other peoples' children, at home, while caring for their own. There was therefore a potential demand for daycare places from just over 30 percent of mothers—half the stated number—and no information on the level of actual demand. A recent American report on fathers' role in childcare shows that the real picture is at least as complex in the United States. Sixty-five percent of families did not pay for childcare even if both parents were employed, not only because many used unpaid care by relatives, but also because many parents worked part-time or worked later shifts so as to be home when a partner was at work.

Official forecasts of demand usually assume that the children of any *woman* in the labor force will require formal full-time daycare, completely ignoring all forms of joint parenting, all informal arrangements and the range of work options (such as part-time work and flextime) which are preferred by many women wishing to combine working and caring. Furthermore, such forecasts have to be carefully read if questions concerning *women's* participation in the labor force are not to be compounded with questions specifically concerning the participation of women with childcare responsibilities. The European Childcare Network, for example, speaking of the European Economic Community to the year 1995, states that demand for daycare ". . . will increase over time. Even without any additional measures to assist with childcare, labor force participation rates among women and their share of the labor force are expected to continue to rise. . . . Demand will also increase because the supply of alternative sources of childcare—particularly relatives and other women caring for children in their own home or in the child's home—will fall as more women enter the labor market. . . . Demand for publicly funded childcare services will therefore increase even without any attempt to respond to this demand. It will increase still further where the attempt is made . . ." That statement is not based on the expected increase in the number of *mothers* participating in the labor force while their children are of particular ages; indeed it is not based on figures that are concerned with mothers at all. It is based on the expected increase in the percentage of *all women, aged 15 to 64,* participating in the labor force by 1995 as compared with 1986. Interestingly, even on that blockbuster basis, the actual predicted increases are surprisingly small: 0.1 percent in Germany, 1.0 percent in the United Kingdom, 1.6 percent in Ireland, 1.7 percent in Spain. The highest predicted percentage increases are around 6 percent in France,

Italy, the Netherlands and Denmark. They will leave a high percentage of women outside the labor force and therefore still theoretically available for childcare at home: Denmark is expected to have 82 percent of all women (not only mothers) working by 1995, and France and the United Kingdom both expect just over 60 percent. No other EEC country expects much more than 50 percent. Such forecasts, and the conclusions drawn from them, tend to overestimate the importance of childcare responsibilities in keeping women's participation in the labor force down, and therefore to overestimate the extent to which that participation would be increased by increases in daycare provision. Looking at the twenty-five to forty-nine-year-old age group, within which childcare responsibilities are most common, figures for the whole of the European Community in 1991 show that 84 percent of all single women without children were in the labor force (working or seeking work) but only 67 percent of married women *without children*. This difference between being single and being married was insignificant in Denmark and the United Kingdom, but in Spain, Greece, Ireland and Luxembourg it was as much as 30 to 35 percent. For all these countries, the fact of being married rather than single reduced women's labor-market activity far more than having children. In fact, in Spain, Greece, Belgium, Portugal and France, women with children were *more* likely to work than married women without. Only in the United Kingdom and in Germany did having children reduce women's work activity by as much as 10 to 15 percent. As the recent report "Employment in Europe" puts it: "There are various reasons for this difference in labour force participation between single and married women over much of the Community. As well as social and cultural factors, they include the fact that family responsibilities are not confined to bringing up children but extend to caring for a household and carrying out the domestic chores which this entails." It may also, of course, extend to the care of the old and the sick.

The European Childcare Network statement quoted above is no doubt correct in its conclusion that "such measures [responding to the demand for daycare] will change attitudes and expectations, making employment more acceptable and attractive, and encouraging more women with children to enter or remain in the labor market." But the difference such measures might make are easily overestimated.

Western media, fed both by those who make and by those who must live with policy, play a substantial part in convincing people that "everybody goes out to work," and that whatever the ages of her children, and his, everybody should do so. Media have glamorized the career woman who is also a loving mother, and the supermom who can do everything at the same time. They do not ask who is holding the baby while these admirable females outsmart males in the boardroom. A baby is a big plus to the image of a North American TV commentator but not if she stays off the screen to take care of him or her. Indeed, many women's magazines and columns have survived their sexist identity by cleaning babies off their screens and pages altogether except as professional extras or fashion props. Almost all the public role models available to girls and women are now seemingly (though not always actually) childless career models. Parenting, the perpetual and prime concern of millions of adults, only becomes interesting if it is in some way unusual—a gay adoption, perhaps, or a woman who turns the tables by leaving a lone father holding the baby.

Media make myths and are then just as likely as the rest of us to believe them. There is selection and slant (unconscious as well as sometimes deliberate) to even the most "factual" reporting of daycare issues. Reports concerning the numbers of mothers working outside their homes, for example, almost invariably draw attention to the vast numbers who do, rather than the (often similar) numbers who do not. A recent New York headline, typical of many, read "54 percent of mothers now in the workplace," and the story began "Homemaking is on the way out. More than half of all American mothers are back at work . . ." Equally accurate would have been a headline reading, "48 percent of mothers still home-based" and a story that began "Almost half of all American mothers but many fewer fathers . . ." Britain's *Guardian* newspaper, in a serious article in its education supplement, recently published comparative statistics of female disadvantage in various European countries. Tables contrasted the numbers of men and women in government and in management under factual headings— "There are no women Cabinet members in John Major's government" and "Men dominate the higher levels of management in all countries." But the table contrasting the numbers of male and female parents of children under four in the work force was uniquely and unstatedly speculative: "Lack of child care facilities prevents women, as opposed to men, from pursuing their careers."

When media report, even editorialize, on the effects of daycare on children, they usually pick on positive studies and select their most positive results. Jerome Kagan, author of an important American study of daycare, took pains to explain that his experimental daycare facility was as good as unlimited funding, professional expertise, highly trained staff and (middle-class) parental involvement could possibly make it and that *under those circumstances* the daycare children did as well (*on specific measures*) as the matched group of home-reared children. None of his provisos was widely reported at the time or has been since. The study was interpreted as an authoritative pro-daycare statement and remains a classic for its proponents. There are equally authoritative, sometimes more subtle recent studies that raise serious concerns about the effects of daycare on very young children; none has received comparable coverage. The most recent studies convincingly suggest that neither a pro-daycare nor an anti-daycare stance is tenable, because the effects of daycare on children depend on the caring institution and its personnel and on the age, family experiences and characteristics of individual children being cared for. There are many complex questions still to be asked and many subtle answers to be interpreted and tested. Nevertheless, the accepted and acceptable message is that good daycare is OK for kids and more good daycare is better for everybody.

It is easy to see why governments and their institutions are eager to believe that message. They want the best for children, or say they do. But children are nations' "most precious resource" in more than the obvious sense: their individual care is very expensive. Daycare can offer economies of scale on the one hand and jobs on the other. Naturally parents who are seeking more and more daycare for younger and younger infants are looking for economic improvement in their own lives, but not many would do so if they believed that they earned money at their children's expense. Why do they believe that daycare is OK? What sad and subtle subtext tells them that money earned away and spent on their children is more important than time at home spent with their children?

People in Western societies still grow up believing that they will and should be important to their children, but not that the importance is manifest in their reliable presence and constant influence. Of course nobody can say, "At such and such an age your child needs you to be around this many hours a day and any fewer will be disastrous for him or her," but it would be fair to say, "The more you are around, the better, and the younger the child, the more it matters." Yet very few people say that. In North America, especially, there is increasing pressure on parents not just to work while children are very young, but to work from a few weeks after they are born; and not just to work a few hours, but to work as if they were childless, including the commute, the after-work drinks and the expense-account travel. The snappy American term "quality time" tells parents that they can pack all the desirable interaction with their children into a single hour of each working day provided it is a *good* hour. There is just enough truth in the idea to convince those seeking reassurance about what they feel they have to do anyway: of course an hour is better than no time at all and if time is scarce of course it is better not wasted on chores. But still, the concept of "quality time" is absurd. The younger the child, the more impossible it is to schedule togetherness times. You cannot make a tired baby stay awake for a day's worth of cuddling, and trying may be a selfish attempt to salve adult consciences and conflicts at the expense of overstimulated infants. You cannot easily persuade a one-year-old who wanted you to play with him this morning to take his one and only chance and play right now; if he is angry at your desertion he will not let you off the hook that easily. And if you are not there when your toddler's first rhyme is spoken, you will not hear it or see her face as she hears what she has made. Magic moments happen when they happen and the painful truth is that the ones that are missed are gone forever.

People are expected to feel strongly about their children, but not to act upon those feelings. Everybody sympathizes with the pain mothers suffer (only mothers; fathers are seldom mentioned) when they leave their babies to return to work, but there is little sympathy for those who avoid that pain by staying close. Indeed the fact that babies do not have to have their mothers' exclusive care twenty-four hours a day, seven days a week, is increasingly taken to mean that they *should not* have it. There is another snappy term—"smother love"—for that, and it is just as nonsensical as the first one. It is clearly and certainly best for babies to have something close to full-time mother care for six months at least—conveniently linked with breast-feeding—and family care for a further year and better two. Using financial or career penalties to blackmail women into leaving infants who are scarcely settled into life outside wombs that are still bleeding is no less than barbarous.

People are expected to do their best for their children but not to assume that they know best, or are best. The widespread Western cult of the professional teaches that "expert" advisers and "trained caregivers" often know better than parents because parents "are too involved to be objective." The last quality children require of the adults who care for them is objectivity: it is parents' unique tendency to consider their children uniquely wonderful that makes them so special. Professionals can be helpful to parents but they cannot replace them because however much they know about children in general, they know almost nothing about this particular child. Benjamin Spock opened his famous childcare manual of the forties with the message to parents: "You know more than you think you know." Almost half a century later that message urgently needs elaborating: "You know more than you think you know *and a great deal more than anyone else.*"

Agenda Item Three: What Kind of Daycare?

Most of the parents who must leave their infants with outsiders and most of the governments who encourage them to do so favor professional childcare over the arrangements with private individuals which currently provide most daycare places, especially for babies and toddlers. In recent years many countries have controlled "other family care" through various forms of regulation and licensing, and there is no doubt that excellent work is being done by some British childminders, North American daycare mothers and variously named European equivalents. But even the best of this type of care is not generally regarded as desirable or satisfactory. Spokespeople—gray-suited or not—generally explain this by referring to scandals about babies being kept confined in cribs or tied in chairs, dirty, ill-fed and unattended; about toddlers and older children being crowded into inadequate rooms without toys or supervision, and about physical or sexual abuse. They admit that there have been similar scandals in daycare centers and nurseries, but point out that licensing and inspection are more effective in those contexts. They say that licensing of individual caregivers cannot easily prevent these horrors because the demand for places outstrips the supply. Thus unlicensed caregivers (who often undercut the cost of licensed places) stay in business, in the United States, for example, catering to at least three times as many children as regulated caregivers, according to 1991 estimates. Unlicensed caregivers can provide excellent care, of course, just as licensed individuals, and inspected centers, can provide poor care despite meeting minimum physical standards. If "other family care" is wanted, the problems of inspecting and supervising it are not insuperable, and the better they are met, the less likelihood there is that a black market in unlicensed care will operate. In the United Kingdom, for example, a caregiver, rather unfortunately known as a "childminder," has a great deal to gain from registration. She will have opportunities for training, and encouragement to specialize, if she wishes, in the care of children with a variety of special needs. Families seeking childcare may be referred to her by health and welfare workers in the neighborhood. She will receive advice and assistance with matters such as insurance, and in many areas there will also be various backup and social facilities available to her, ranging from a toy library through a play center for all local caregivers and children, to emergency backup in case she, or one of the children, is taken sick. The truth is that institutional daycare offers advantages to adults that have nothing to do with infants' safety or happiness.

Policy-makers assume that there are major economic advantages to institutional care, especially the economy of scale achieved by having one worker looking after, say, five infants or ten preschool children, instead of an individual caregiver who typically looks after only one or two in addition to her own. Furthermore, nursery workers are fully integrated in the labor market, where individual caregivers are often peripheral to it. The individual who takes a child into her home frees his or her parent for employment, but she is often not fully "employed" herself in the sense that she is not "trained," would not take any other kind of job (wishing to remain at home for her own children) and is paid minimal—sometimes undeclared—wages for her childcare services.

These arguments are specious if they are not actually dishonest. The more economy of scale a daycare institution offers, the worse that care will be for the children. Although imaginative organization can make the best of limited resources, a high ratio of adults to children is crucial to quality of care and the younger the children are, the higher that ratio needs to be. The ideal ratio is certainly one adult to one *baby* or six adults to six. Caregivers, like parents, may be able to meet the needs of a baby and of older children at the same time, but where age groups are closely segregated, even the highest ratio recommended in any country for this age group—one adult to three babies—is too low. Good care does not only depend on how many infants each adult must care for, though. It also depends on the qualities of the adults. High(er) pay is crucial to that, of course. But childcare is so labor-intensive that any increase in salaries has a marked effect on total costs—and rapidly reverses economies of scale. Daycare centers are always expensive to run and the better they are, the more they cost. An expert estimate from the United States said that they *ought* to cost $150 per child per week in 1988. At that time parents who were paying for daycare were paying an average of around $55 per week. Perhaps childcare institutions appear economical to policy-makers because, unlike state benefits to unemployed mothers, any public funding can be recouped from parents and/or their employers, and because many centers, especially in North America and increasingly in the United Kingdom, are commercial, profitable concerns. For-profit nurseries increased by more than 60 percent in London between 1985 and 1988.

For parents, daycare centers have both practical and emotional advantages over "other family care." Children are a center's business, so parents assume that their child will be basically well cared for by people who know about safety and hygiene, nutrition and health, education and play. Because a center is a business, it can be more reliable than any individual: always open for its stated hours and days; never down with the flu or pregnant and unlikely to decide that it cannot keep even the most-terrible two. And centers place few personal demands on parents who are already overstretched between home and work. Where a daycare mother has to be made into a friend and kept feeling needed and appreciated, a center asks little more of parents than their money, reasonable punctuality and a few civil words twice a day.

That relative impersonality may be more important to some parents than they themselves realize. Most parents are ambivalent about leaving children with outsiders. When mothers delegate the care of babies or toddlers, they often feel an uncomfortable mixture of guilt because there is not enough love between caregiver and infant, and jealousy because there is too much. Such a mother may find it far more comfortable to leave her child with someone whom she can see as a trained professional in an institutional setting (and therefore quite different from herself at home) than to leave him with someone who is just like herself—except that she is willing to care for the child all day.

Most important of all, though, to policy-makers and parents alike, may be the perception of institutional daycare as "educational" and therefore positively advantageous to children. The popular image of group daycare is a nursery-school image. Whenever daycare issues are publicly debated, television screens are filled with pictures of three- and four-year-olds happily playing together in an enchanting child-scale world of bright rooms, tiny furniture and brilliantly colored "educational toys." These are the images that inform campaigns for more daycare places. This is what people want their children to have.

Parents are right to want their *children* to have that kind of experience, but they are not right to assume that the experience is, or can be, equally valuable for babies. By the time children are around three years old, most of them enjoy and almost all of them benefit from being part of a close-knit group of other children, from close contact with nonfamily adults and trained teachers, and from a wider and more carefully planned range of opportunities, activities and equipment than most private homes can provide. Every child should have the opportunity for preschool educational experience. Its provision in settings variously termed nursery schools, prekindergartens, play groups, play schools or *écoles maternelles* should indeed be a real priority. Much of Western Europe has made it a priority, but in the United Kingdom "preschool education" is still one of the many broken promises of the Thatcher years, while in America, less privileged children, especially the under-fours, are still waiting for the chance of a Head Start.

Babies and toddlers are not waiting for groups to join, though. What is good for most children of three years is not necessarily appropriate for children of thirty months and may be downright harmful to any child of thirteen, let alone three months. The educational tradition that legitimizes preschool centers has no relevance to infants, and their corporate nature—so desirable to policy-makers and reassuring to parents—is developmentally inappropriate for them.

Agenda Item Four: What Infants Need

Older babies and toddlers do not need their mothers every minute; the necessity for "full-time exclusive mothering" has been exposed as a myth of the postwar West. We know that having their care shared between parents and other adults is not damaging to children and may be enriching; that shared care—albeit of many different kinds—has been the norm in every time and place and remains so in many. And we know that lack of people with whom to share childcare is a major problem in Western maternity. Daycare *is* shared care, so why is it not ideal?

The answer comes from a lot of other things we know about children—things that are being conveniently forgotten in the daycare debate. Perhaps the most important is that developmentally infants are *not* children and neither are toddlers—quite. The spiraling strands of development that transform helpless newborns into sociable and socialized small people are plaited into their relationships with known, loved and loving adults. Those adults do not have to be parents or relations but, unfashionable and unpalatable though the fact may be, it is much easier if they are. Mothers start out with an irreplaceable bio-emotional advantage in relating to their infants, and fathers start out with a lesser one that still puts them ahead of any outsider. That does not make every natural mother or father a "good parent" nor handicap every infant raised otherwise, but it does stack the odds and should inform the debate. Whoever it is who cares for infants, they need to have permanence, continuity, passion and a parentlike commitment that is difficult to find or meet outside the vested interests and social expectations of family roles and cannot be adequately replaced by professionalism.

WHY CONTINUOUS INDIVIDUAL CARE
MATTERS TO BABIES

If a new baby wants to suck, she will suck your finger or her own, whichever is handiest. She does not know that she is separate from other people; she recognizes no boundaries between self and other.

The long, slow realization of her separate self starts early. As well as using other people as extensions of herself, the baby uses them as mirrors that reflect her own behavior back to her. In her first days, for instance, she smiles and frowns more or less at random, but within a couple of months she smiles only when she is pleased and sociable and frowns only when she is not. It is the consistently pleased or concerned responses of adults that have taught her which is which.

Responsive and overtly affectionate adults are crucial to all aspects of infants' development. Every time a baby's very existence is celebrated in another spontaneous hug; every time her sounds, expressions and body language are noticed and answered; every time somebody does something just because she seems to want or enjoy it, a tiny piece is added to the foundations of that baby's future self-image, self-confidence and social competence. The more of that sensitive, tuned-in experience a baby gets (and the less of its opposite), the better. We cannot measure out "enough" but we know the likely consequences of strict rationing. After the Second World War, thousands of orphaned and refugee babies were kept in institutions where their care was physically excellent but wholly impersonal. Many of those babies failed to thrive; some died for reasons nobody could quite understand. The researchers of the day eventually concluded that those babies were suffering from "maternal deprivation" but while being with their mothers would certainly have saved them, it was not separation from their particular blood-mothers that removed their will to live but deprivation of individualized, responsive, sociable care. Western countries learned to avoid residential nurseries when they could, and organize those they had to have differently. But the same syndrome became apparent in 1990 when Romania's packed orphanages were revealed to the world. Impersonal residential care is only the greatest, not the only, risky situation. Any personal indifference is damaging to infants, even that of a potentially loving mother who becomes so submerged in postnatal depression that it is all she can do to keep her baby fed and warm and clean and more than she can do to offer herself to him, respond to him, glory in him. An outside caregiver has less reason than a mother to celebrate an infant and therefore needs less cause to be indifferent to him. A nursery worker has less reason still to celebrate this infant because she has others to care for who may overload her or whom she may prefer. How well an infant thrives despite any of those situations probably depends on how much time he also spends with someone who cares not just *for* but *about* him. Three hours a day in an understaffed nursery where he is special to nobody is far from ideal for a newborn, but nine hours a day is far more likely to damage his development.

By around three months or so, infants realize that they are separate from the mothers and others on whom they are totally dependent and then only sensitive and consistent responses can protect them from the lonely fear of being abandoned and from anxiety about their needs being met. If circumstances allow her to do so, a baby will now learn to recognize and distinguish all the people who regularly come and go within her small space, learn what responses to expect from each person and, gradually, learn how to evoke the responses she wants. A baby who expects particular people to respond to her particular signals in their particular ways is confused and distressed when they do not. If a mother who has been smiling and chatting to her three-month-old baby suddenly becomes impassive and silent, the infant will quiet, sober, stare and probably cry. It is not that the adult's silent, serious face is frightening in itself (it certainly would not bother the baby if she was studying her mother who was watching TV, for instance). What upsets that baby is her unexpected failure to manage and control the interaction and evoke a response. She reacts as we react if somebody cuts us in the street: as if the mother had snubbed her, hurting her feelings.

Many people dislike the notion of babies "managing" adults; it makes them sound manipulative and raises peculiarly Western fears that they will become spoiled. But it is only by being allowed, even helped, to find reliable ways of controlling some aspects of adult behavior that a baby can build vital competence and confidence in her own powers of communication. Whether they are six or sixteen months old, most babies try to keep a beloved adult with them all the time and while they are awake, many are successful. Once they fall asleep, though, they cannot prevent adults from leaving; like it or not, they usually wake up alone. If a baby is to accept that calmly—neither fighting to stay awake so as to prevent it, nor panicking when she awakens—she needs to know, from repeated experience, that she can get a parent or accepted substitute (not someone unexpected or strange) back again with a cry or call. All babies are physically helpless, but the babies who *feel* damagingly helpless in the longer term are the ones who cannot trust their special adults to be there and to respond to them.

In the first half-year or so babies are seldom alarmed by strangers (though they may be alarmed by what strangers do). Introduced to an admiring male visitor, for example, a baby will usually try to interact with him as she does with her father. If she does not get the responses she expects she may be puzzled, or obviously turned off, but as soon as she is handed back to familiar arms she will switch on again, and after a while she may willingly give the new person another try. That familiar interlude is vital. She can cope with a stranger for a while, but not with an unbroken succession of strangers. Each presents her with subtly different intonations, expressions and body language and without re-confirmation from someone she knows well, she gradually loses track of who she is. Handed from one stranger to another, a baby may even panic as an adult can panic in a fairground hall of mirrors, seeing a different distortion of himself wherever he turns. When a baby in his third hour in the temporary childcare facility set up at a conference, or third day in a daycare center, suddenly cries and cannot be comforted, he is usually assumed to be crying for loss of his mother; in truth he is more likely to be crying for loss of his own identity and control, vested in his mother and not yet assured by a sufficiently known worker.

Only adults who know, have known and will go on knowing an individual baby can provide that vital sense of trust and growing empowerment. Even the best-intentioned and qualified stranger cannot do it because however much she knows about babies in general, she knows nothing about *this* one. The baby eats lunch; the caregiver goes to put her down for a nap but she cries. Training or experience suggests questions but not answers: Is she crying because she is tired and this is her idiosyncratic way through to the relaxation of sleep? Is she crying because she is not tired and therefore does not, today, want to nap? Or is she crying because some minute difference between the stranger and her accustomed caretaker—her smell, her tone, her arrangement of cuddly toys—has broken the usual progression from full belly to slumber? It does not hurt a baby to have to get to know someone new, especially if someone familiar can stay around while she does it. By tomorrow the stranger will seem less strange; if she is still there in a week or two she will be a known friend. But what if someone else is there tomorrow and someone else next week?

Even beloved adults cannot always understand a baby's messages. When they do understand them, they do not always choose to do or give what the baby wants. That's fine. Babies have to learn to communicate more and more clearly (and eventually to speak) and of course they cannot always have what they want. But adults who are tied to infants in reciprocal affection will always *try* to understand and they will always answer, even if the answer is "no." That is what matters; that is what assures infants that they are real, individual people who can act upon other people, and that is the assurance that will keep them going forward. However carefully she is fed, washed and protected, and however many mobiles are hung for her, a baby's overall care is not good enough to ensure her optimal development unless she is constantly with people who know her as an individual and who always have the time (and usually the inclination) to listen to and answer her, to cuddle and play, show and share. Those are the people she will attach herself to and that attachment matters.

Every baby needs at least one special person to attach herself to. It is through that first love relationship that she will learn about herself, other people and the world, experience emotions and learn to cope with them, move through egocentric baby love into trust and eventually towards empathy and then the altruism that will one day enable her to give another person what she needs for herself now. At least one person. More is better, safer. Babies do not have a fixed quota of devotion: if there are several adults around and available to an infant, she will usually select one for her primary, passionate attachment (and, even today, that will probably be her mother), but each and all of them will be special to her and any one can serve as a life raft when the mother's absence would otherwise leave her drowning in a sea of deserted despair. Every baby will sometimes need a human life raft. The grieving of a baby who loses her one and only special person—her lone mother who dies, for example, or the lifelong foster mother from whom she is removed—is agonizing to see because we know we are looking at genuine tragedy. But the pain of the separations we arrange and connive at every time we change caregivers or leave a baby in the daycare center that has new staff—again—or with an agency babysitter she has never seen, may not be as different as we assume. In her first six, nine or even twelve months, that baby has no way of knowing that the parent who leaves her will come back, no way of measuring the passage of time, no way of holding the parent's image in her mind so as to anticipate her or his return. Only another known and beloved adult can keep her happily afloat.

WHY NURSERIES AND DAYCARE CENTERS SELDOM MEET THOSE INFANT NEEDS

That vital continuous one-to-one attention can rarely be achieved in group care, however excellent the facility may be. Babies in their first year need one primary adult each, and while that may be inconvenient, it is not very surprising. Human beings do not give birth to litters but almost always to single babies. Women can only just feed two at a time (ask any mother of twins) and cannot singlehandedly care for more (ask any mother of triplets). No amount of "training" enables a nursery worker to do better. If one baby is sucking a bottle on her lap when another wakes from a nap and a third drops a toy from his highchair, she cannot respond adequately to them all. If one is unwell and one is tired, she cannot cuddle them both in a way that makes them feel she cares, let alone keep the third busy and safe. And that is three. How many daycare centers really offer a 1:3 adult-child ratio? A recent survey of eighteen British nurseries produced an average ratio of 1:4.6, while data from the comparative licensing study of American states showed that *recommended* ratios for infants ranged from 1:3 in three states to 1:8 in four states. And as all researchers acknowledge, even these figures may overestimate the adult attention available to each baby—as, for example, when two adults have charge of six infants, one will often stay with them while the other cleans up.

In most countries, the majority of daycare centers for infants are not excellent. How could they be? The work is underpaid and undervalued, as well as demanding, so it neither attracts nor keeps high-quality staff. As a recent report to the European Commission put it: "Childcare workers . . . are amongst the lowest paid of women workers. . . . The conditions of work are also often very poor. . . . Often the pressure of work is such that workers are too exhausted to even think about their work, let alone improve it."

Although both parents and policy-makers assume that center care is professional care, this is seldom true for children under three. In this one respect, the United Kingdom fares better than much of the European Community because it has a well-established diploma-level Nursery Nurses' qualification. In those eighteen British nurseries, only 20 percent of the staff lacked any formal training. In most EEC countries, however, it is rare for those who work in daycare centers with this age group to have childcare qualifications of any kind, and in many countries even the basic educational requirements for entry to the work are minimal. In the United States, where federal standards have been abolished and each state makes its own childcare regulations, the current situation is best summed up by the researchers who studied comparative licensing: "The possibility of having a 'qualified' staff is virtually non-existent. . . . In a majority of states, the existing regulations allow these very young children to be cared for by a staff that would have a mean age of 18, has not graduated from high school, and has no previous group day-care experience."

Although higher salaries are desperately needed, and might help to attract higher-caliber staff (although they would also raise the costs of care), a real improvement in standards would also require training, better working conditions and career opportunities. Unfortunately, every such concession to adult needs further reduces fulfillment of the children's. The daycare center's working day, for example, has to be longer than a full office day to allow for parental commuting. Center staff's working hours can be reduced by splitting the day into two shifts, but that immediately doubles the number of people with whom infants must interact. As soon as nursery workers are also given proper lunch hours and breaks, sick leave, vacation entitlement, in-service training, educational leave and encouragement to relocate for promotion, there is such constant staff movement that babies are likely to be handled by several different people each day and are unlikely to be handled by those same people all week: some will inevitably be strangers to some of the children, filling in for the known caregivers who are already filling in for parents. And still nursery workers leave. In North America the annual turnover of childcare staff is around 42 percent, and aides come and go even more frequently. It is not uncommon for a group of children to have three "mother figures" in a year. If each baby is not fully attached to each successive caregiver, she will spend many days in limbo; if she is fully attached she will spend many days in grief.

WHEN INFANTS BECOME TODDLERS

When somebody of eighteen months in jeans and sneakers struts across the room yelling "No, go 'way!" the unwary onlooker may easily mistake him for a child—and one who is ready to leave his mom. But the autonomy of the toddler is as much an illusion as his toughness. Both are to be fostered but neither can be relied upon. Treated as a clinging baby, he fights, but treated as the sturdy child he sometimes seems to be, he instantly becomes—a clinging baby. The drive to grow up—to become an autonomous child—constantly conflicts with the need for the safe dependence of infancy.

This is the stage in children's lives when adults rightly begin to demand new, socialized behavior, from using a potty instead of a diaper, to *saying* no instead of grabbing and hitting. Those demands are appropriate (if gently made) because they are within the toddler's developmental repertoire and important to his eventual acceptance in a wider and less tolerant world than family, but they offer him no obvious reward. His socialization depends on that conflict-laden desire to grow up, and the only way to foster it is to resist pushing him forward but to let him lead the way and fall back when he frightens himself. "Me do it! Go 'way!" he yells, faced with his coat. But he does not mean "Don't help me and don't stay with me"; he means something like "Give me space (about eighteen inches) and time (about thirty seconds) to have a try and then help me so that I can feel successful instead of being overwhelmed by frustration and fury."

Toddlers live on an emotional seesaw between babyhood and childhood, tears and tantrums. They need their special adults to stand on the center and balance it, to let them try but still be willing to help, to let them express their sharp new feelings but to control their actions when they cannot control themselves, to let them disagree without finding them disagreeable. Out of all that comes yet another kind of trust—the toddler's trust that his special adults will not only control him when he feels like a murderous monster but will go on accepting and loving him when he behaves like one. If unconditional love is important to the biddable baby who means no harm, it is vital to the balky toddler who must pit himself against parents to see whether the limits of their patience with what he *does* also mark limits to their acceptance of what he *is*. Only when he is certain that there are no limits to that will he be sure that it is safe to be himself—to become a genuinely autonomous (if still very small and inexperienced) person.

The toddler will not be ready for a classroom (or even a "toddler room") until he has crossed that bridge of trust into early childhood. Parents and the other people who are special to him are the pilings of that bridge and it will not hold steady beneath him if they keep being pulled up and replaced. Unfortunately, even parents who have given or arranged for individual one-on-one care during infancy are often overwhelmed by the pressures towards group care in the second year. Sometimes a substitute caregiver who loved a baby is unwilling or unable to cope with what she sadly labels a "terrible two." Sometimes some of that terribleness looks like boredom and the educational value of the group that would stop him being bored becomes more credible and more tempting. If school is going to be good for him when he's three, won't sending him at two be a head start (as well as a convenience)?

The fact that a toddler is bored with a caregiver (whether or not she or he is his mother or father) does not mean that he is bored of being adult-centered, but only that he is ready for new activities. He finds other children fascinating and will enjoy spending time playing near and alongside them, but that does not mean that he is ready to make real friends and be their classmate. His toddler activities mimic those of preschool children: he, too, wants to paint and climb and sing and cook, but, unlike those three-year-olds, his enjoyment and his learning depend on adult participation or at least adult support and commentary. And, far from being even a partial replacement for that individual adult attention, a group of other toddlers—each as needful of the adult as himself—introduces competition and social stresses he is not yet capable of dealing with. Of course he will have to learn to deal with them—learn to share toys, to take turns, to argue his case with words rather than blows and to give way gracefully—but he cannot do so without the trusted control of his own particular adult until he is capable of putting himself in another child's shoes so as to "do unto others as he would they should do unto him." For most children, that is a third-year development. In the meantime, and especially as the numbers of only children and of isolated caregivers increase, there is a real need for places where they can go together to meet and play with others as they can in the United Kingdom's extensive (though scattered) network of adult-and-toddler clubs and drop-in centers.

Everyone who lives or works with toddlers knows that they are not well adapted to group life. Nevertheless many people believe that joining a group before he is developmentally ready can accelerate a toddler's readiness: that the experience and the teachers will help him grow up and, above all, help his speech, his independence and his sociability. Research suggests otherwise. A major British study, for example, showed that under-threes talk and are talked to far less in group than in domestic situations, even where the preschool teacher was well trained and the mother or caregiver at home was not especially child-centered or communicative. As for learning to be sociable, outgoing and independent: Zigler's 1988 paper on the effects of daycare summarizes many studies to suggest that early daycare may foster those "virtues" to excess: "From the research carried out to date, a tentative consensus emerges that . . . children who have experienced early group care tend towards assertiveness, aggression, and peer rather than adult orientation." A 1990 study from the Institute of Human Development at the University of California even suggests that, beloved though they are of North American adults, those virtues may not be virtues at all in small children. Looking back over the lives of mature adults who had been studied from infancy the researchers found that "men who were rated as dependent in childhood emerge in adulthood with a quite distinctive catalog of impressive attributes . . . calm, warm, giving, sympathetic, insightful, undefensive, incisive, consistent across roles, comfortable with ambiguity and uncertainty, and socially poised."

It really does seem that the appropriate use of professionally staffed daycare centers is for children who are well into their third year or more, able to cope with the inevitable discontinuities of care and to benefit from the group life and the educational tradition that are premature for younger age groups.

So who *is* to care for infants and young toddlers when family members are not available?

Agenda Item Five: Buying Individual Care

There is nothing new about paying women to look after children, but there is something new about using money as the sole motivation for the task. Generations of privileged Western children have been reared wholly or partly by housekeepers and nannies, at home and all over empires. But being a traditional nanny was something closer to a way of life than to a job as we know it and the tradition depended on an ample supply of women for whom a lifetime spent suspended somewhere between the drawing room and the servants' hall (or the native or slave quarters) was preferable to the available alternatives. A children's mammy in the southern states of America or their ayah in India had contact with, and protection from, the ruling race and often some advancement for their own offspring too. In Britain, the First World War killed so many men that thousands of women were left with no prospect of marriage and homes of their own, at a time when it was scarcely possible for females to earn and live independently. Becoming nannies—or governesses if they had some education—was a dignified alternative to domestic service. Such women valued their autonomy in the nursery domain and the household's protection and reflected status. Wages were scarcely relevant.

Employing a nanny (or any in-home caregiver) no longer implies great wealth and in countries where wages are low and unemployment rates high, their numbers are booming. It is estimated that there are more than 100,000 trained nannies employed in the United Kingdom alone, and according to Fallows, 6 percent of American under-fives were already cared for in this way in 1985. Many more children in both countries are cared for by "au pairs." So is an individual caregiver who comes to, or lives in, the child's own home the answer for women who want to work outside it? It may well answer the childcare needs of fortunate individuals but it cannot answer society's because the system cannot be comfortably translocated into the supposedly equalitarian marketplaces of modern Western life.

Paid one-on-one care by someone brought in from outside the family offers no economies of scale: the mother simply replaces herself with somebody else. If the household is to make anything out of the arrangement, she must pay the nanny less than she herself can earn, after taxes, outside the home. But who is going to want to fill, as a job, the role with someone else's child that the mother does not wish to fill with her own? The answer, of course, is only someone of lower earning potential than the mother and that almost always means someone lower down each society's own educational and status ladder. Whether that matters to the child or not, it does not suggest a high valuation for children as a group, or high respect for the job of caring for them. Perhaps we have not moved as far as we like to think from those old colonialist traditions.

The system does not only affect the employer's children, either. Many caregivers have children of their own. What kind of care are those children getting while their mothers care for the children of other people who are doing something different? A pregnant California mother of a one-year-old explained to me how the system works with Mexican nannies and added: "I nearly fired her when she got pregnant soon after me, but she's got a sister with five kids and when she's too big to work, she'll take care of them and the sister will come work for me. Then when she's had her baby, she'll leave it with her sister and come back. Bring the baby with her and care for them both together? No way. I'm not paying her to look after her own child, I'm paying her to look after mine." There were eight children, three mothers and one father involved in those arrangements. Was *any* of the children going to have as good a childhood—let alone a better one—than he or she would have had if society had taken it for granted that parents care for their own?

Attempts have been made to dignify the role of paid caregiver by making childcare into a professional, specialized job and, above all, by separating it from domestic responsibilities. A trained British nanny will not expect to undertake anything but childcare and will not expect to work all day and then get up for night feedings and nightmares. So, at the end of the working day the employer finds herself doing household chores that would have been done while the baby napped if she had been in charge, cooking a meal for the nanny who is now off duty and facing yet another broken night. The truth is that no single salary can pay an individual to do everything mothers are expected to do for love, and no single salary ever has. Traditional nannies had nursery-maids of their own.

So what about the less professional, less specialized "mother's helper"? She certainly commands less money and accepts more chores; she may even accept a job description that says she will do anything the mother would otherwise do. But why should she want to? Surely she will find being at home with the baby just as lonely and boring as the mother would? There is a difference between them—she gets paid a small wage where the mother gets paid nothing—but does that really counterbalance the other difference: that it is neither her home nor her baby? Mothers do what they do because, overall, they like it, or like some parts of it enough to put up with the rest. If they do not, nobody else is likely to, and money alone is not going to make them do it well and go on doing it.

Of all the kinds of purchased daycare currently available, the kind that is most likely to meet the needs of infants, as opposed to preschool children, is not institutional group care, not pseudo-professional care by nannies and their like, but the best of the licensed "other family care" that parents and policy-makers tend to regard as second-best.

Women who take children into their own homes on a daily care basis—daycare mothers in North America, childminders in Britain—mostly look after other people's so as to be able to go on looking after their own. They tend, therefore, to be people who recognize the value of their parenting to their own children—which is why they do not want to ration or withdraw it in a hurry—and who are confident that the parenting skills learned on those children can be valuable to others. Such women often see the "mothering" of one or two other children at a time as the continued exercise of skills they are proud of, within a life-style they enjoy, or at least prefer to other currently available options.

It is often easier for parents to make, and keep, a comfortable relationship with a caregiver in her home than in their own because the caregiver functions more like a member of the extended family than like their employee. The relationship is an equal partnership focused on what really matters—the child's well-being and happiness—rather than diffused over other concerns that can seem to matter (like whether she runs up the telephone bill or uses the best coffee). The baby joins an ongoing household where his new caregiver is clearly in charge and has her own routine into which he is welcomed. It may take him a little longer to settle with her than with a babysitter or nanny who comes into his own familiar home, but once he has done so her busy household may feel less lonely and strange than his own does without parents. Her household responsibilities can be an advantage too. Any nine-month-old would rather go shopping and then play while watching someone cook than be with someone who has nothing to do but watch him—or the soaps. And her own, older children may enrich his life as brothers and sisters might. Unlike the other infants in a daycare center, they are not at his age stage and therefore direct competitors for her attention; rather they are objects of fascination and admiration whose comings and goings keep his days varied and interesting.

Such arrangements do not always work out well, of course, but where they do the similarities with extended family care are inescapable. Although daycare mothers are paid for their services—and should be paid more—their motivation is only partly commercial and their involvement with individual children and their families is a large part of their reward. Some come to function as extended family not just for children but for their parents, especially for those who are alone. Sometimes the relationship outlives infancy and toddlerhood. Some childminders take children to playgroups, just as their mothers might, and to nursery schools when they are ready for preschool education. When geography allows, it is even sometimes that original infant caregiver who provides the six- or seven-year-old with after-school care.

Although this is an idealized picture of other family care as it is in many countries, experience in the United Kingdom suggests that it need not be unrealistic. Offered some training, and community backup along with registration, some British childminders can, and do, offer daycare that is quality care for infants.

Agenda Item Six: Own-Family Care

The more closely the search for alternatives to own-family care for infants is studied, the more absurd it seems because the kind of daycare that works best is the kind that most closely approximates it.

Babies and toddlers need individual care, consistently given by the same known and loving adults.

The needs of the youngest among them can only be fully met if much of that care is given by their mothers. Most daycare advocates gloss over babies' need to be breast-fed and to establish the primary attachments on which later development depends, but I am aware of none who deny it. Regular all-day separation in the first six months means that the baby cannot be fully breast-fed; furthermore, it means that the nursling relationship between baby and mother (which can, of course, be maintained if she uses bottles rather than her breasts) is diluted. The baby will be fine if he has a single, continuously available, long-term alternative person to attach himself to (his father, perhaps, or the rare kind of in-home caregiver who really is psychologically part of his family). The mother will be fine if she feels no sense of long-term loss. But those are large ifs.

As the first months pass, infants' care can gradually be more and more extensively shared with other consistent, individual caregivers, but there is not yet any positive advantage to the infant in it being so, and if the only "sharing" available to the mother means substituting an outsider's care for her own, there may well be disadvantages. However taxing an infant's care may be for his or her own family, few other caregivers are ever going to do it as well as most parents because nobody will ever do as much for money alone as they will do for that atavistic mystery we call parental love. So why are Western societies so sure that the future lies with daycare rather than with parent care?

If the search for alternatives to parental care is absurd, so is the popular belief that there must *be* widely available alternatives because parents cannot and do not want to care for their own infants. It is true that many two-parent families cannot manage on one income and that lone parents cannot manage on none. It is true that many women, still underprivileged in the work force, do not want to leave it to be part of a specially underprivileged subgroup called stay-at-home mothers, and that few men even consider it. And it is true that it is difficult for parents to put children first if doing so ensures that they themselves come last. What is not true is that those are the inevitable results of making one or two children the major commitment of two or three years of a forty-year working life.

We need to think again, not from where we are into a nostalgic past, but from where we are into where we could choose to go. How can young children's needs best be met in the socio-economic circumstances of today?

New Models for the New Debate: Sweden

Mention Sweden in a discussion of social policy with North Americans or the British and everybody sighs. They are tired of having Sweden held up as a model, certain that it must be living off the fat of a small population and large resource base and sure that its welfare policies must mean that it is a "welfare state" in the sense that is anathema to Western free enterprise. So great is some people's irritation that they raise the old myth of Sweden's high suicide rate, or the new failure of her social democratic party to hold on to office, as if any evidence of Swedish discontent could somehow invalidate her family policies. Such issues are irrelevant because nobody is suggesting that other nations should model themselves on Sweden in every respect. Swedish family policies—and those of other Scandinavian countries—are a model in a different sense: a model of new ways of thinking about women and men, about families and especially about children—the best example there is of the new alternatives that are opened up by different priorities. In this sense it matters not at all whether Sweden's new government will hold the same priorities. What matters is that a similar shift in *our* priorities might work for *us*.

Like most Western nations Sweden has been hard-hit by world recession but, relative to others, it remains an economically successful country with a strong and internationally competitive industrial base built on labor force concerns such as getting more women into the work force and investing in training, retraining and, where necessary, job creation schemes.

Sweden is not a welfare state in the sense of relying heavily on state benefits. All adults are expected to work; earnings, rather than national insurance–funded benefits, are the assumed source of income for everyone of working age. But employment is seen more as a means of funding a desirable life-style than as a way of life. Wider concerns such as equality for all, family life and child welfare are considered crucial to the whole society's well-being, and both individuals and policies demonstrate a determination to balance paid work with leisure activities.

Children are not regarded as a leisure activity for parents, though. They are both seen and treated as citizens, as clearly entitled to have their needs met as any other group. Parenting (by fathers as well as mothers) is considered to be something children need and the arrangements for parent care are organized as children's entitlement rather than for parents to use on their behalf. For example, daycare (almost universally available to follow parental leave) receives direct public funding so that it benefits all children equally rather than operating selectively, as the cash and tax benefits channeled through parents in other countries so often do. Yet this is not the nanny state dreaded by the West's more conservative governments. As a matter of policy, central provision and administration of services are avoided. Daycare is not provided in state-run nurseries but largely by local authorities, with public funding also going to voluntary associations, parent cooperatives and even individual initiatives.

In order to ensure that all children have equal access to their parents, irrespective of the jobs those parents do, all employment arrangements affecting parenting are universal legal entitlements rather than something left to collective bargaining or to individual firms. This is a vital point. It means that unlike children in many Western countries, Swedish children cannot lose out on parental care because their parents work for unsympathetic employers or in high-status competitive fields, such as the media, where even if a maternity leave is offered, a mother may dare not risk dropping out of view. Nor can children in Sweden benefit unfairly from having parents who are privileged to set their own hours and terms. It is accepted that children need their parents; the existence of a child is therefore the sole qualification for employment arrangements that free parents to meet that need.

Swedish employment arrangements are based on two important Scandinavian assumptions. The first is that men and women are equally responsible for their children, not only financially but in terms of their daily care, their well-being and happiness. Some people in North America believe that mothers and fathers *should be* equally responsible; some countries of the EEC are trying to *make* them equally responsible, but only in Scandinavia is it accepted, in attitudes, policy and practice, that it *is* so.

The second important assumption is that parenthood must not disadvantage people either in terms of their present earnings or in terms of their future prospects. There are other societies that protect the *earnings* of parents but they do so at the expense of their active parenting. China, for example, expects parents to continue working as if they were childless and thus provides universal, publicly funded daycare—even residential care or boarding school if work involves travel or irregular hours. Other campaigns in the West would like to see parental *income* protected but at the expense of participation in work: by parents caring for their own children and being given a state childcare allowance. Either approach disassociates the role of parent from the role of worker: Scandinavian policies crucially integrate the two.

Sweden's policies acknowledge the importance of personal parenting to children, the importance of work outside the home to adults and the importance of both to the whole society, by making the care of their children something that parents do *within* their ongoing outside work. Parents do not give up work, they take parental leave. Their parenting is not supported by state benefits paid at a special (and especially low) rate, but by a universal tax on employers that pays for the continuation of 90 percent of the wage or salary they had already achieved. And since mothers do not leave work, they do not face a problematical return. Parental leave is like the temporary assignment of a professional or the sabbatical of an academic; it is not at all like being unemployed.

Every baby born brings an entitlement to eighteen months' parental leave. That leave can be taken by either parent (after a two-week paternity leave that enables both parents to be together with their new baby) or shared between them. It can be taken in one immediate full-time block, spread part-time over a longer period or taken in shorter blocks. Parents can, for example, stay at home until children are fifteen months and keep three months' further entitlement for use at particular times such as school entry. If there is more than one child, of course, there will be sequential parental leave entitlements and the first child may benefit from the period that "belongs" to the second. That parental leave need not be used for everyday problems such as illness, though. Each child also entitles his or her parents to leave of up to ninety days per year for "family reasons" until he or she reaches the age of eight. This very generous entitlement protects the small number of families with a chronically sick child, a child with special needs or one who has undergone physical or emotional trauma, but is not abused by others. The average number of days taken per child per year is under ten—no more than is taken by many British or American parents who can only nurse sick children by pretending to be sick themselves.

But there is more to come. Once parental leave has been used up, parents are entitled to work a six-hour day until their youngest child's eighth birthday. This not only deals with the problem of after-school care for the most vulnerable age group, it can also dramatically reduce the hours younger children must spend in daycare services. The promised extension of parental leave to cover the first thirty months of life, rather than the first eighteen, is not likely to be honored in the near future, but many parents of toddlers stagger their working hours so that one goes late and the other comes home early and only the hours between, say, 10 a.m. and 3 p.m. must be covered by nonparental care.

All these leave entitlements are paid at 90 percent of the parent's wages. Allowing for some probable savings on work-associated housekeeping, clothing and transportation costs, there is virtually no financial loss to an individual parent who stays at home. Even in Sweden, though, there is still a tendency for less well-paid jobs to be done by women and this means that it is sometimes more expensive for families when men undertake the at-home role. If a man earns $50,000 per year and his partner earns $30,000 per year, 10 percent of his salary loses the family $5,000, where 10 percent of her salary loses it only $3,000. Those financial differences do not prevent full-time fathering but probably limit it. It is the male partner who takes parental leave in about 30 percent of Swedish families.

Generous financial arrangements and job security make it comparatively easy for Swedish parents to stay at home with their babies and toddlers but, judging by other countries, they are certainly not the whole reason why parents do so. In most Western countries, poverty prevents millions of people from giving their children personal care, but nowhere does wealth alone make them feel that they can. In North America, for example, there is no positive correlation between wealth and the willingness to undertake full-time childcare, though there is a negative correlation with poverty. At least as important in the Swedish system are the attitudes of employers, colleagues and friends and the actual quality of home-based life. Swedish women who want to be with their young children do not have to give up work and its associated status and financial independence: they merely take an expected and accepted break in an ongoing career. In doing so they do not revert to a traditional "woman's role" but move forward into a modern parental role that is considered equally appropriate to men. And by being at home they do not isolate themselves in solitary stress or in exclusively female company; every community contains many households where one or the other parent is at home with a baby or small child and suffering no financial or social loss of status for being so.

Of course new parents in Sweden still have difficult decisions to make about the timing, caring and sharing of their children, but they also have genuine choices. So what do they choose? Most couples, and lone parents, avail themselves of almost all the provisions available to them: to put an infant into daycare is very unusual; to work a forty- (let alone fifty-) hour week while children are small is rare, and not to stay at home when a child is sick, needs a medical or dental appointment or has a birthday or a function at school is unheard of.

Scandinavian countries have conducted a debate about children's care rather than daycare, about people as parents rather than women as mothers, about people's perpetual right to earn and care rather than their right to choose one or the other. Swedish policies, built up over sixty years, have worked for Sweden. As I write—in 1993—they are under threat by an insecure coalition government pledged to improve the country's finances at their expense. But that coalition faces powerful opposition from another: a coalition of women spanning the political spectrum who have formed themselves into The Women's Party, pledged to defend the social welfare system and the jobs within it that have brought them closer to gender equality than women anywhere else in the world. Sweden's debate and the attitudes and the thinking behind it are available to every country in the Western world. Contained within them is an answer to all the policy-makers and politicians who say "we cannot afford it." Let us hope that it will not be *only* women who finally convince them that we must.

Children are people with needs as real as, if different from, our own, and with an equal right, as citizens like us, to have them met. Parents are people too with special needs, for the moment, because their children need them and they need to meet their children's needs. Ask them.

— 5 —

Growing Up Takes Time

At a party, late on and liquored, a father describes the results of his two-year-old son's routine developmental assessment and ends, " 'Coming along nicely' just won't do and 'average' is an insult. I don't want him to be average, I want him to be best."

All parents everywhere want the best for their growing children, but parents in Western societies are particularly inclined to confuse that with making them *be* the best. Once children reach adolescence, such parents cheer (or yell) for them to make the grades, pass the exams and get into the jobs or colleges that usher in adult success. Even while their children are babies, many parents find it hard to accept that the best a child can have is every possible, peaceful opportunity for optimal personal development, and "the best" he or she can be, at any time, is the person that development has produced. Too many Western parents treat the few testable benchmarks of aspects of development as measures of "progress," emphasizing what babies can *do* rather than glorying in the people they are becoming.

All age groups have been invited to the party. A smiley baby girl is carried from adult to adult, and after the obligatory "Isn't she lovely?" almost everyone asks, "How old is she now?" Two older babies crawl among the crowd; one uses the couch to pull himself to a standing position and the mother of the other quickly points out to anyone who will listen that her baby—who does not do that yet—is "younger than he looks." A three-foot person pushes over a two-foot person and someone remarks that she is "old enough to know better" while, over in the corner, smothered but admiring laughter greets the child who thanks his hostess for a "'ceptionally nice party." *How* old is he now? Just as the adults seem unable to interact with each other until each knows what the other "does" ("He works on Wall Street but I'm just a mother, I'm afraid") so they seem unable to relate to any child until he or she has been slotted into an age bracket. The parents are not surprised; exact answers—"three months and four days," "four next week"—trip smoothly off their tongues. Their children's position on the calendar is never far from their consciousness, being used, from the beginning, to judge the legitimacy of their needs, the appropriateness of their demands and the adequacy of their progress. A new baby's cries at 3 a.m. say she is hungry but it is the calendar that says whether or not she ought to be. An older baby crawls across the floor or gets to his feet, and again it is the calender rather than his face that tells his parents how to react. If he is "only" six months or nine months old they will be triumphant; if he is "already" twelve or eighteen months old their dominant emotion will be relief at this evidence that their beloved baby is catching up. Catching up with what or whom? With "age norms" from a book or developmental chart, with the expectations of a daycare center or grandparent or with the "superior" performance of a niece or neighbor who, horror of horrors, is younger than he is? This father's frankness may have been unusual but his sentiments are not.

It is not surprising that parents demand excellence from their offspring. Rearing children is a major pragmatic and narcissistic investment. All parents expect a return on it and all returns relate to children's performance. There is always a bargain between the generations although its existence is not always acknowledged or its nature understood. In times and places where the work of even very young children has economic value, and grown ones are obligated to support their aging relatives, outsiders see an obvious pragmatic return for parents and often underestimate or ignore the narcissistic return which is part and parcel of it. In modern post-industrial regions, where economic resources flow from parents to children rather than the other way around and parents may face peak financial commitments to children (such as college fees) just as their earning power dwindles towards compulsory retirement, the absence of a pragmatic return on procreation throws the narcissistic return into high relief, though insiders usually deny it. Citizens of "advanced nations" like to believe that they have babies for altruistic rather than selfish reasons. But when parents across the globe are asked why they have children, what their children are for, all their answers are remarkably similar. We all have children for ourselves and our pleasure. We all want them to make us feel good, to raise our self-esteem and self-respect and therefore the esteem and respect accorded to us by others. In order to make parents feel good, children must succeed according to whatever cultural values are locally prevalent, and it is here, in the nature of the success that will make people proud to be parents, that the real differences lie. Children may succeed in their parents' eyes by contributing to family survival or prosperity with labor, marriage or procreation; by honoring gods, ancestors or traditions; by fulfilling a range of duties and obligations to other people, implicit in their names or membership of the group into which they were born. But for those steeped in the ethos of the post-industrial West, the dominant values are primarily individualistic and competitive.

Our children have not only a right but a duty to fulfill their "personal potential." Membership on the team is fine, but being its leader is better. And whatever our particular code of ethics and morals, ends justify such a wide range of means that "let the best person win" easily elides into "one who wins is the best," according to a lexicon that often equates personal initiative with sharp practice.

For parents living here and now, then, within that broad value system, a desire for children to achieve not only individual excellence but excellence relative to others is readily understandable. Nevertheless, their determination to demonstrate it from day one in an endless series of nursery comparisons is unfortunate. The evaluation of childish accomplishments by the speed with which they are achieved, rather than by their quality, range or utility, contradicts much of what is known of the nature of human development and is demonstrably counterproductive.

Child development is a process, not a race. In the first years each infant recapitulates the evolutionary stages that produced humanity, so major landmarks like walking and talking are important and exciting. But that does not mean that it is necessarily better to reach them faster and pass them sooner. The modern infant *is* human and therefore *will* become a biped and communicate in speech. She is not a better example of her species because she does these things at an earlier age than average, nor does infant precocity predict adult excellence. We behave as if the child who walks earliest will run fastest, as if exceptionally early single words predict meaningful later sentences and as if children's prospects as intelligent, independent and socialized people can be improved by speeding them through age-appropriate illiteracy, dependence or incontinence. It is not so, and there is abundant research evidence to prove it, even though much of it is based on testing procedures that do indeed measure performance against the calendar.

Developmental tests for infants try to cover the whole child by considering his development in each of several areas. "Motor development" covers progress towards walking and beyond, via those best-known milestones: sitting alone, crawling and standing. "Language" covers progress towards fluent, grammatical speech via listening, responding to and understanding the speech of others, and via communicating in sounds, labeling familiar objects with names, using single words and phrases. "Social development" ranges from smiling in the first weeks and give-and-take games in the first months to self-care in the second year, while "cognitive development" (often misconstrued as a baby IQ test) attempts to assess aspects of thinking and reasoning via play tasks with standardized objects. The child's score in each area is related to the average of scores achieved by large samples of other children of the same chronological age, and his individual result is then presented as an age score. Children always produce a scatter of scores from area to area. A ten-month-old may perform at thirteen-month level on motor items, at eleven-month level on verbal items and at the nine-month level on social or cognitive items. Does that mean that he is "advanced" in walking and talking and "behind" in social skills? Yes and no. The scores may be valid for today (though nobody can know whether the performance he gave was the "best" he could give or merely the best he felt like giving at this particular time and with this particular person) but that does not mean that they are a valid statement of his development even relative to the other infants whose scores make up the norms. If that child is tested again six months later he will again produce a scatter of scores but it will probably be a different scatter. Now, at sixteen months, he performs all motor items at sixteen-month level so that he is no longer "advanced" but "average" in motor development. His verbal development has also "dropped back" and he now tests out at the thirteen-month level, which is below rather than above his chronological age, but both his social and his cognitive scores have risen to scores of sixteen months and eighteen months, respectively. Test him yet again when he is two and the natural peaks and lags of development will probably produce equally unpredictable scores.

Babies are born already programmed with a map of the long and complex route towards maturity and beyond, and with the drive to travel along it. The route is the same for every child in the world but the scale of the map is too small to show the millions of minor roads and scenic routes, diversions and disasters, roadblocks and resting places that make each developmental journey unique within unimaginable human diversity. Just as a road map states total distances between major cities but neither predicts nor prescribes individual journey times, so the developmental map is confined to neuro-biological distances between sequential landmarks. Babies cannot dance before they run, run before they walk, walk before they stand or stand before they sit. But exactly how long each one will spend at or between these stage points on the track nobody can know. Nobody should care, either, because it is not a racetrack and there are no prizes for the one who gets there first nor, barring serious long-term physical problems, penalties for the one who gets there last. Babies do what they have to do when they are ready to do it whether or not adults try to motivate or teach them and even if circumstances seem against them. A heavy plaster cast may delay a baby's first attempts to pull herself to her feet but it will not long delay her walking because, if she is developmentally ready to walk when that cast is removed, she will make up for any lost time by spending less on the preliminaries. Released from casts and sitting position at twelve months, some such babies pull themselves to supported standing, cruise around furniture, let go to stand alone and then walk independently before they are fifteen months old. It should not surprise us. Our pushy passion for leg-strengthening floor play, for baby walkers "to give him the feel of his feet" and for spending hours holding small hands while we cry, "Walk to mommy, darling," is a parallel route rather than a shortcut on that map. Navajo Indian babies who had been kept more or less immobile in cradleboards throughout most of their first year walked at exactly the same average age as other American babies reared in California or Boston.

A baby's performance today says very little that is useful about his likely performance next year. As long ago as 1970 the psychologist who developed the most widely used of all infant development scales, the Bayley Mental Development Index, wrote: "The findings of these early studies of mental growth of infants have been repeated sufficiently often so that it is now well established that test scores earned in the first year or two have relatively little predictive validity." But that does not mean that developmental tests are useless; it simply means that we tend to misuse them. Skilled assessment of the development of populations of infants, or of specified subgroups within populations, is an invaluable research tool. Without standardized scores we should never have discovered, for example, that many aspects of the development of groups of infants tested by the Gesell Institute during the 1970s were advanced by almost six months over the development of similar groups, similarly tested, during the 1930s—invaluable findings to policy-makers concerned with childcare or education. Such testing can also be a potent weapon in the hands of those who seek to establish the ill-effects of specific kinds of deprivation and then to measure the efficacy of intervention programs such as Head Start. It is the testing of individual children that requires such caution. Useful as a way for professionals to screen for difficulties, such as deafness, that might otherwise go undetected for long enough to cause global developmental problems, such testing is a misleading procedure for parents seeking confirmation of their children's "intelligence" or "advancement" and a dangerous tool in the hands of those looking to speed up the "progress" of children whose overall development gives no realistic cause for concern. As Gesell, father of developmental assessment, pointed out, it is not superior performance in one or all fields that differentiates even highly gifted children from others, but a far more nebulous quality of vividness and vitality: "the infant with superior equipment exploits his physical surroundings in a more varied manner, and is more sensitive and responsive to his social environment . . . the scorable end-products may not be far in advance, but the *manner* of performance is superior."

If parents would look at their children's "manner of performance" rather than at *what* is performed or its date on the calendar, they would see individuals in all their complexity rather than in their age bracket, see all the things they do that have never been studied rather than the things they do not yet do and "should," see who they are rather than how they compare with others. Achieving head control, rolling over, sitting up, crawling and standing, for example, are genuine milestones along the road to becoming a biped but while being a biped is a necessary condition for being a person, it certainly is not a sufficient one. When a two-month-old baby begins to roll himself over, he is not just demonstrating an achievement in neuromuscular control, he is experiencing the vital new autonomy of being able to change his own view from the crib or changing table, to release an arm that has been trapped beneath his body or to keep his mother in view as she moves around the room. When he can sit alone he is not just halfway to an upright posture but freed from the restrictions imposed on him by having to lie down or be propped, so that he can more easily reach out for things with his arms and coordinate his hands and eyes in manipulating objects. Being a sitter enormously enriches his interaction with people and playthings. What he does as he sits has real importance; it matters far more than the speed with which he stops "just" sitting and begins to crawl or stand. Continually looking for further accomplishment, parents deprive both themselves and their children of peaceful pleasure in their joint present.

The assumption that children who go fastest go farthest is so deeply entrenched in our society that it is not surprising parents accept it. It is there in the baby books that tell new mothers their babies "ought" to sleep through the night at six weeks old, sit at six months and read at six years; it is there on the packaging of "educational" toys that say "suitable for ages 9–18 months" and imply that the baby in that age group who disregards them is backward rather than uninterested or busy with other things. And it is there in the time-framed obstacles some childcare workers and teachers set up: "we cannot take your child until he is out of diapers . . ."; "we expect our three-year-olds to know their colors and the days of the week." Talk to individual parents about their children's separate accomplishments, and most will agree that it does not *really* matter if a baby prefers crawling to construction toys, or if a preschool child has learned a lot of nursery rhymes but no colors. But most of them still believe that *overall* "advancement" must be a

Good Thing. The angry father we met at the beginning of this chapter certainly did: "He's quick at *everything* and always has been. He walked sooner than most; he talks better; he draws well, washes his own face, does puzzles meant for older kids—you can't tell me he's not bright." Nobody had told him his child was not bright. The pediatrician had told him he was normal and since he wanted to be told his child was a genius, he found that insulting. How he would have envied the father of a five-day-old baby I met last year: "Isn't he really great?" he responded to my congratulations. "The pediatrician told us he was the best baby in the nursery."

All any parent can be told with confidence is that a baby has no apparent developmental difficulties and that is all any parent need hope for. An infant whose development is accelerated in all fields and re-mains so over a year or more *may* be highly gifted; certainly plenty of gifted adults were rapid developers in infancy, though some were mark-edly slow. But plenty of "average" adults were rapid developers too. A baby's present "good performance" shows that his or her environment, care and fortune have been fine—so far—and that she or he is unlikely to be of much below average intelligence when grown up. But average the child may well be. By definition, most people are. What a tragedy if a child's normal abilities when it is time for school disappoint parents because they were convinced they had produced a prodigy and had al-lowed themselves to think that a prodigy was what they wanted.

Parents have enormous influence over their children but many people misunderstand its nature. Some still see infant development as Watson or James saw it—see babies as "blank slates" for adults to write upon, formless and functionless creatures that must be shaped and cast by adults. Others, culturally adapted to improving on nature, are con-vinced that any parent who can repair a car or make over a company can surely exert the same kind of power to perfect one small child.

Such misunderstandings put a burden of responsibility onto parents that is like a novice hiker's rucksack: heavy with the latest trendy gad-gets, light on basic necessities and so badly balanced that there is no pleasure in the walk. Parents do not need to shoulder active responsibil-ity for bustling children from helpless newborns to competent people; they can trust the developmental process to move them along at the rate that is appropriate for them. Children do not forever suck instead of eating if nobody weans them, fail to learn language if words are not taught, remain incontinent unless they are "trained" or grow up in ignorance of what is right unless they have been punished for doing wrong. Encumbered with all that unnecessary activism, many parents jettison some of their vital but more passive responsibilities as models, caring companions, unfailing supporters and facilitators of children's own overall development as individual people. An imbalance between those two reduces parents' pleasure in the whole child-rearing expedition and puts both the child's performance and long-term development at risk. Nobody's baby will starve because granola and broccoli are not forced down her reluctant throat, but a few people's children will later starve themselves in anorexia nervosa because foods and overwhelming concern were forced on them. Nobody's toddler will grow into an aggressive psychopath because he "got away with" biting other toddlers, but a few people's children will still bite others in kindergarten because, bitten back by a parent "to show how much it hurts," they learned the unintended lesson that hurting people is a legitimate way to exert power over them.

Inbuilt sequences of development do not only render parental pressure unnecessary—because children will do what they need to do as and when they are ready—they also make that pressure pointless, or worse, because children cannot do things until they are ready. Like every other mammal, babies and toddlers instinctively protect themselves and their possessions with teeth and claws. In group care with a shared caregiver, physically aggressive behavior makes for chaos and parents press for more socialized ways with outraged cries of "Don't hit—ask" and "Be nice to your little friend." But until the second, or even the third year, children cannot "be nice" to each other on purpose because it takes that long for social and cognitive growth to bring toddlers to awareness of other people's feelings and to compel them to experiment with putting themselves in other people's shoes. Once that awareness takes root, there is much that adults can do to facilitate and encourage the flowering of empathy and related impulse control, but nothing they do before that will hurry the growth of altruism and relieve caregivers of the necessity for protecting their charges from themselves and from each other.

This inbuilt developmental protection from pushing is important because if parents really could accelerate children's achievement of particular goals the results would often be disastrous. Imagine the fate of a one-year-old who really had learned to respect the feelings of other infants and "ask nicely" while they ignored her pacific gestures and snatched at her toys and hair. Or imagine parents who really concentrated on teaching their baby to walk and succeeded in rushing her past that milestone at seven months. Apart from their own glow of pride, what would they have? A baby who walked around rooms before she had mapped them visually, and who met phenomena like steps and dogs from a perilous upright posture without first having come to terms with them from the relative stability of hands and knees.

But the fact that children cannot do what it is developmentally inappropriate for them to do does not protect them from adult efforts to make them. Parental pressure does not have to be successful to be unfortunate. A child's energy and waking hours are limited and the time adults will spend with her is almost always rationed, so the very process of pressuring her to do something she is not ready to do is likely to deprive her of time to do and enjoy what is appropriate. Hours spent in a baby walker cannot also be spent crawling on the floor with toys. Time adults spend holding her hands and exhorting her to walk cannot also be spent cuddling her, showing her things and telling her she is wonderful. And even if there is, overall, enough of everybody's time for everything, time that is spent orienting infants towards achievements that are still in the developmental future is time wasted, or worse. Look at early potty training. Diapers almost always become family history in the daytime during a child's third year whether the parents start "training" him when he is twelve or twenty-four months old. Wait until he is developmentally ready and the process may take three months; start before he is ready and it will take all the months until he is, plus that same three months. If it takes three extra minutes to pot as well as change a baby-in-training and that is done four time a day, the difference between starting at one year or two is twelve minutes a day for 365 days, which is over seventy hours or almost two working weeks with nothing to show for them except extra stress. And if the stress of that year of unsuccessful/impossible potting has been considerable, the difference may well be even greater because the one-year-old who did not know how to do what the parents wanted has become a two-year-old who does not want to. It is even easier to pressure children into problems with nighttime dryness. Living with a child who wets his bed, night after night, is not easy: how is the mattress to be dried or kept dry? How is the laundry to be coped with? How can the child be taken on vacation or left overnight with friends? Aware that the child wets in his sleep and therefore cannot be blamed for it, parents may try to be understanding and sensitive to his feelings, but they cannot conceal those practical problems or their own desire for the child to change. Enuresis quickly becomes a major factor in his life and self-image. But what made that little boy into a bed wetter? Whatever the complex physiological, genetic and emotional explanations for his failure to con-centrate his urine and hold it through the night, the direct answer to that vital question is simply "leaving off the diapers that kept the bed dry." The calendar may say that a child is three years old; the develop-mental charts may pinpoint that as the proper age of nighttime dryness, but parents' only real cue to the right timing for their child comes from his personal development. As long as he still wakes with a soaking dia-per each morning, putting him to bed without one guarantees a soaking bed. Should diapers that have been prematurely abandoned be reintro-duced? While the parents could solve their practical problems that way, a simple reversal seldom solves the problems that pressuring parents have caused their children. That child has been told that he is a "big boy, not a baby who needs diapers any more"; how will he feel when he finds himself clad as a baby all over again? How do children who have been coached into the very best nursery school and pushed into kindergarten a year early feel when they are kept down to repeat the class the following year? And how do they feel when after months of unavailing home tuition in reading, parents suddenly take the teacher's advice to withdraw and leave literacy to her?

Parents whose own egos are directly invested in children's forthcom-ing achievements are distracted from enjoying them as they are today and disappointed when they fail to meet their aspirations for tomorrow. That is sad for the parents but it is much worse than sad for the chil-dren. Their ego development depends on parental pleasure and ap-proval; to find themselves a disappointment is disastrous. If children are to develop the self-esteem and self-respect that will maximize their fulfillment of their potential, their resilience and their ability to esteem and respect other people, they need to feel loved, respected, even celebrated, for what they are rather than for what they do. That means that they need to be as sure that extra achievement could not earn them extra love as that failure could not deprive them of the love they have. Unconditional love in infancy and early childhood, from at least one adult who is both consistently available and emotionally involved, seems a mondial prerequisite of mental health throughout life. Putting conditions on that love may be as risky as putting limits on adult availability. Today's families often do both at once.

Children in the post-industrial West have the longest compulsory childhood the world has ever known. With all those years of enforced dependence ahead of them, we have to learn that letting them take their own time over growing up is what is best for them now and what will best help them to fulfill their own potential when they are grown. It will not be an easy lesson. The tyranny of time works powerfully on adults and the more time children take, the more parents must give. As well as seeming to spell progress and promise success, a speedy passage through developmental phases means that parents can quickly be rid of bottles and broken nights, diapers and nightmares, toys and testing, mess and muddle, explanations, exhortations and endless demands for vigilance, responsibility and love. But all those things are the stuff of childhood. If adults experience childhood as something for children to be put through, and parents to get through, as fast as possible, no child can ever experience their love as belonging by right to the person she is today; it will always seem conditional on her being a different person tomorrow.

"Have yours all left home now? How old are they now?" Only in the lonely peace of the finally emptied nest is there time to realize just how little time it takes children to grow up, and to wonder what the rush was really all about.

— 6 —

Discipline, Self-Discipline and Learning How to Behave

Good discipline" is close behind health, happiness and success on parents' most-wanted lists for their children, and it often tops their to-do lists. Advice columns, radio call-ins, even pediatricians' office hours overflow with "How can I make them . . . ?" queries, and in the crowded market for how-to-parent books, the one that promises sure-fire ways to get kids to lay off candies or go to bed, clean up their language or their rooms, will always find takers among parents who try everything because nothing seems to work. Those parents get little public support or sympathy. Talk to teachers, scan the media or get into conversation with people watchers like cab drivers, supermarket checkout clerks or restaurant managers, and most will describe rising indiscipline among young children, predict yet further increases in juvenile crime and blame most of it on parents. Even allowing for the historical fact that every generation considers the one that follows it worse behaved than itself, it does seem that parents are worrying and working at discipline yet signally failing—in their own eyes and the eyes of others—to instill it; why?

The explanation does not seem to lie in any confusion over what dealing out discipline means. The *Oxford English Dictionary* defines the noun "discipline" as "the order maintained and observed among persons under control or command; a system of rules for conduct; correction or physical chastisement," and the *Oxford American Dictionary* defines the verb as "to train to be obedient and orderly . . . to punish." Parents who are asked to describe a mother or father who is a good disciplinarian usually come close to those dictionary definitions with descriptions like "someone who gives clear orders and punishes consistently if children disobey." That is exactly what most observers want parents to do and complain that they do not. Primarily concerned with the childish behaviors that make them personally uncomfortable here and now—crying in buses and planes, running around in restaurants, being noisy and argumentative in public places or disrespectful and disruptive to their elders—they say that parents allow children to "get away with murder"; any child who is unruly, disobedient, willful or defiant should instantly be punished: "A good slap is all it takes." Teachers are less inclined to recommend physical punishment and, being primarily concerned about their own role with children, they tend to use more positive and future-oriented phraseology, but their concept words are similar: parents should ensure that children are "orderly," "ready to pay attention," "able to concentrate" and "accepting of authority." There is broad agreement, then, on what good discipline *is*.

There is considerable, possibly crucial confusion, however, about what discipline is actually *for*. Although parents describe the means to good discipline in phrases redolent of the word's ecclesiastical and military origins, they describe its *ends* in quite different terms. Parents want their children to know right from wrong, to do what they should and avoid doing what they should not, to be pleasant, helpful and polite and to avoid letting them down in public. Those are qualities involving not just obedience but ethical judgment and choice, not just order but cooperation with a friendly face, not just submission but sensitivity to the feelings of others—subtly socialized stuff and surely not amenable to shouts and smacks. On a parade ground—or perhaps in a Victorian schoolroom—where adults have decided exactly what children should and should not do, watch them every moment and punish every lapse, they can impose order, keep control, ensure obedience—or at least keep disobedience furtive. But life in most modern Western families is not at all like that. Most parents find it difficult enough to invent an observable code of conduct for themselves amid a welter of conflicting values; few have, or would wish to have, simple codes of behavior children are expected to perform like automatons. Furthermore, with parents' time at a premium and much older siblings almost as rare as parental delegates like nannies or servants, few could arrange for young children's behavior to be constantly monitored—and therefore their misbehavior to be instantly punished—even if they wished to. From a very early age children spend much of their time alone or with groups of other children, under distant supervision rather than individual direction. Instead of being managed, they are expected to manage themselves. Instead of depending on enforced obedience to external controls their behavior has to depend on voluntary obedience to the internal controls we call "conscience." If parents want to cultivate self-discipline in their children but are trying to do so in the growth medium of that good disciplinarian, it is not surprising that they are finding it an anxious struggle.

Self-discipline is a slow-growing plant that roots in children's identification with parents or parent substitutes. Learning how to behave— and to be more comfortable behaving that way—depends on parental influence rather than power, on the warmth of the relationship adults offer rather than the clarity of the orders they impose. Children need to be shown what they should do and prevented from doing what they should not, and they need honest explanations for each piece of everyday advice and instruction, praise and reproof so that they can generalize from one tiny incident to the next, gradually incorporating clusters of behavior into a vast jigsaw puzzle of values that is building up inside them. The unquestioning obedience so beloved of disciplinarians contributes nothing to the learning process; the punishments that are supposed to ensure it are irrelevant, at best, and physical punishments, like spanking, actually sabotage it.

There is little immediate prospect, though, of that heavy word "discipline" being sent back to the parade ground where it belongs. Its punitive connotations and practices—including spanking, imprisoning and shaming children—are still deeply embedded in the puritan ethic of most Western cultures and in those made subject to their imperialism or colonial rule. Up to 90 percent of British, North American, Australian and Caribbean populations "believe in spanking," according to national opinion polls; according to less formal media polls, two thirds of parents put that belief into at least weekly practice, especially with younger children and by no means excluding babies under one year old. During 1992 and 1993 the percentages of parents in the United States, the United Kingdom and Canada who reported spanking their children seemed to be diminishing, although no national polls have recently been taken. Corporal punishment may be becoming less socially acceptable, whether or not it is yet becoming less frequently practiced. Certainly a majority of parents do still hit their children, and that majority must include many millions of parents who also believe in, and try to foster, cooperative, even democratic, styles of child rearing, not realizing that in families (as in nations) physical punishments, or the real threat of such naked assertions of force majeure, confound all the rest. Of course many parents who do not *believe* in physical punishment can be stressed into hitting a child, but for every parent who lashes out and regrets it, there is another who jovially boasts that "nothing ends an argument faster than a good smack on the butt" and yet another who truly feels a disciplinary duty to punish children that way. It is not surprising. Children learn how to be adults, and eventually parents, by modeling themselves on their own parents or parent figures so the child-rearing attitudes and practices of one generation tend to be incorporated in the belief system of the next. Parents who do not spank are a minority, and almost always people who were not passed this particular tool in the parenting kit they received from their own parents. Those who do spank almost invariably were spanked. Of course change is possible; there is free will in parenting as in everything else, but there is a heavy personal investment ringing through the good disciplinarians' chorus line: "It didn't do me any harm." As children, we all have to identify with our parents and that means that we have to believe in them and what they do. If the children parents hit today are not to hit their grandchildren in twenty years' time, they will have to come to terms with the painful possibility that they *were* harmed by those parents. Only by accepting that their own parents were not perfect, and therefore are not perfect models for their own parenting, will they be free to see that their very different kinds of family function better with different and more positive kinds of discipline.

Negative discipline is built on the assumption that babies are born full of original sin (or inherently antisocial) and that virtue—however a family, school, community or culture defines it—must therefore be forced on them. The contrary assumption underlying positive discipline is that human beings are born morally neutral but inherently social animals who gradually learn the values and associated behaviors of their parents or parent figures, just as they learn everything else.

Learning acceptable behavior is more difficult and takes longer than learning any specific skill because what has to be learned is complex, involves control of powerful impulses, and often demands that children act against what they see as their own best interests. The child who refrains from grabbing the last cookie, after all, does not get to eat it; sharing a toy means losing sole possession of it; refraining from bashing other children over the head may allow them to win a playground battle. Nevertheless small children will learn almost anything that adults try to teach provided they are physically, mentally and emotionally mature enough to understand the lessons, and provided they experience some success to keep them motivated. Socially acceptable behavior is no exception. Children like to learn because they want to know—everything there is to know about their world—and they rather particularly want to know how to behave because they want to be like their parents or parent figures and to have their approval. So when there are problems with discipline they are usually in the expectations and the methods of those doing the teaching rather than in those doing the learning. Busy parents, pressured by the disapproval of observers who neither understand nor enjoy young children, often expect too much, too soon. Instead of adopting in their families the principles of modern early education they expect in daycare centers, nursery schools and kindergartens, and practicing with their own children the patience they preach to "real educators," taxed parents are tempted towards traditional discipline, and especially punishment, because it seems like a shortcut.

Whether their cultural roots are in the Bible and its hellfire or in behaviorism and Pavlov's dogs, most people believe that punishment is so basic to discipline that there can be no discipline without it: the notion that people will desist from behavior for fear of punishment is uncritically accepted as commonsense. In fact punishment is a very inefficient way of bringing about lasting change in peoples' behavior and, as those behaviorist psychologists soon found with their maze-running rats, vastly inferior to rewards. An individual who knows how he should behave and has choices open to him may avoid parking beside a fire hydrant for fear of the fine, but he will still park wherever he thinks he can get away with it even when he has *been* fined. Punishments do not inspire remorse or motivate effort; they seldom reform people—criminals, citizens or children; indeed they often backfire and make people angry and obstinate instead. There is nothing original, let alone revolutionary, about that statement. Modern management techniques are based on it. Employers who want to increase the output and loyalty of staff are not advised to police them, yell at them and withhold wages when they arrive late, but to treat them as responsible people, thank them for their work, and pay bonuses when they stay late. We all work to gain rewards rather than to avoid punishments and the basic reward we all seek is a boost to self-esteem. Even in the workplace where the tangible reward of money underpins life-style, even ensures survival, earnings are often even more important as symbols of self-esteem. Many individuals would rather have a promotion without a raise than a raise without a promotion, and even a gleamingly golden handshake seldom compensates for the damage done to self-image by early retirement.

Children depend on parents or their substitutes not only to *maintain* their self-esteem but also to *build* it. Babies piece their self-image together from the myriad reflections of themselves they see in the mirrors of adults' reactions to them. If nobody reacted at all they could not come to feel themselves real, so social responses are crucial to psychological development and adult attention is, and remains, not just something children crave but something they truly need. From the first months of life their sense of themselves as valued and valuable, loved and loving, clever and competent, or the opposites of all those qualities, comes primarily from the people who care for them. As they grow, the esteem in which they can hold themselves depends on the esteem in which they feel themselves to be held. Like the rest of us, children bask in approval. But where mature adults may be self-sufficient enough to prefer to "keep themselves to themselves" rather than attract unrewarding attention, most small children cannot *be* themselves with no attention at all. They would rather have disapproval, anger, even punishment, than be ignored and will often provoke negative attention if that is the only kind available to them. That bane of the kindergarten class, the "attention getter," is not a child who has had too much attention and should be given less; he is almost invariably a child who has had so little that he will settle for any kind he can get. He needs more, much more. Only when he knows that the sum total of available attention is more than he needs will he begin to discriminate between pleasant and unpleasant kinds, changing his behavior so as to minimize scoldings and maximize praise.

There are many children in need of more adult attention because it is one of the scarcest commodities in our materially rich homes, as well as in understaffed daycare facilities and schools. Although modern parents usually have only one or two children to attend to rather than the larger families of earlier generations, most have a great many more things that they must do separately from their children and fewer other adults around to share children's lives and therefore dilute the demands made on them. Instead of accepting children underfoot (or hopefully "at heel") like puppies, many parents adopt the principle of "let sleeping dogs lie," often leaving children to their own devices or electronic entertainers until misbehavior compels their attention. Which child has his hand held, is talked to and eventually handed M&M's in the supermarket check-out line? Not the one who is peaceably sucking his thumb but the one who is playing up and being an embarrassment in front of those people watchers. How can children ensure that they will be taken to the park on a Sunday morning? Not by asking nicely and waiting patiently, but by giving parents no peace to sleep late or to read the papers. And how can a child most successfully interrupt adult conversation and divert it to himself at the dinner table? Refuse, mess with and spit out the food. Negative attention is still attention and any attention is better than none; used in the absence of the positive kind, or as a shortcut to it, disapproval inadvertently rewards children for being a pain instead of for being a pleasure. If we want children to "be good," we have to ensure that they have a more enjoyable time when they do as we want than when they do the opposite.

Traditional disciplinarians argue that "virtue is its own reward"; parents ought not to reward children with friendly attention and praise just for behaving as they should. It is enough to punish them when they behave as they should not. But in the first two or three years of life, children are not mature enough to be able to be "good" (or the opposite) on purpose. If they are to understand virtue—a prerequisite, after all, for choosing it—they must first discover and understand its constituents in terms of the behavior that is wanted from them in a myriad of different circumstances. They cannot acquire that understanding entirely from being told off when they get things wrong. The two-year-old who has spent the morning in the sandbox turning out pies, turns out her dinner and gets her hand smacked because she "ought to know better." Ought she? If nobody keeps explaining the arbitrary and inconsistent differences between food and playthings, and between the behavior that is acceptable in kitchens and in play places, how can she? A red hand will not help her. Only through understanding can children generalize appropriately from one piece of behavior to the next. "Is this *church?*" a four-year-old loudly inquires as his embarrassed parents beg him to sit still in the airport departure lounge. Making connections is not the whole story either: what makes children willing to do what they have discovered parents want them to do during the years it takes them to internalize that wanting and make it their own? Only consistent experience of a pleasanter time when they do than when they do not. The "ought to know better" and "because I say so" school does not only sow injustice and sad confusion, it also misses prime opportunities to educate and to motivate.

When children live as integral parts of adults' lives nobody has to have a policy to ensure that they have more fun when they are nice than when they are horrid. It just happens. When children are meeting the demands of the moment—enjoying a treat, helping with a chore or managing to keep the noise down because somebody is on the phone—adults feel, and therefore are, pleasant and companionable with them. When they are being a pain adults are irritated, disapproving or cross. With adult attention freely available to them either way, those children prefer the pleasant kind, so they experience the change to cross faces and reproving voices as a cost. Such children absorb parental values and the behaviors that fit with them rather as adolescents used to learn skills through apprenticeship to craftspeople. They learn how to behave by being around parents and aspiring to be like them; by watching what they do, listening to what they say, imitating them and being praised, being shown how to do things and getting them wrong, then less wrong, then right enough to feel proud; being rewarded with a try at something on their own initiative, getting that right and being promoted to something new. Even on a two-week vacation, a parent who offers a child a genuinely shared activity rather than one that is just for him—fishing, perhaps, instead of those educational games in "quality time"—may suddenly find himself with a faithful and enormously hardworking follower instead of the beloved but boring burden he is accustomed to at home.

Few children in the West can have a full-time apprenticeship to their parents or substitutes, though. Most are extra to adult lives that are already too crowded with child-excluding activities to be fully shared. Children have a tiny part of adult life set aside especially for them, and a special ration of parents' attention, but the working parent, the adult person with activities, concerns and values of her own, remains a stranger to them. Under these circumstances the business of learning how to behave is necessarily self-conscious and easily distorted. Instead of being the behavior that enables everybody to do what they have to do and enjoy it as much as possible, desirable behavior for children becomes the behavior that allows adults to ignore them. It is but a short step from "virtue is its own reward" to "children should be seen and not heard" and from there to the common assertion that, irrespective of how they behave, children should not have "too much attention" in case they get "spoiled."

The concept of a spoiled child, redolent of the insidious and disgusting taint acquired by good meat if it is wrongly handled, hangs over many parents like the sword of Damocles. For fear of it babies are left to cry without comfort, late-returning fathers are denied hugs, grandparents are denied visits and whole families deny themselves the pleasure of children's joy. And it is all a sad misconception. There is no such thing as too much parental attention for children; it is parents who may need to limit the supply, and their guilty replacement of it with material goods that may start the rot. Children cannot have too much companionship, talk, play and laughter, too many smiles and hugs, even too many presents and treats, provided they are freely given because parents want children to have them. The charming baby who becomes a selfish, insatiably demanding, bratty four-year-old has not turned out that way because she has been given "too much"; she may indeed have been given comparatively little, materially or emotionally. Whatever she has had, though, she has turned out that way because she got most of it by bullying parents to give, against their better judgment, as that toddler in the supermarket got the M&M's. Spoiled children have learned an effective but undesirable way to behave: they have learned to blackmail for the attention they crave, or at least for material things to symbolize it, parents who will neither give generously nor refuse convincingly.

Whatever the composition of a family, parents or parent figures are the grown-ups, and the children need them to be grown-up enough to take charge. No child of any dependent age can be safe, or feel secure, without the certainty that irrespective of her knowledge of how to behave or her desire to behave that way, "her" adults will not let her go beyond the pale. Parents fail a child if they allow her to do anything that makes them dislike *her* as well as her action. They also fail her if their tolerance much exceeds her community's norms so that everyone else dislikes her. Unfortunately, deciding where to place their particular limits, in the light of what it is reasonable to expect of their individual child, and then ensuring that those boundaries effectively contain her, eats up those scarce parental commodities: time and attention. Faced with the boredom, inconvenience or embarrassment of enforcing their own limits, many parents stand by and watch, or even connive, while they are overstepped and then blame their *children* for not observing them. The mother of that toddler in the supermarket said, "He knows he's not allowed treats at the check-out—we have a rule about that— but today he just would not stop crying and carrying on so I had to buy him something." She did not have to, though: she had several other—more or less unenviable—choices. She probably could have prevented the scene by being more companionable with her child earlier on so they arrived in the boring line in mid-conversation, or by foreseeing the problem and handing him a roll out of the cart without waiting for him to fuss. Failing prevention, she could have completed the check-out *while* he fussed or, if she really could not stand the embarrassment in front of other shoppers, she could even have sacrificed her place in the line and removed him until he calmed down. The M&M's were quicker and easier; often a smack is quicker and easier too, for the so-called adult. But making sure that limits limit is a prime adult responsibility and reneging on them with bribes and punishments is a betrayal. Nothing young children can do can actually force parents into acting against their own convictions if those convictions are strong enough, but are they? Parents often maintain that they "cannot stop" crawling babies playing with the TV, but how many turn up at the hospital because they failed to prevent them playing with the space heater? The difference is not in the relative difficulty of keeping babies away from TV sets and fires but in the relative importance of doing so. Many parents assert that preschool children "will not do as they are told" and cite as an example their difficulties in sending the children to bed on time. Many children have indeed learned to defer bedtime almost indefinitely, but only because parents are too tired to follow through. If those same children need medication for a chronic illness such as asthma, they take it without a murmur because parents are convinced that it really matters and are therefore clear, confident and consistent in their insistence.

Children have to test the limits put upon them—how else can they find out where those limits are?—but when they meet one that is firm and clear, a no that does not mean maybe and never changes to yes (or even to the drama of a scene) because of the lengthiest nagging or the loudest screams, they stop, because pointless pushing is boring. The children who keep probing are the ones who cannot detect the real limits amid endless cries of "no," "stop it" and "don't" that experience tells them are meaningless; the ones who cannot make sense of the limits because nobody explains that "don't hit your sister" means "don't hit *anybody*"; the ones who find that if they push hard enough they can move the goalposts even if they do get punished for it.

Although it is easy to understand how parents come to find physical punishment acceptable, and to find setting effective limits effortful, it is still surprising that so many allow themselves to base their discipline on the one in place of the other. Almost everyone in Western societies agrees that it is morally wrong for people to settle arguments or impose their will on each other with blows. When a big kid hits a little kid in the playground, we call him a bully; five years later he punches a woman for her wallet and is called a mugger; later still, when he slugs a fellow worker who insults him, he is called a troublemaker, but when he becomes a father and hits his tiresome, disobedient or disrespectful child, we call him a disciplinarian. Why is this rung on a ladder of interpersonal violence regarded so differently from the rest? Is it the motive: the claim that he spanks "for the child's own good"? He may (or he may not) but even if he does, why does a parent's good motive justify him in using violence when a police officer's desire to convict criminals does not justify violence to suspects? Is it the parent-child relationship: the private, loving, family context in which the spanking is administered? That argument is useful to parents who want to hit their own children but do not want to delegate the "right" to schools, but it is shaky. Husbands and wives are also in private, loving, family relationships but that does not make wife- (or husband-) beating acceptable. It used to, of course. Physical punishment was once an accepted part of any relationship that gave one individual legitimate authority over others—master over slave, servant or wife; officer over lower ranks; law enforcer over law breaker; employer over apprentice—but that is history; we have universal human rights now—universal except for children, that is. If the whole concept of punishment is foreign to the self-discipline parents want children to acquire, then physical punishment cuts at its very foundations, highlighting people's reluctance to regard children as fully human—as people just like themselves except for youth and inexperience—and their ultimate readiness to abandon cooperation for the naked assertion of painful power.

Many parents regard the assertion of that painful power as a necessary part of keeping small children safe, rather on a par with stair gates or car seats. The argument is that when a crawling baby reaches for the iron or a toddler runs off the sidewalk, a slap or a spanking is justified—almost a duty. The argument is as curious as it is common. Stair gates and car seats *prevent* injury; they do not *punish* children for risking it. When a baby or toddler is heading into danger he is saved by being grabbed, not by being hit. Some parents maintain that the blow teaches the child not to take that risk again, but few can believe that. Babies are incapable of judging which household objects it is safe to touch and when. Even the most disciplinarian parents know this and babyproof their homes accordingly. And nobody assumes that a toddler will stay safely on the sidewalk after enough spankings rather than enough growth in understanding, foresight and self-control. This kind of punishment is not education for children but post–traumatic stress relief for parents.

Some parents reserve corporal punishment for extreme situations, often to discriminate "moral offenses" like lying, hitting a smaller sibling or using bad language to a grandparent, from "mere naughtiness." Children cannot readily see that difference, though, and a spanking certainly does not help them learn it. Moral ideas require careful explanation to an interested child who is listening, rather than to an angry child who is crying. And no wonder. Why is "it wasn't me, it was him" a lie, when "I can't come; Mom won't let me" is just an excuse? Why is it worse to say s- - - to Grandma than to a friend, and anyway why *is* it worse than sugar? And how come it is bad to hit your little sister when Mom (who is always right) hits you?

Other parents see a spanking or a whipping as a final, smarting boundary for children who keep testing limits. But punishment—by definition—takes place *after* the boundary has been broken. Do they all lock stable doors after horses have been stolen, or blame the horses rather than the thieves? The most honest and insightful among spanking parents admit that the punishment is usually given for the last in a run of trivial misdemeanors which ultimately broke their patience. The child has been out of line so often and in so many ways that a swipe seems easier on him (on *whom?*) than yet another lecture. Although the reasoning is understandable to anyone who has been there on a bad day, it is too complicated for small children. If children are asked what they were hit for, their answers almost all fall into one of three categories, each as uneducational as the last: the parental-guilt-inducing and literal "for spilling my juice," the unfortunately accurate "'cause you were angry" or the confused and hopeless "I don't know." How *can* such children come to understand what is out of line and learn to be their own linespeople? In any normal home, the carelessness or showing off that gets a blow today may have gone unnoticed yesterday and raise a laugh tomorrow. The reality of family life is that only a minute part of learning how to behave is about learning absolutes; most of it is a matter of learning to adapt impulsive childish behavior to adult moods and circumstances: to judge the moment, gauge their moods, be sensitive to their feelings and therefore be careful enough, respectful enough, obedient enough and neat enough to pass muster *right now.* There is no way a spanked bottom leaves space in a child's head for such subtle stuff.

Increasing numbers of younger parents are trying to get away from slapping and spanking but that does not necessarily mean that they are moving away from negative discipline and towards the positive kind that is loosed from the stranglehold of all punishment. The fashionable alternative to a spanking is a "time-out" which banishes a child who is misbehaving until he earns restoration to adult companionship and his previous activities by giving up the "wrong" behavior—by stopping yelling and kicking, for instance. As a concept a time-out has much to recommend it. Loss of social interaction until the child himself changes specific unacceptable behavior both motivates and explains: he cannot stay at the table and spit because the spitting spoils the meal for everyone else; his mother cannot go on playing with him if he is rude and horrible because his behavior stops her feeling playful. Adults take a time-out (they call it "some fresh air") when they feel their manners threatened by the heat of cocktail party arguments. Many children accept, even instigate, time-outs to escape the kind of vicious circle that used to leave my daughter furiously wailing, "I *can't* get nice." That was my cue either to suggest that she run around the yard or to take the pressure off by turning away and busying myself with something else until we had both simmered down. Her brother used to rush off to his bedroom yelling, "I'm going away, so there," as if I were the one who would mind being left alone. A few minutes later he would emerge, the argument forgotten, back on track just as the proponents of time-out suggest. But not quite: he had gone away voluntarily and he had kept his dignity intact so *he had not been punished.* "Good disciplinarians" do not accept that a time-out can be disciplinary if the child does not perceive it as punishment; indeed proponents of this technique advise parents to ensure that time-outs are unpleasant, or at least boring. The child must not be sent to his room if he does not mind going and will simply play; time-out chairs should be placed so that occupants see nothing but a blank wall; children who refuse to go to, or remain in, time-out must be taken and kept there by force. The agreed purpose of a time-out is to enable a child to regain *self*-control and make a fresh start: why then is heavy control by an adult appropriate? And if force is used, time-out becomes a physical punishment, and a dangerous one, even if it hurts only dignity and feelings rather than bottoms as well. All physical punishments are potentially dangerous, not only because there is risk in a large person using any physical force on a small one, but also because since they are not an effective way of changing children's behavior, they tend to be repeated again and again and that means that they are likely to escalate over time. When the child who is spanked repeats his offense, he is likely to be spanked again—harder—and there may come a time when open hands give way to belts or canes. When a child will not stay on a time-out chair, he is liable to be put in his room; if he comes out before the allocated time is up, there will be an undignified struggle. Eventually the only answer seems to be to lock the door, but what if it has no lock? There may come a day when a time-out is being locked in a cellar. Parents who have never done such things in the name of discipline usually cannot imagine that they ever would, but we know that some people do, because they tell researchers so—and why would they make it up?

Should there be any punishments, then? No, not if "punishment" is seen as the deliberate infliction of pain, physical or mental. There are many kinds of action parents can take in the interests of children's safety, social acceptability and eventual social learning. Many of these are punishments in the true, psychological sense of reducing the likelihood of the child offending again, but they do not have to be perceived as punitive to be effective. A toddler who keeps biting others in the sandbox is removed by her mother. Held a protesting prisoner, she is punished; distracted to the swings she is not. A five-year-old begs to use his new skateboard on the sidewalk; after much discussion about safety he is allowed out, goes straight over the curb into the street and is immediately confined again to the yard. Whether he sees that as punishment or as protection depends on the parents' attitude and tone. An eleven-year-old girl has not completed her homework by the time her favorite TV show begins so she is not allowed to watch it. A punishment, or just a restatement of parental priorities and a reminder that limited time needs planning?

Difficult though it may be to admit it, even to ourselves, there is an element of power play, even revenge, in this discipline business and that is why it remains trammeled in the concept of punishment. We do not only want children to do as they should; we want them to think we can force them to do so. We do not simply want the naughty child to stop behaving badly; we want her to pay for our inconvenience or embarrassment. Parents like to believe that their relationship with their children is 100 percent "loving" so they find it painful to acknowledge such primitive reactions to them, but when one partner in a love relationship is dependent on the other, loving and controlling are inevitably intermixed, and never more so than in parenting. Somewhere inside themselves many parents are uneasily aware that their control is tenuous and their power has limits: they cannot literally *make* children do as they are told, and every sign of defiance raises the specter of a child who gets "out of control," endangering not only himself but also their self-image as "good parents." Specters are not real, though. The reality is that what parents lack in power they more than make up in influence, and influence is founded on love, not fear, and on identification and respect rather than on authority.

Parents do not have to earn children's love: it is implicit in infant dependence and amazingly difficult to lose, as those who seek to protect the children of abusive parents know. Parents do not have to stand on their dignity to gain children's respect: as their primary models, they already have it to such an extent that it is difficult for later models, such as teachers, to compete. As parents keep children safe and keep others safe from them, children learn to keep themselves safe and care for other people. As parents control their behavior, children learn to control themselves. And as parents explain, again and again, the few and vitally important values that underpin their everyday exhortations about trivia, children measure their words against their actions and take the values that they see truly held into themselves. "You *must* not *ever hit* people," chants Father as he spanks his son. But the child will do as Daddy does, just as Daddy does what his daddy did.

The Preschool Years: Learning and Lessons, Education and School

When is a toddler no longer a toddler? When a confusing, unpredictable and balky person-in-the-making becomes a comparatively cooperative and recognizable human being who is both eager and easy to please—at least 50 percent of the time.

Nothing is sudden in human development, but this shift is as close as it gets. Parents of three-year-olds often talk of caterpillars turning into butterflies and frogs turning into princes and then they say guiltily, "It's not that we didn't *love* her before . . ." No, of course not; it is just that she is great deal easier to live with and to love now than she was then. So what is that "now"? We call it the "preschool period": a mundane name for a magic time and also a powerful misnomer.

The years between three-ish and five-ish are not just a waiting time before school or a time of preparation for school, but a period, properly called "early childhood," that has its own developmental agenda. The agenda has nothing to do with school and is exactly the same in societies where starting school happens much later or not at all. The vital education of early childhood is concerned with managing feelings, emotions and relationships. Children acquire it less by listening to adults' "lessons" than by listening to themselves, in play.

Babies have feelings; we can see (and hear) their strength; we even know that the part of the brain that controls them—the limbic system—is more fully developed at birth and grows more rapidly than the areas that control thought and language. Thought and feeling begin to connect up for the toddler, and people take shape, too, as through her struggles to balance dependence with autonomy she eventually arrives at a sense of her self that acknowledges basic characteristics like gender, and recognizes them in others. As "I" enters the child's consciousness as well as her vocabulary, it brings with it self-consciousness and therefore the beginnings of shame and pride, the capacity for empathy and the potential, at least, for altruism. But even though she is leaving toddlerhood behind, the child is still at sea in a storm of feelings that are intense, wild, crazy sometimes, in adult terms. Connections between feelings and language still have to be forged so that the feelings can be integrated. Finding words for feelings, and a more or less reliable match in feelings for other people's words, takes many more hugs and yells, smiles and frowns, and all of early childhood.

It is easy to be fooled into thinking of early childhood as more mature than it is because the three-year-old seems so dramatically different from the toddler. The three-year-old *looks* different. She loses the fat pads over her cheeks and the resulting round-eyed look which is part of babyish appeal and a powerful evoker of protective feelings in adults. In a single year she may grow as much as two and a half inches in height for only five pounds' gain in weight, which gives her a leggier look and more fluid, graceful movement than the dumpy toddler whose center of gravity is set safely low. Hair has grown and coarsened so braids have point and ribbons purchase. And, for a while at least, all the baby teeth are in and none is out. Between neuromuscular and cognitive developments, the three-year-old comes to behave more like a child too. She is better than the toddler at remembering and therefore looking forward—and that means she can (sometimes) wait thirty seconds for that drink *and* choose painlessly between orange and apple juice. She is just as likely now to want to pour it herself but a great deal more likely to do so, and to drink it, without spilling. And some things she may now willingly do not only for herself but by herself, whereas the toddler always needs a parent to go along and watch admiringly. It is not until children begin to rush off to the toilet alone that parents realize how constantly their lives have been punctuated by that particular trip. Most important of all, though, the child's swift development of language not only makes her *sound* like a child but allows adults to interact with her as they do with everyone else and therefore encourages them to expect her to be like a child.

When adults interact with each other they *do* very little and *say* a great deal. We use words instead of actions, explaining instead of demonstrating, quarreling instead of fighting, telling troubles instead of howling, making lists rather than ten trips to the store to buy ten separate items. Babies, of course, say no words at all. Their lack of language is an important factor in the special treatment they receive from adults, and the beginnings of language, in the toddler, are always exciting. But even toddlers mostly say comparatively little, do a great deal and force adults into showing rather than explaining, taking rather than sending, preventing bodily rather than verbally. Now, almost suddenly, the verbal fluency of early childhood allows parents to talk and listen to this child and they can all hear and understand each other—or can they? Parents certainly can and should talk, listen and try for understanding, but they should not assume that words are enough—as they would be with an adult and will be in middle childhood—or that information or explanation, given by either party, will be received without distortion and that all the taking and showing and holding used in infancy is now redundant. Young children say what *they* mean but their meanings are seldom based in an adult mind-set. They hear what adults say but often miss or misinterpret meanings that spring from adult logic. The primary importance of first fluency in language is not in fact but in fantasy. Language does not just double a child's world by adding words to the objects she must understand, manipulate and manage; it enables her to come to grips with the vital emotional intangibles of her world.

If the use made of words in early childhood can be misleading, so can the use made of objects—of toys. During these years there is no distinction between learning and playing nor between educational toys and any other plaything. Play is any activity a child engages in for himself because he enjoys the activity whether or not he also enjoys the results. If he persists for two minutes or two hours, it is because he enjoys it for that long. And if he is enjoying himself he will be learning—whether or not adults can see the point of his activity or his loafing.

Amid the thousands of studies of early childhood play, there are many that illuminate the cognitive developments of this age stage but very few that stress play's equally vital role in emotional development: in empowering young children and enabling them to grow. The clearest statement is still one made by Erikson almost two generations ago. He was writing about play therapy, but what he said is true for every child because each must find in play his or her own therapy for the dis-ease of being three or four years old: "The small world of manageable toys is a harbor which the child establishes to return to when he needs to overhaul his ego. . . . Mastering toy things becomes associated with the mastery of the traumas which were projected on them, and with the prestige gained through such mastery." When young children play with toys, they are doing more than pretending that the cars are crashing or the dolls having dinner. Their play is a replay, in fantasy, of their own experiences and the feelings they evoked. What it is too frightening to feel themselves, they may fantasize onto another being. What they dare not do or be, they may manage as or through the stronger, braver, invincible somebody they can become at will. What they cannot understand or even allow themselves to think about or see, they may be able to creep up on in play. Playthings are useful. Children find them in every culture whether adults provide them with "real toys" or not. Playmates are invaluable, though they do not have to be the carefully arranged "peer groups" beloved of our culture. But early childhood play does not depend principally on any of these. Most of its goes on in children's heads, peopled by an imagined self in relationships with invented others. This is the age of imaginary friends and scary monsters, of heroic or horrific deeds, of "mothers" and "fathers" whose rigid roles and punitive characteristics may amaze the flexible and friendly parents who are listening. As children play—with objects, with each other or simply in their heads as they follow adults through the supermarket or swing on a gate—they talk, and thus give us (if we are listening) clues to themselves and their world as they see and feel it. But they are only clues. Much of the language of early childhood is as meaningful and illogical as a stream-of-consciousness novel—and that indeed is what it is. Through fantasy and the stories that are fantasy-with-words, children (like all human beings everywhere and in every time) construct kaleidoscopic versions of themselves and of reality, shaking them together in their growing brains to produce myriads of different patterns and versions until, like historians, they arrive at a story that others will share as true. Until they have done so, much of our information and explanation passes unnoticed: "this one is green"; "there aren't really any monsters"; "he didn't mean to hurt you"; "you're cold; you need your coat"; "it's nice to say 'please.' "

Meaningful truth depends on a stable and shared reality which only gradually accumulates during early childhood and cannot be hurried with evidence and proof. Here is the three-year-old's mug of juice, and here are her other identical mug and a much taller, thinner beaker. Pour the juice from one mug into the other and she "knows" she still has the same amount, indeed she may volunteer that it is the same juice—"my juice." But pour that same juice into the tall thin beaker while she watches, and she "knows" that there is more. Let her do it for herself, pour from one container to the other, use a marked measuring jug, drink it; let her prove your "fact" to herself any way she can, and still she will not share it with you before her reality incorporates the principle of conservation. Be glad that demands for "more" can be satisfied by "making more" of what she has already, and face the fact that this is not yet the age of reason!

When the term "preschool education" was freshly coined, it did recognize early childhood as a developmental period in its own right and the importance of facilitating it with richly varied and largely social play. Indeed it was recognition of the difficulty of providing for play in small families and urban homes that inspired the first preschool play groups. In the 1950s in Britain, for example, the Pre-School Playgroups Association set up groups designed specifically to provide all kinds of play under the guidance of play leaders (rather than teachers) and with the active participation of parents. British preschool play groups, many still linked to the original association, still provide for more British children than all other forms of preschool provision put together, but the philosophy has changed with the times—and in many the play has changed too. Here, as in other countries, the popular interpretation of preschool has evolved from "before school" to "waiting for school" and in some play groups, nursery schools and even daycare centers, parents expect their children to get preparation for school.

Preschool groups vary, of course, within and between countries, but in most, preparation for school is not direct, or directly academic. Provision for "free play" (meaning that children choose whom and what they play with), for "creative play" (meaning arts and crafts materials) and for "imaginative play" (meaning encouragement to use now-standard nursery items such as a home corner and dress-up clothes) are essential elements in all modern Western facilities for young children. But just by recognizing them as essential elements, we acknowledge that they are not the whole. They are parts of a curriculum containing other activities that may not be called work and may not be compulsory, but are certainly not play. Inspired, directed and rewarded by adults, all those table-top activities (puzzles, bead stringing, card games), all those group projects (making cards for Christmas or Mother's Day) and all those "circle times" (for telling news or performing action rhymes) form the part of children's day that is regarded as directly educational. By stimulating persistence and practicing problem-solving, providing "preliteracy exercises" and encouraging "communication skills," preschool education prepares children for school.

Schools are an educational tool, and a very useful one—the best we have to help children who have accomplished the five-to-seven shift into reasonable, middle childhood along the road towards a good education. But education and schooling are not necessarily the same thing at any age, and the younger the child the less likely it is that they will prove to be so. The equation of the two in people's minds has made schools into goals and made doing well at school into an end in itself, and that trend has had two very unfortunate effects. The form that schooling takes—daily attendance in age-grouped classes within large multigroup institutions, for example—and the formal kinds of learning that go on there (such as reading, writing and number work) have overshadowed, even eclipsed other modes and kinds of learning. Secondly, the age frontiers of school attendance have been pushed further and further back on aphoristic grounds such as "you can't have too much of a good thing" and "it's never too soon to learn." Many Western parents—and not especially pushy ones either—think about early-childhood education rather as this American mother of a one-year-old does: "When my child starts school he will learn to read and write and that's what his promotion will depend on. If he makes a start on reading and writing in nursery school or daycare he will have a head start in school. If he is going to start reading and writing in preschool, he needs to be well ahead in preliteracy skills when he gets there, so if he isn't already at a daycare center, he will need to go to a play group first. He'll have to be at play group or play school by the time he is two if all that is going to fit in, and they won't take him if he isn't potty-trained—we're working on that—and talking well and socializing with other kids, so we're taking him to Gymboree and to a really neat 'bright baby' class. . . . But you know, the one-year-olds' curriculum at our local daycare is fabulous and some of my friends' babies are ahead of Jo-Jo. Maybe we'll have to let the au pair go, and find the money to send him in the fall."

Focused on the future, and school, many parents have lost sight of the intrinsic value of preschool, and of any group experiences that come before it. Play schools or play groups are not meant to prepare children for preschools; in fact they are not meant to *prepare* them for anything at all. They are intended for adults' companionship and children's fun; the social learning that may go on there or the stimulation provided by extra equipment and toys is just a useful extra. Preschools should not require any preparation anyway, other than children's own graduation from toddlerhood: it is their challenge to cater for the reality (and the fantasy) of early childhood. They are not, or should not be, designed to prepare children for school either. Nursery schools do children no favor if they offer a similar curriculum to the American kindergarten or the European intake class: starting ages for formal schooling are set where they are because that is the period in most children's development that educationists recognize as appropriate for the introduction of formal learning. The five-to-seven shift is that landmark period. The law still says that American and most European children must start school (or suitable alternative education) soon after their sixth birthdays, with Scandinavia a year later, Britain a year earlier and Northern Ireland a year earlier still. But whatever the locally compulsory starting age, more and more children are actually starting school around their *fourth* birthdays and some even earlier: right in the middle of early childhood, then, and more than a quarter of their whole lifetimes earlier than those educationists intended.

Parents and pragmatics are working together to pull school further and further back into early childhood. Falling birthrates have left many Western countries with empty classrooms while increasing demands for daycare overwhelm available facilities. By sending the older members of that "surplus" daycare population into schools, policy-makers ameliorate two problems simultaneously and generally receive popular support. Schools and teachers do not only enjoy higher status than childcare facilities and workers; a place at school is usually free where in many countries a place in a daycare center is not.

Early school entry means different things to different proportions of children in different countries, but everywhere in the West it means more children entering formal education earlier in early childhood, and therefore more children receiving a preparatory introduction to some of the form and content of elementary schooling even earlier. Neither the form nor much of the content of elementary schooling is likely to be appropriate before the beginning of the five-to-seven shift, and much of it can be limiting, even detrimental, to younger children's development. Group membership for those younger children needs to be early-childhood education in its own right, rather than pre*school* education.

Early childhood learns by playing and therefore optimal learning means freedom to play: to choose what to do, with whom, when and for how long; to touch, manipulate and experiment as well as look and listen; to move about and involve the whole body and, always, to talk. Attempts to teach three- and four-year-olds directly, making them sit still and keep quiet while they are shown and told things, are doomed. Indeed attempts to teach them by *making* them do anything are pretty well doomed: as every experienced parent or play leader knows, you have to make them want to, because while early childhood knows no difference between play and learning it often makes an important distinction between play and lessons.

There is a real difference and it is exactly this difference that eventually justifies the role of schools and teachers. Formal education— whether in academic or nonacademic subject areas—involves the acquisition of a range of knowledge and skills wider than any child could learn for himself by hands-on investigation. Furthermore much of it must be developed and perfected by more practice than most children will always enjoy. Even the best teachers cannot ensure that every child enjoys every lesson he must learn, but a good teacher in a supportive school setting will make it as easy for him as it can be to devote effort today and tomorrow to something like legible handwriting, which seems pointless to him and will not give him pleasure for years. Learning to exert that effort—to work for a future goal set by somebody else and get pleasure from mastery—is undoubtedly important in middle childhood: often more important than what is learned. But it is not an appropriate challenge for early childhood. Teaching a preschool child what she does not especially want to know, getting her to achieve a performance that looks good to the adult but means nothing to the child, is at best a meaningless waste of everybody's time and at worst a turn-off. "Can she count?" inquires one mother of another. "Oh yes, she's up to twenty," comes the proud reply. Twenty whats? Not twenty things, just twenty; you know, the one that comes after nineteen and eighteen. Children's capacity for rote learning improves rapidly during early childhood but exercising it that way tells them nothing they want to know—a pity, because they do want to know about the numbers those words are names for.

Young children's learning leads from experience of the objects themselves: one apple for you, one for me and one for Daddy; "three" is a useful answer to "How many apples do we need?" and "four" suddenly comes to life when there is an extra child coming on the picnic. It is not just *called* four; it demonstrably *is* four: one and one and one and one, or one and three or two and two: two *groups* of two. A five-year-old who has been playing with numbers since he was a toddler will scarcely need teaching that multiplication is only a quick way of adding. Dividing, even "fractions," just happen too, because apples get cut in half to "share out" and he can see that the two halves make that one apple. The head start is real, but it is in play-learning, or having fun understanding something you are doing, rather than in "math." The three-year-old bangs the piano with concentrated enjoyment. She is probably "being Daddy" or the entertainer from a recent TV show. The sound she makes is probably irrelevant to the role-playing and the concomitant enjoyment of noisy banging. Still, she may be delighted if Daddy shows her how to pick out a familiar tune, and who knows whom she becomes as she plays and sings it? But now Daddy, delighted by her delight or her performance, arranges piano lessons for her and explains that she must practice ten minutes each day "because then you'll be able to play better and better." What happens? Nothing whatsoever. The child's interest in piano playing comes to an end and if lessons or practice are imposed on her she resists. Playing the piano "better" was not on her agenda; her "me-playing-the-piano" story was already perfect. She wanted to play at playing the way she could play now, not work at playing so as to play differently in an inconceivable future.

When parents ask how much they should teach their preschool children, the answers they get often depend on the schools for which those children are bound. The entry test for an oversubscribed Manhattan kindergarten, for example, may require children to know the sounds of some initial letters; the "look-and-say" teaching methods of an English state infant school may require them not to. Rephrasing the question as "How much should children be taught in early childhood?" produces something much closer to a universally truthful answer: "As much as they want to know, and no more."

Young children cannot be taught too much by people who are following their lead, but they can be put off the business of being taught altogether by people who drag them along towards invisible objectives. Reading is a case in point. The adult objective is understandable, heaven knows; come middle childhood there can be little formal education without literacy. But many children, dragged towards literacy with flash cards and preschool reading schemes, dig in despairing heels long before they are comfortable enough "reading" pictures to be ready for the further abstraction of words. Allowed to lead, most children go a long way towards reading by and for themselves. Although most Americans do not read one book per year, and many British households use the word "book" to refer to magazines, Western urban environments are dominated by printed words from captions and comic strips to instructions and advertisements. Children notice that—notice adults' interest in what the mailman brings, in the squiggles on food packages and in the boring-looking newspapers they hide behind on Sunday mornings. Reading excludes them, and they want to know what is going on. Let into the secret of reading—the fact that those squiggles are coded messages—they may accept it as interesting information about something older people do (and therefore nothing to do with them just yet) or as an interesting idea to experiment with. If it is the latter, they may ask for the messages on advertising billboards and signs (many untaught four-year-olds can read "restroom," "exit" and "don't walk"), demand their names on everything from bedroom doors to T-shirts and eventually share the comics in those Sunday papers. Is that teaching? Well, it is not lessons, but it is certainly learning.

Often children lead adults verbally towards the next thing they want to be taught. They want to know, so they ask. It is a pity if they are not allowed to talk, if there are twenty of them to one harassed adult so nobody hears, or if a preconceived syllabus dictates the availability or content of answers. "Why is his willie big?" inquired a four-year-old in the preschool bathroom. "We don't talk about that, Andrew," replied his teacher. What a pity: penises—by whatever name—are central concerns in the early childhood of both sexes even if sex education is planned for later.

With the child in the lead and playing, adults cannot go too far or too fast, but neither can they go in all possible directions because children do not know the way. A three-year-old cannot invent the idea of a swimming pool: in order to lead adults to help her swim she needs to be introduced to the possibility. Showing children the possibilities that exist in their environment, the places and activities they might find interesting and the skills they might wish to acquire, is one of the most enjoyable and educational aspects of being the parent or the play leader of a preschooler. But introductions do not always lead to love affairs as every matchmaker knows. The child who is taken to a swimming pool does not have to go in the water, let alone take her feet off the bottom or join a swimming class. Introduced to a library and the idea of borrowing as many books to look at and listen to as she pleases, she does not have to learn to read, and taken to the zoo or a museum, she does not have to study the exhibits rather than the pigeons or passersby. The more ideas, activities and skills children are offered, the better, but only if those correlations between play and having fun, and play and learning, are respected. Major family expeditions that cost more time, effort and money than parents can easily afford often turn into disasters because of the pressure that parental investment puts on their children. The story of the British father overheard telling his two-year-old, "I've brought you here to paddle, now damn well *paddle*" is apocryphal but I heard it for real in Boston recently: "He loves the beach, but if his father comes with us he stays well away from the ocean so his dad doesn't get the chance to carry him in." More subtle pressures can be just as powerfully counterproductive: pressure to use toys "right"—the way the manufacturer or the teacher intended—instead of using them for play, which is, by definition, personal; the pressure of those questions—"What's that you've painted?"—which imply it must be something other than an exploration of the medium; the pressure of unasked-for help—"Oh, you're feeding your teddy! Shall I get him some milk?"—and the pressure to *do* something when you are wandering about *being* somebody. A French teenager once told me that watching TV is "what you do when there's nothing to do"; in early childhood it may often be the nearest adults will let you get to doing nothing.

Preschools or daycare groups can reveal possibilities to children and offer them activities—and playthings—that might not be available in the environs of home. Their most important offering, though, is one that rolls all those into one fascinating package: playmates. All children are interested in other children. Given the opportunity, babies often look at other babies more than at older children and more at them than at any adult other than a parent figure. The reputation second or later children have gained for being "easier" than first or only ones is largely based on their fascination with their older siblings. Even the parallel play of toddlers is far more than simple imitation, and it changes, in any case, as soon as each toddler has someone older or younger to play with instead. Where children have the opportunity to play freely in mixed age groups, all ages mix and play. In small rural villages the few children form into loose-knit groups ranging from toddlers to teens. Even in the urban West, where such opportunities are rare, all the children in one lakeside vacation community or around one hotel pool may run in a single, shifting pack. Most of the time, though, many of our children have no regularly available playmates at all outside daycare or preschool groups. By the time early childhood begins, they truly need to spend time with people who slip in and out of fantasy as easily as they do and will sometimes weave daddies around their babies or accept cops for robbers. In a play-group "circle time" a little girl recounted her nightmare with such obvious residual horror that the play leader found herself drawn into one of those "there aren't really any monsters" statements. Looking around the group, she could see the idiocy of what she was saying: there *were* monsters in these children's heads, they showed in their eyes as they listened in unusual silence. "Was it one of the slimy ones?" a boy inquired of the dreamer and at her shuddering nod a sympathetic susurration ran around the circle; they all knew the slimy kind.

Even this vital provision of playmates, though, can suffer from preschool groups being modeled on schools or seen as preparation for them. In most Western schools, children are gathered together in large groups with an age range of little more than a year or so. Teachers say that such peer groupings can be taught more efficiently than mixed-age or family groupings. Whatever the validity of their arguments for formal teaching, they cannot apply to preschool play. Indeed much of the drama and difficulty we associate with peer relationships and social learning during early childhood is caused by our curious assumption that children should play and learn exclusively with their peers. Even within families we are quick to decide that an older child "cannot be expected" to play with his younger sibling, that she is "not old enough to go with the big children" and that if four has a friend in to play, six must invite another six-year-old.

Spending all day in the exclusive company of twenty or more age and status peers is stressful for everyone: for adults in open-plan offices as well as for children in school. It is not only extremely stressful but often counterproductive for very young children. They must continually compete with each other and for the adult attention they all need; there is no inbuilt hierarchy to guide their continual jostling, nobody smaller to patronize so as to grow again after being made to feel small and nobody bigger to follow, or to challenge that edge between leadership and bullying. There may not be much kindness or tolerance, either. When acceptable socialized behavior is an effort for every member of a group, the one who fails to keep the rules about making lines and waiting, taking turns and sharing, can expect little forbearance from the others who are succeeding—at this moment. When that group is both inescapable and irreplaceable, the threat of rejection by it is so heavy that "do as you would be done by" or you will "be done by as you did" may compel kinds of conformity that are quite inappropriate to early childhood. All two- and three-year-olds have to learn to take part in competitive games for example: learn to play by the rules (because the game is no fun otherwise), enjoy being a genuine winner (because winning was the object of the game), yet tolerate being a loser without disastrous loss of self-esteem. Studies have shown that under these circumstances learning may be distorted because children learn to dissemble their pleasure in winning for fear of provoking rejection by all those who lost.

The more the social world of a preschool group is structured as a blueprint for the world of school, the more of it will be premature for children who are not developmentally ready for school. But even where preschool groups, inside or outside daycare centers, are structured to meet the needs of this age group in its own right, they cannot meet them all because the prime learning of early childhood is about the real world and no preschool group is that. It is not a family, tribe or community in which adults as well as children pursue their own ends; it is a group designed exclusively for children in which the only adults have the children themselves as their ends. Since the adults do not spend their time doing adult things, the children cannot learn adult things from them; instead the children learn from the adults how to do childish things in a more grown-up way. Emotions between the adults and the children are not real, either, because they are not people who love and hate each other but people involved in the pallid imitations that are professionally permissible between a teacher and a child. Furthermore the objects, activities and lessons of the group are symbolic rather than actual: snack times representing meals; Play-Doh for mud; pretend stoves for pretend cooking; gold stars for praise; jungle gyms to challenge muscular effort and simulate risk; even, perhaps, a reusable plaster birthday cake, with only the candles to symbolize individual celebration. Such a pretend world can neatly meet early childhood's need for play as a safe haven in which to rehearse and refine its narrative self. But the sanitized specialness that makes the preschool suitable and safe prevents it from feeding the narrative itself: only the outside world can do that.

The long childhood of human beings is not for finding the way from daycare through high school, but through infancy into adulthood, and for this children need to serve an apprenticeship to parents or parent figures in the business of growing up. Just as individuals who are apprenticed to craftspeople are sent to a technical college to acquire the academic aspects of their practical skills, so children are sent to school. But at any age stage, schooling can only be truly educational within the context of lived learning, and in early childhood, there is a lot of living that must come first.

If young children are to fit in enough of the living that is the real preparation for everything that is to come, not even groups that are truly oriented towards early childhood rather than towards preparation for middle childhood and school should take up most of their waking time. They need to be released from group life with energy still flowing and then to experience parents—or other *personal* adults—not as teachers, with special games and quality time, but as people, with shared activities and reality time.

In early childhood children are newly fledged into self-conscious individuality and gender identity, wild with emotion and imagination, wondering and afraid, aggressive and romantic—and continually flummoxed and frustrated by how things work and will not work for them. Through self-motivated play and endless talk they must incorporate the puzzlements of themselves, other people, feelings, processes and objects into a constructed reality which they can share with adults. Early childhood education can help them do all that—help them towards the shared reality and the dawning ability to think about it conceptually that will mark their first readiness for school and lessons—and the five-to-seven shift. What it cannot and should not seek to do is hurry children through these necessary processes of growth and maturation. Good early childhood education has its own validity. "Preschool" may describe its time frame, but it does not describe its purpose.

— 8 —

7-Up: The Years We Ignore

> When they have passed their fifth birthday they should
> for the next two years learn simply by observation what-
> ever they may be required to learn. Education after that
> may be divided into two stages — from the seventh year
> to puberty and from puberty to the completion of
> twenty-one years. Thus those who divide life into peri-
> ods of seven years are not far wrong, and we ought to
> keep to the divisions that nature makes.
>
> Aristotle, *Politics*, c. 345 B.C.

If only one span of years was important in a child's development, it
would be the first. But if those years of infancy and early childhood
shape the individual, this next span of middle childhood meshes that
individual into his society. Seven—or six or maybe eight—is acknowledged as some kind of watershed by almost every school of thought in
Western culture. Freud's latency period, Piaget's concrete operations
and Kohlberg's conventional morality are all located in this time frame,
and classical learning theory pinpoints it as the period when mental
processes, including speech, begin to mediate between the stimuli children receive and their responses. Whether the focus is on children's feelings, understanding or thoughts, their judgments, beliefs or reasoning,
the beginning of middle childhood promises a new maturity and a new
desire to learn that is recognized in every culture. All over the world, it
is at about seven years of age that children become increasingly aware
of a wider society surrounding family. They want to acquire its knowledge and skills; they need to learn its history; they strive to understand

its concerns and aspirations. And because children are, above all, social animals, they do all that learning within the context of social value systems and come to behave as others in their social group behave.

Although Western social institutions acknowledge the watershed in a number of ways—using it to mark the transition from kindergarten into academic education, for example—Western parents tend to regard the seven-and-up years as an "easy phase": a rest between the exigencies of babyhood and early childcare and the upheavals of puberty and early adult-care. Early childhood and adolescence take up the childcare shelves in bookstores and libraries, the call-in shows and the dinner-party conversations in Boston, Birmingham or Brussels; middle childhood is marked only by sighs of relief. When children are eight or nine there is surely little parents need worry about (unless there is trouble at school) and little they need do, either (because children's lives are focused on school).

But far from being a well-earned rest pause in parenting, these are the years that give parents vital opportunities to influence the children they have made towards being the kind of people they want them to be. Why are those opportunities not being fully exploited? Are they not recognized? Are they dodged because they are personally demanding and difficult? Or is it simply that, unlike the urgent demands of the baby or toddler, or the potentially dangerous excesses of the adolescent, the latency child's socio-intellectual demands *can* be ignored, in favor of her "busyness" with skills and school and peers?

Those unvoiced demands should not be ignored. Children's identification with parents or parent figures is the basis of all social bonds and at least as important in middle childhood as it was earlier on. The relationship that was the basis for the child's development of socialized behavior now becomes the basis for her dawning social morality, and the simple guidelines—such as "do as you would be done by"—that were useful in early childhood are no longer adequate. This older child is no longer concerned only with herself and her family, or only with outward behaviors. She is concerned with the internal workings of people and the world. Seven does not just watch and notice; she thinks. Seven still loves us and believes we are wonderful, but she also wonders how we can do what we do when we say what we say. And seven will remember. The fog of forgetting that mercifully blankets adult short-

comings, injustices and mistakes on the first part of the path from infancy to adulthood is thin and tattered now, no longer to be relied upon
as wool to pull over children's eyes or as sand for parents to play ostrich
in. Middle childhood calls on the adult world to account for itself, and
much of what it sees and hears will remain in conscious memory, or
easily available to it, through adolescence and into adulthood. Whether
we think of what we have to do as transmitting social values or simply
as explaining ourselves, the responsibility is awesome. When my
daughter was eight she watched me wielding an insect spray. Because
she was only eight, she did not avert her eyes and think of other things
as I had long learned to do, but watched a targeted wasp buzzing back-
wards, frantic, poisoned, dying. And then looked at me. Because I loved
her I could hear her unsaid words, and because she loved me they were
incredulous: "How could you do something so terrible?"

The temptation to sidestep such value-laden questions—even to divert children from asking them—is obvious. Unlike older generations
with clear-cut and socially accepted ideals of Church and State, few
people under middle age have packages of received wisdom ready on
ice until they are needed, like convenience foods in the freezer. Parents
who want to serve their children a moral meal have to invent a personal
recipe and put it together out of fresh ingredients—and that takes time
and courageous introspection. Is it necessary? Is it even desirable to
serve up that moral stuff to children? Concepts like right and wrong
are out of fashion, the words sometimes trotted out on political plat-
forms, but mostly reserved for sums or multiple-choice questions. Good
judgment is something everyone wants, but nobody wants to be judgmental. Even values are tricky to handle and usually kept as impersonal
as "value for money," or as distanced from individuals as "conservative
values," "Christian values" or perhaps a deprecating "good, old-
fashioned values."

Parents can let the moral stuff go by default but cannot completely
avoid it because they have an enormous input into their children's value
systems to which authoritative instruction at Sunday school or little
talks at bedtime have scant relevance. Children's ideas about what
people should be like, what they should do and how they should relate
to each other are already rooted in what they have experienced at home.
Those roots are due to start sprouting into conscious personal values,

and they will do so, with, or without, further deliberate input. If parents withhold deliberate input, children will be exposed both to untempered influences from the outside world and to *unintended* influences from their parents. Children learn about the issues that are important to adults (like employment and money), about relationships and ways of relating and about causes of conflict and their resolution, by listening to adults talking to each other. Parents cannot prevent that kind of learning because children hear what they say even when they do not appear to be listening, overhear snippets of the most intimate and acrimonious moments in a marriage however hard adults try to keep them private and *always* notice if Mom's been crying. Parents who try to keep adult business private, and family secrets secret, risk children picking up misheard, misunderstood or misinterpreted fragments. Parents who keep family communication open, share their own opinions with their children, trust them with their own feelings, can deliberately feed important items into their children's agenda.

Children arrive at value judgments, and eventually at value systems, via the processes of active reasoning they can increasingly bring to bear on life's conundrums. All human beings tackle moral dilemmas, real or simulated, most effectively in discussion and argument with people they perceive as equals, so a lot of middle-childhood debate goes on among peers, in the playground, where parents have no vote. Nevertheless it is parents who, willy-nilly, set much of the agenda: "My dad says hunting's cruel." "It's not. My dad goes hunting. . . ." "Your dad's a nerd!" By using the reasoned discipline that demands not just obedience but understanding and progress towards self-discipline, they constantly generate a rich network of issues from everyday life: "I'll have to ask my mom . . ." "Why? She'll never know . . ." "I have to ask . . . she might worry . . ." Parents whose children are sure that they will listen to them with respect and talk to them with honest conviction may even be used as a checkpoint for playground lore ("Jessica says boys can't have babies . . .") and honored by having their responses taken back for further discussion.

Not all parents realize that having their breakfast-table conversation debated on the swings is an honor. Many parents are less concerned with listening to children than with having children listen to them, less concerned with being understood than with being obeyed and very disinclined to waste time on debate that seems like argument by a liberal name. They know right from wrong. If their children would only do as they tell them, they would stay out of trouble and the principles would take care of themselves.

Unfortunately the principles do not take care of themselves. Children cannot learn to "be good" (in anybody's terms) just by carrying out instructions, any more than babies can learn to talk just by imitating adult word sounds. Understanding of the general behind the specific requires social context and adult models. Where the orders children are asked to obey happen to reflect behavior they observe among adults, children will go a long way towards deducing virtuous principles for themselves, but where there is discrepancy, they cannot. Why *did* I kill that wasp, and by a method designed for my convenience and its torment, when I had told my children every living creature has a right to life, and taught them that deliberate cruelty is always wrong? Because I hold competing beliefs about the importance of hygiene in kitchens? Because I am too self-righteously squeamish about killing to use the kinder open violence of a rolled-up newspaper? Because I am scared of wasps? Because it is what everybody does? Children will not easily learn to draw appropriate later lines between their own compromises and crimes, and to come to terms with whether or not ends ever justify means, if we will not allow them to engage with us, their model adults. And we certainly cannot assume that they will understand, let alone adopt, social values that are vaunted but contradicted wherever they turn.

Most hear a great deal about honesty, for example, but live in societies where it is only selectively demanded. Children must not lie or cheat or steal, but adults tell "white lies" all the time and are often dishonest with children for their own convenience or the "children's own good." Adults are supposed to deal honestly with one another, rail against thieves and con artists, and can be penalized for libel and slander, traveling without a ticket or falsifying a tax return. But children see those same adults voting for politicians who lie with statistics, beg people to watch their lips while they make promises they have no intention of keeping, and slander their rivals.

Explaining differences between public and private morality, between faults of omission and commission or between identical acts with different intentions is never easy, but we can only get them onto children's agendas if we try. Until adolescence, at least, children have to understand principles in terms of behavior, even though they are not the same thing. But where the three- or four-year-old is content within absolute limits and clear guidelines that easily translate into the sort of homespun personal honesty that keeps most people from cheating individuals, middle childhood brings both internal and external complications. The four-year-old's access to a complex outside world is still controlled by a few adults; he is likely to believe what he is told and to live by it—sometimes to an embarrassing degree. One woman abandoned her European habit of tasting fruit before buying it because "my son always tells the stallholder and begs him to charge me for one extra grape." She is not exceptional. Many parents find it essential to ensure that their behavior is not only honest, but also *seen* to be honest while they have preschool children. The seven- or eight-year-old, on the other hand, is quick to realize that both black and white are shades of gray and to notice when those who set out the guidelines do not live within them. Now parents must face issues like the inflated insurance claim rather than the tasted grape. Claiming the old dent in the automobile's door as well as the new one caused by this accident is not *exactly* dishonest because insurance companies set inflated premiums ("They cheat, do you mean?") since they know everybody will overclaim ("You mean they're stealing from us so it's OK to steal from them?").

If the issues parents must address inside families become increasingly complex, so do the issues that arise outside. The child's safety in the outside world is an issue in itself. Many communities are so overwhelmed with motor vehicles and cowed by crime that children are scarcely allowed out without an adult. In middle childhood, going to the playground with friends, visiting back and forth, walking—or even cycling—to school, become developmentally appropriate pieces of independence. The child who must always wait on the convenience or whim of an adult to take him and pick him up and make formal arrangements for him to get together with friends is deprived of autonomy and of confident self-reliance. The lives of children who often wait in vain may be so limited that outside school hours most of their time is spent passively, in front of a screen.

However isolated they may be from the outside world, though, its impact on them will increase as children get older. Indeed, skills we are trying to teach them give them increasing access to everything we are trying to protect them from. Once a child can read, he will—and not only his storybooks either. Once he can manage the TV, the VCR and the telephone, and visit other households, the media, commerce, and a range of strangers will become increasingly influential in setting the curriculum for his social learning, and in teaching that curriculum, also, unless parents stay in charge.

The danger of strangers, for example, is part of the social curriculum for most children in urban areas. Unless parents also make positive efforts to help them develop a sense of themselves as members of the community, children are likely to grow up with a basic suspicion of anyone they do not know and a fight-or-flight reaction to any unexpected social contact. "What should I do if that lady talks to me, Mommy?" "Scream, honey—just as loud as you can." Parts of that curriculum are dangerously confusing, and nowhere more so than in attitudes towards personal violence. Outside extremist political and religious groups, Western culture uniformly expresses nonviolent ideals while living beset by violence and displaying a fascination with blood and pain and terror that dominates both entertainment and news media. Two generations ago only a few unfortunate children ever *saw* anyone hit over the head with a brick, shot, knifed, rammed by a car, blown up, immolated, raped or tortured. Now all children, along with their elders, see such images every day of their lives and are expected to enjoy them. The jury is still out on the direct effects of violent entertainment on children's behavior, but familiarity with those images undoubtedly reduces their horror impact. The seven-year-old who hides his eyes in the family cops-and-robbers drama is desensitized four years later to a point where he crunches potato chips through the latest video nasty. Will the next generation learn not just to *watch* unmoved, but to take part in the horrors, courtesy of "virtual reality"? It seems terrifyingly likely. Commerce is well practiced at blurring the lines between horrible reality and profitable play. How many preschool children truly distinguished between the endlessly televised hi-tech precision bombing in the 1991 Gulf War and the lookalike Nintendo game? And how many children will really play Sega's "Mortal Kombat" without its exploding brains, and hearts ripped from living chests and held up still beating?

Much has been made of the "gore code" that is needed before those exquisite touches are revealed. It is supposed to enable parents to control the violence of the game (and to make sure that violence does not dissuade them from spending their money). But the publishers of magazines want to make money too. The code was revealed in "Sega Megatec" before the game was even available in the United Kingdom.

Middle childhood has known reality from fantasy so far, though. While personal experience of violence has the greatest effect on children, followed by personal observation of it, newscasting and documentary reporting almost invariably have more impact than entertainment, and many children remain easily moved by war reporting. But that part of the curriculum on violence is troublesome, too. If children are not often taught that Might is Right, they certainly get the message that Right is Might, as the major powers police the world, celebrate victory in the Falkland Islands or the Gulf and decide what sanctions should be applied to whom in Eastern Europe. And if we truly reject *real* personal violence, and only report the details of "ethnic cleansing" in order to express righteous horror, why have real American serial killers become folklore heroes, depicted on playing cards with their totals of real, and very dead, individuals listed on the back?

Other parts of the outside world's curriculum for children are wrongly paced, with much to which parents have no objection on adult principle being offered objectionably early in children's lives. Most of today's parents believe that sex education, for example, is a good thing and must include information about HIV/AIDS. But surely children should have time to come to terms with the concept of sexual activity as a life-enhancing, life-creating pleasure for the future, before they face it as a life-threatening danger? Should prepubertal children who are not yet comfortably familiar with the practical workings of any kind of sex nor yet at risk from it really be exhorted to "safer sex," complete with condoms?

Most parents reject outright censorship, but that does not mean that they are grateful to the American Comics Code Authority for giving the Marvel comic "X-Men" a positive endorsement as "suitable for children."

And what about music? The enriched fantasy world of popular music, with its heady mixture of visceral rhythm and fantasy sex, has been big business for generations, but the targeted audience has changed. Today's principal buyers of hit recordings are nine- to fourteen-year-olds. The top hits of 1991 included Color Me Bad's "I Wanna Sex You Up," and the album produced by rapper Ice T, star of the movie *New Jack City,* includes the voice of a woman saying "I am totally and irrevocably on his dick." Since then some of the stars who make their living from it are beginning to draw the line at the nineties' "slack" music that has replaced the smoochy lovers' reggae of the eighties. In 1992 Carlene Davis indicted slack lyrics for being as sexist as they are sexual: "Slackness is frightening because kids from the age of five are listening to it. . . ." Listening? Rasheda Ashanti, editor of *Candice* magazine, hopes not. "Judging by the way these girls dance to them, you'd think they weren't hearing what's being said. We don't mind a man complimenting our bodies but we do object to him describing the shape, size and smell of our vaginas."

The social curriculum on sex is not so much contradictory as hypocritical. While the hidden horrors of child sexual abuse are slowly revealed, and fathers and father substitutes all over the West wonder if they can change their toddlers' diapers or bathe their little daughters without their intentions being misinterpreted, a leading greeting card company calmly mass-markets a photograph of a flirtatious three-year-old saying, "I hate to bother you with my little personal problems . . ." Open the card and she concludes ". . . but I'm horny." So what about the sexy lace lingerie, make-up and perfume now marketed for very little girls in every Western mall? Some condemn it as likely to increase sexual abuse but others condemn *that* argument as sexist: a small girl's equivalent of exhortations to big girls to avoid sexy clothes in public for fear of provoking rape. The chances of a six-year-old being sexually assaulted are probably no higher if she is wearing black lace panties than if she is wearing pink cotton briefs, but there are subtler and even more sexist dangers to come-on gear for small girls: it might make them feel that somebody ought to. Manufacturers, anxious to expand this profitable extension to the saturated teenage market, are scornful: "Every little girl dresses up in Mom's clothes, tries her lipstick. What's the difference if she has her own?" The difference is between fantasy and reality: between *playing at* being a grown-up—with no attempt to convince the world outside your head—and *pretending to be* a grown-up with the connivance of that outside world. The first is an important developmental strategy, the second a dangerous developmental distortion.

In theory, commercial and societal values need not conflict because people do not have to buy what they do not want, and parents, holders of the purchasing power, do not have to buy for children what they do not want them to have. In practice, though, there is conflict and it haunts many families. The advertising arm of commerce does not simply ask people what they want or show them what there is: it teaches them what to want. Not many parents can withstand children's pleas for consumer goods or fashions that are desirable in their social group because however much they disapprove that game or garment, video or record, they do approve the peer-group membership that it has come to symbolize. As I write, there are families in Britain who are not eating enough because children feel that sneakers that cost a week's wage are the price of acceptance at school, and children in the United States who are not only wearing the price tag on the outside of their new jeans, but stealing tags off more expensive garments to attach conspicuously to their own.

If we notice, we all know that this is all horrible.

Most of the time most of us do not notice. We take our environments and behaviors, attitudes and life-styles for granted, too busy living to think much about how we live. But the inquiring eyes of middle childhood force parents to look at themselves and their lives, and many do not like what they see. Asked to account for themselves and the world by small people whose faith in them is not yet blemished, who are trying to be like them, and would like to be with them, many parents realize that they want a safer present and a better future for their children. Education seems the key. Most parents cannot teach and protect children themselves; their own work has no place for child apprentices and leaves precious little time for companionship or guidance. Furthermore, the dirt and danger of the environment they themselves face every day is not what they want for these loved and vulnerable small individuals. Parents want children prepared for success somewhere safe and supervised: they want them in school.

There is nothing uniquely Western in parents' passion for schooling, but there is something special in what Western parents expect of schools. All over the world education is recognized as the door to personal and social development and to socio-economic success, and wherever and whenever societies have been able to give children leisure from subsistence labor, they have established schools. It is difficult to imagine more culture-bound institutions than junior high schools in the American Midwest, provincial French lycées, British public schools, Japanese kindergartens or rural Kenyan primary schools, but they all share a worldwide and ancient idea: that formal education—"book learning"—is most efficiently delivered in educational institutions, where students can be gathered to share teachers and resources. Schools are never *only* for academic learning, of course, because the groups into which children are gathered are important in themselves. Many aspects of development depend on the mutual aid of peer interaction—pleasant and unpleasant—and the eventual formation of a fresh older generation to be responsible for society depends on children and young people growing up through shared experience. New adults, who can show and tell and teach different things from family, are important too, and wherever groups of children are given teachers, they always take more from them than the subjects they mean to teach. But although peer groups and teachers in schools are universally important, they are more important in Western countries than anywhere else in the world because they are expected to fill and fulfill a larger part of children's lives.

In most times and places, that expanding experience of friends, enemies and mentors has many different sources in the community, the neighborhood, the village, clan or tribe. In most societies a child or young person has a place in many interlocked or separated social groups: temporary groups (like those that form for festivals or as families follow work); recurrent or seasonal groups (like those that re-form each time a move is made to summer grazing); permanent groups (like the lifelong ties formed by co-initiates in many cultures). In the post-industrial West, schools often replace all those so that, for many children, nonfamily peers and adults are almost exclusively classmates and teachers. Western schools are therefore expected to provide not just formal or book learning but all learning; not just fuel for intellectual development but for all development; not just work but also play; not just a part of life for a few years but the major element in children's life-style for a decade or more and often a dominant influence, and source of social networks, into adulthood. The more schools dominate young lives, the more important it is that they not dominate *children*. Many Western schools do. And although the proponents and practitioners of child-centered education fight hard against that standpoint, conservative education policy often suggests that schools *should* dominate children. During a House of Commons debate on Britain's recent Education Bill, for example, an amendment was put forth to provide for the views of children with special needs to be ascertained in special education procedures, as they are ascertained in social matters under Britain's Children Act and should be, in all matters, under the United Nations Convention on the Rights of the Child. The Minister, Eric Forth, commented: "The [Children] Act ranges much more widely on welfare issues, inter-personal relations and the child's existence in a social environment, whereas the [Education] Bill deals with more strictly educational matters. . . . There is a difference between taking full account of a young person's attitudes and responses in a welfare context and asking the child to make a judgment, utter an opinion or give a view on his or her educational requirements." Is there, or should there be, a difference? Schools *are* social environments. The sharpest criticism that can be leveled at a school is that it does not see itself as such—does not see children as people with whom teachers are involved in reciprocal interpersonal relations, but as objects to be taught if they will listen, controlled rather than consulted if they will not.

Can schools serve as children's main source of socialization as well as of academic learning, guardians of their physical and moral as well as intellectual growth, principal agents of each generation's acculturation? Perhaps some can, and do, but most clearly cannot, do not and should not be expected to. Teachers are taught to teach a range of subjects from math to music, geography to gymnastics, but they are not selected for their social and cultural attributes nor trained to convey manners and morals to their pupils. It is rare to find an educational establishment—as opposed to some individual schools—that has even agreed upon the values that should be offered to the young, much less attempted to build them, and the skills needed to communicate them, into their teacher-training programs. We therefore expect most Western teachers to be what nothing in their selection process suggested they must be, and to teach to children what nobody has taught to them. And, increasingly, they are supposed to cultivate this marshy cultural fallow without allocated time or resources. Teaching a group of nine-year-olds "education for family life," "personal studies," "sex education" or that traditional British grammar school favorite "civics" is often the responsibility of an individual from a different culture, subculture and mother tongue from most of her pupils; a sexual orientation different from any accepted by their communities; a political or religious affiliation, or lack of one, that some of their parents find offensive. She may never have lived within the society in which the children are growing up, yet she is somehow expected to play a major part in outfitting them for it, and she may have a single session per week, shared with practical matters like scheduling and homework, in which to do it. Of course social values, and behaviors appropriate to them, are not learned only from individual teachers and in special lessons— on the contrary—but they are not inculcated just by being at school either.

Active interaction with peers is a necessary but by no means a sufficient condition for the development of personal value systems in middle childhood or for personal happiness. Without constant input from adults with whom they have a personal as well as a public relationship, children in groups will not socialize each other, indeed they will often deny each other the rights, and trample over the values, their societies hold most dear. Groups of seven-year-olds, confined in a given room or playground without an adult or adult-suggested activity, do a lot of playing, certainly; a lot of talking if they can hear themselves shout. But they do a lot of less desirable things too. The girls boss and criticize each other; the boys knock each other about and trade insults; the genders scarcely mix except in warfare. It is easy to assume that it is all good-humored, that trivial physical hurts are accidental and teasing should be taken in good part. Easy, but dangerous. Along with interpersonal violence, physical and emotional, mixed sex groups will display powerful sexism, with the boys overrunning more than their share of territory, the girls retreating behind barricades of scorn and obloquy, and both genders making group membership conditional on "sex-appropriate" behavior. Little boys dash around trying to get a look at little girls' underwear. Fourteen little girls pile onto one small boy in Kiss and Tell. Parents who complain are told that these are universal playground games—part of childhood and, therefore, somehow legitimate. But these are the games and the childhoods that have legitimized generations of sexual harassment. *How* can they be legitimate? According to recent research compiled across many countries, about one in five children in this age group will suffer from bullying and about one in eight will bully. Bullying may take the form of racism, or the equivalent singling out of any obviously "different" minority or individual, including the physically disabled, the extra small, the extra fat and the noticeably underprivileged.

Adults know that many children sometimes dread school. It is the rare parent who never has to soothe a psychogenic bellyache on Sunday night or help avert dreaded tears on Monday morning. But somehow we go on believing that this unhappiness is not quite real, not quite the equivalent of an adult's dread of factory hazing, military "initiation rites" or an office whispering campaign. We make children go to school, leaving them no options, no appeal, but we do not insist that somehow or other schools must be places where everyone can feel safe and each valued individual can flourish. Our belief in the rightness of school life is so strong that even when children are acutely unhappy there, we tell ourselves that they are learning valuable lessons about getting on together.

Under skilled adult direction, they may. But who is providing that outside lesson periods? In most countries teachers increasingly—and very understandably—resent extracurricular duties such as playground supervision. Teachers are often so overburdened that the time taken by such duties is desperately needed for lesson preparation, interaction with colleagues and relaxation. But lack of time is not the whole story. There is often a much sadder subtext. Would the teacher be happy to join her students to eat lunch and to play if she then had an alternative time for a personal break? Probably not. Just being with the children is often seen as unskilled work (and therefore insulting within a professional context) and is usually extra-contractual and can therefore be regarded as unpaid. Children certainly suffer from their awareness that teachers do not like them enough to want to spend nonteaching time with them, as well as from inadequate alternative arrangements. The employment of nonteaching staff for extracurricular duties is common and increasing everywhere, but the caliber of the people employed is vastly variable. Some large French schools, for example, employ teams of graduate students from relevant university courses to undertake play-leadership roles on a part-time basis; some American schools have highly qualified pastoral care workers who act as well as advise. But most British schools, and many in other countries, treat the care of children outside the classroom as entirely "supervisory" and regard playtime duties as on a par with the domestic work involved in serving school meals. Two or three hundred children may therefore spend an hour or more each school day confined to an asphalted—and often almost featureless—space under the supervision of people who are not expected to organize and entertain them and who have been given neither the training and status nor the facilities to do so. For many children, especially the very young, the very shy and the current victims in a group's dynamics, "playtimes" are the most stressful parts of the school day and "dinner ladies"—as children in the United Kingdom often know them—the most important adults in it. Almost all these undervalued, underpaid members of the school's staff know that it is neither possible nor desirable to "supervise" children as if they were prisoners in an exercise yard or animals in a zoo. Many provide not only a haven and hands to hold, but warm, ongoing relationships. Some do organize and entertain children, on their own initiative, and in a few schools they have won recognition for their vital social role. In the north of England, for example, a few "dinner ladies" who had been teaching the traditional group games and good manners of their own childhood produced such an improvement in recess happiness and behavior that the school district made their work into an official playtime program for the first four grades.

Even for children who are currently happy there, though, a school can rarely provide the whole range of experiences that constitute a rich world for middle childhood, or the principled protection from, and preparation for, their own world that parents want them to have. Being in a large group all day, every day, is stressful for most children just as it is for most adults, and the larger the institution that group is in, the higher the potential stress level. Children want peer-group companionship and interaction, but what they get at school is often more like a conference reception than dinner with friends, and vital pair friendships must be conducted so publicly that they are often constituted as much according to the relative status of each child as to their mutual attraction or sympathy. Children want and need to learn about and from each other, but rigid age grouping denies them the flexible shifts between asking and knowing, being nurtured and nurturing, following and leading, that are so effective in informal, mixed-age family or friendship groups. Children acquire skills, as well as doing most of their social learning, by playing together, but if there is play on the school curriculum at all it will usually be in the form of competitive sport, which is not truly play even when it is referred to as "playing games."

When laboratory rats are overcrowded they stop doing what scientists intend and do all manner of nasty things instead, like attacking each other. Overcrowding heightens competitive stress. In many classrooms children compete with each other in the very areas parents would like schools to protect them from. Social acceptance may depend on the right clothes and possessions (including the right parents); popularity may be bought with a currency ranging from gum to swear words and soft porn to hard drugs, and assured by behavior that adults regard as antisocial. The behavior of children at school is mostly crowd behavior—anathema to the exploration and development of individual value systems and singularly resistant to adult influence. Even where a teacher has the time and inclination to offer children individual attention, and the personal relationship on which personal social learning depends, children may have to reject it or risk rejection by the group as "teacher's pet."

In the Western world middle childhood development is being distorted by an overvaluation of the peer group relative to individual relationships with adults. By committing children so wholeheartedly to the world of school, we have reduced the influence of home- and community-based adults to a point where it is often impossible for them to override peer-group influence with their own. How can we deny children the activities, acquisitions and attitudes of "everyone in my class," when we have structured their lives in such a way that being just like everyone else in that class is essential to survival and self-image? Within that world of school, there is usually no adult who is psychologically part of that class in-group. By first grade, if not in kindergarten, most teachers have ceased to be parent-substitutes or pack-leaders and have assumed a version of professionalism that easily becomes detachment. Once children sense a divide between "us" and "them" the ethos of the group may easily become anti-authority, anti-effort and anti-education, and if it does, teachers will find it difficult to provide even the academic education that is still a large part of schools' purpose. Despite endless arguments about teaching methods and content, both within and between countries, there is something approaching general agreement about what that education should do. Children should not only study math or science but also learn how to study; not just complete work assignments but acquire a work ethic; not just enlarge cognitive and intellectual skills but learn to respect and strive for them. Countries differ, of course, and so do regional and local educational areas within them and schools and teachers within those, but on the whole Western schools are not remarkably efficient in achieving the narrow goal set for them by politicians: the production of an internationally competitive work force in a world "with most new jobs demanding more education and higher levels of language, math and reasoning skills."

Debates about whether or not educational standards are falling are perennial in most countries, but few have objective ways of assessing even this limited aspect of their schools' success over time and many educationalists are concerned about the limiting effect standardized achievement tests, such as those currently being pressed forward by the British government, may have on education in a wider sense. They argue, and convincingly, that even where "objective measures"—such as the American Scholastic Aptitude Tests (SATs)—have been long established, it is difficult to be sure of the exact nature or significance of what they measure.

Nevertheless, any apparent decline in "educational performance," such as the recent evidence that the SAT scores for American college-bound students have dropped by 70 points in the last twenty years, puts schools under pressure; any suggestions of "poorer performance" by the students of one country than by those of its economic competitors tends to cause panic. In 1989 the International Assessment of Math and Science studied students in eleven post-industrial countries. American students attained the lowest scores of all, and British students scored next lowest. Fewer than half of American seventeen-year-olds, for example, knew whether 87 percent of 10 was the same as, more than or less than 10, and few of them, or of the British students, could write and punctuate a simple description of themselves correctly. Another study, comparing the school performance of American seven- and eleven-year-olds with carefully matched Japanese and Chinese counterparts, also showed the American children trailing, despite the comparatively excellent resources available in their schools.

Unfortunately, panic over arguably oversimplified comparisons, especially with the high-pressure, achievement-oriented educational system of Japan, produces pressure for arguably counterproductive measures. There is little doubt that many young people in the West, especially in the United States and the United Kingdom, are leaving school with levels of literacy and numeracy below those that should be achievable much earlier, in middle childhood, by every child without special educational difficulties. But it is very doubtful indeed that Western education would be improved by a return to "traditional classroom teaching"—meaning sitting children in rows in front of a blackboard to rote-learn tables and spellings—and to endless competitive assessment of children's performance. If our schools are failing children, it is not by neglecting to force-feed them with skills and facts but by failing to provide educational food for which they feel hungry, and dining facilities in which they are eager to take it in. As one professor of education with wide experience of grade school teaching in several countries put it: "For early primary children, especially, parents want security, happiness, imagination, flexibility and social skills to lie alongside—say to dominate—the basic skills. The lessons of the last 50 years are now to be ignored, or worse, lied about."

We cannot afford to ignore those lessons about how children learn and about the personal relationships and social circumstances within which they can want to learn. Above all we cannot afford to believe that better measurable performance by children who are driven and drilled means that they are better educated for modern life. Today's industry does not only require an increasingly literate and numerate work force; it also requires responsible, self-motivated, self-directed and flexible employees, and that means tapping children's in-built desire to learn. Western schools are not doing that. The most notable finding in that comparative study of American and Japanese children was that "American children were the ones who regarded elementary school less positively. . . . [Their] expressions of dislike for school must reflect, in part, their belief that school is not an interesting place." Findings such as these seem to parallel the personal experiences of some Western volunteers who teach in developing countries: "I've got sixty kids, from eight to eighteen, three to a desk, no books and the roof leaks. They won't take a break when it pours; they won't let me go home at the end of the day. They're there because it's a chance to learn; they want to learn and do they ever learn!"

Meeting a challenge with genuine effort, doing something because it is worth doing in itself rather than because it is fun, and finding *that* fun, are important—and peculiarly middle-childhood—aspects of experience. But who sets out the challenges? In the West, the challenges children set for each other within that single, overwhelmingly important school peer group may soak up most of their energy and dominate their learning. We need to replace some of that peer influence with adult influence and enthusiasm.

Teachers cannot do that alone. As the scope of what is expected of schools widens, the personal leadership they can offer to children diminishes. For many teachers, the job on the written job description is hard, the job that is unwritten is harder and the two together are impossible. Most indict lack of resources, and often rightly. But the further resources have to go, the more thinly they must be spread; spread over "the whole child" they are thin indeed. If we are determined that teachers should serve as health educators, personal counselors, social workers, play leaders and sports coaches; introduce our children to art galleries, museums, theater and music; give them some experience of the countryside and of travel; teach table manners, prevent swearing and raise everybody's self-esteem, schools do not just need more teachers, but many more and infinitely better-trained teachers than any country currently provides within an educational system that is free at the point of consumption.

If we asked less of teachers, their efforts would be spread more generously. If families, within self-conscious communities, took back the prime roles in socializing and acculturating children and keeping them productively and creatively busy outside the classroom, those teachers would have more time and focused energy to teach what they have been trained to teach and inspire the enjoyable efforts on which all education depends. And if homes and schools, families and teachers, worked together in close cooperation, we know that they would all work to much greater effect.

Shared aims and mutually respectful links between students and teachers and between school and home are vital factors in school "success" wherever and however that success is measured. Research studies and governmental inquiries in many countries have shown those links to be crucial to outcomes ranging from an easy adaptation to school life to learning to read, and from freedom from truancy and vandalism in secondary schools to success in final examinations. Lack of capital investment and poor resources in schools are important, but it does seem that lack of parental support and involvement may be even more so.

The effectiveness of a shared ethos at school and at home cuts both ways. If neither home nor school puts a high valuation on education and high expectations on students, their performance will reflect it, however well resourced the schools may be. It is hard for any child to concentrate on his homework on a fine summer evening, and *very* hard if he can hear other children outdoors on their bikes. It is intolerable for a child to be stuck inside with his homework on a fine summer evening if it is only his family (not his teacher) or only his teacher (not his family) who cares whether he does it or not. And if nobody cares whether he does it or not, why should he either care or do it?

Many parents are dissatisfied with the way Western education systems are working. A few do look to themselves for solutions. There are an estimated 5,000 British families and 1.5 million American families educating children outside the school system, either because they have rejected it, or because it has rejected their children. Most dissatisfied parents, however, do not see their own levels of involvement as part of the problem or part of the solution. They demand more of teachers, and look to schools to demand more of their children; larger and larger minorities abandon general school systems in favor of special provisions, leaving the lowest common denominator to drift further and further down. Magnet schools, specializing in particular subjects and with highly selective entry, have long played a part on the American educational scene, are well established in Germany and have appeared in Britain as city technological colleges. They attract high-caliber staff and students and produce high-level examination results. Now it is becoming clear that similar results can be achieved without *academic* selective entry provided that schools make themselves appear selective in *some* way. American magnet schools are magnetic enough to attract white middle-class parents to black areas or urban ghettos, even if they demand no entry qualifications other than a special subject to which prospective students must agree to give extra time. Those schools still produce relatively good results because children do well in schools to which parents positively choose to send them and in which teachers want to teach. The policy of the present British government leans heavily on this self-fulfilling prophecy as a way of improving schools. Academic selective entry—a hot political potato in the United Kingdom—is now permitted and schools are being encouraged to opt out of local authority control and become self-administering, specialist and self-advertising, through a government-published league table of examination results. The best will attract the best and become still better. But by exactly the same process, the worst must become still worse.

Money, from parents' pockets rather than the educational establishment, provides another escape route. In some European countries the number of children attending fee-paying schools has grown despite widespread recession. In Britain, for example, the number was higher in each successive year from 1984 to 1992, when a drop of about one quarter of one percent was recorded. The educational standards offered to children by the private sector—especially in early and middle childhood—are not always better than those offered in local state schools and they are often far worse. But parents choose the schools, are conscious that they pay for them and, usually, are more directly involved and more respectfully acknowledged. One British teacher—dedicated, left-wing—was driven by the recession from work in state primary schools to work in a small private school. The school lacked much of the equipment considered essential in publicly funded elementary schools; its buildings were drab, its servings of consumables—from food to drawing paper—were meaner. But the parents were constantly in and out, demanding that Johnnie's reading should be heard every day or that Jane's budding talent for math should be fostered, and the owners, needing to keep them happy and paying, insisted that the teachers should be always available to them. Almost every child read fluently by the age of five and liked school, too. As the teacher put it, "I don't approve of it, but it works." If it "works," why does she not approve of it? Because with parents paying all that attention to the school, and paying for one twelfth of a teacher for each child, the potential for truly child-centered learning is there. But it is not being realized because an intensive focus on reading and math is what the parents are paying for. Five-year-olds can be happy in a hothouse, but that does not mean that it is the most appropriate environment for them. Furthermore, like magnet schools fee-paying schools drain the most privileged and often the most highly motivated parents and their children from the mainstream. A school that is "special," after all, is only especially attractive if it is seen as better for children than most schools, which must therefore be relatively unattractive. No system that improves some schools at the expense of others can help to fulfill middle childhood's huge potential for book learning. And any system that emphasizes academic learning and examination results as measures of schools' success ignores children's largely unmet needs for all the social kinds.

However reassuring—or convenient—it may be for parents to hand middle childhood over to schools, the assumption that schools are the ideal focus for children's lives and the uniquely appropriate setting for their learning is sadly misplaced. There are good schools. But schools as a whole are not institutions organized with and for children, and some are hostile places that they cannot use but must survive. Furthermore, parents' hope that teachers can achieve what they themselves cannot is vain. Schools and homes, teachers and parents share the culture that gradually soaks into children. If there is violence on the streets, just sending children to school will not protect them from it because violence will reverberate in its halls and spill onto the playground. If Bart Simpson is a cultural hero, spearheading a spreading cult of mediocrity, schools alone will not manage to engender a group ethic that makes it enjoyable to strive for excellence. If homes have fashion and porn magazines and no books, few children will seek out the literature they might passionately enjoy, no matter how dedicated the English teacher. And no teacher will ever have enough time to talk with children to compensate for homes where parents are too busy and the TV is always on. If it is really important to us to have children educated to be as we want them to be, as we wish we were rather than as we are, we shall have to change not only our schools but Western cultural values. We can only do that by changing ourselves.

PART THREE

---◆---

Putting Children First

INTRODUCTION

The failure of Western societies to do their best for children has only become apparent as cross-cultural and cross-disciplinary research knowledge of childhood has accumulated. That process has been so gradual and specialized that it is still difficult to see the forest of societal disaster for its separate trees. Millions of adults are troubled about individual children, groups of children and particular aspects of childhood: parents struggling to bring up their own; health professionals and educators whose job descriptions emphasize the positive enhancement of children's development but whose working weeks are dominated by attempts to compensate them for earlier disadvantage; child protection agencies reeling under revelations of institutionalized child abuse; economists and policy-makers watching more and more programs, public money and philanthropy draining through social problems like water through a beach on a falling tide. But most individuals, professions and institutions look no further than their own backyard. We all prefer a rosy glow of wishful thinking to clear vision, and surely *overall* things are not so bad for children? Surely they have better lives here than there and now than then? Of course, it is more comfortable to believe that things are getting better, that "we," whoever we may be, are making some kind of "progress," however that may be defined. I wish I could believe it, but I cannot.

In the first two parts of this book I have argued that the development of post-industrial societies has been inimical to the nurturance of children and that we have all allowed it to be so. We have the knowledge and the resources to facilitate child health, growth and happiness, but while millions of individuals strive to do that on a personal or professional level, society as a whole chooses to ignore the necessity or deny the feasibility of doing so on a public level. To me, this willful refusal to do what we could, and therefore should, do for our most vulnerable and dependent citizens counterbalances the achievement of the individual freedoms that we prize so highly and makes a mockery of Western claims to the world's moral high ground.

Children are the largest minority group in society and the minority that is most subject to discrimination and least recognized as being so. There is no equivalent to equal-opportunity legislation for children. No demands are made on their behalf for political correctness; even those who decry ageism seldom include children, certainly not preadolescents. Somehow we have allowed children to be unthinkingly excluded from otherwise universal human rights, and that means that the special needs that go with being very young are not met as of right but at the whim of adults. It is the nature of childhood to be dependent on adults for present survival, health and happiness, for opportunities that foster future development and for the eventual achievement of competent adult independence. From their first toothless and transforming smiles, children have effective ways of evoking the necessary goodwill from parents or their substitutes. But however solidly those relationships are founded, they alone cannot ensure that children's needs are met because even the most loving and privileged of parents can only do what society arranges, allows and supports.

Post-industrial countries certainly could afford practical measures that would revolutionize all children's lives. In fact, they could easily afford them for every child in the world, not just for their own. What would it cost each year to control major childhood diseases, halve child malnutrition, bring sanitation and safe water to every community, provide basic education for all children and make family planning and maternity services universally available—*worldwide*? Twenty-five billion dollars. Less than Americans spend each year on beer. Half of the money spent on cigarettes in Europe. If we could do all that for all the children in the world out of beer and cigarette money, we could also do anything we wanted for children in our communities. Some of the most expensive measures would require shifts in our immediate spending priorities, but the costs of most needed policies would be balanced by such massive long-term savings that the net expense would range from nonexistent to negligible.

Establishing a moral priority for children's known needs and the political will to meet them as of right is the difficult part of what needs to be done for children. Actually *meeting* those needs, day by day and year by year, is comparatively easy, because the people who have to do it are their parents or parent figures, and almost all of them want to. There are many different ways in which parenting could be facilitated and parents supported and helped—all parents, those who are currently coping, those who are floundering and those who have fallen down. I sketch some simple suggestions in the final chapters. If those, or similar ideas, were actually implemented, every issue raised in this book could be addressed. And they could be implemented. The final irony is that similar ideas *have* been instituted, somewhere, sometime, for a few people, *and they worked*.

Are we ever going to acknowledge that priority which is not only moral but also practical, not just for today's children but for everybody's future? Are we ever going to find the political will as private people to insist on public action? There are around 300,000 homeless children under ten in the United States. Most lose their chance of a good education because they do not attend school regularly. Many lose their families; the older children are placed in foster care, while mothers and babies stay in public shelters and fathers sleep on park benches. Around ten million more Americans are on the edge of homelessness— doubled up with family or friends, at the mercy of a landlord's displeasure or the inexorably growing tensions of overcrowding. The United States dropped its federal support for low-income housing from $32 billion in 1978 to $9 billion in 1988—a decline of more than 80 percent after adjustment for inflation. The resulting housing shortage, described by Barry Zigas, director of the National Low Income Coalition in Washington, D.C., as "the worst since the Great Depression," has left thousands of families who qualify for help waiting for it without hope—44,000 of them in Chicago, 60,000 in Miami, 200,000 in New York City. America is not alone. Australia and the United Kingdom are taking the same path. Homelessness in Britain doubled during the 1980s, and 80 percent of families that become homeless now include children.

Hundreds of thousands of children without addresses, home bases or beds to call their own in the richest nations in the world? Shocking. Clearly it must be somebody's fault; clearly somebody should do something about it. But not us, surely? We are only responsible for our own. Nobody says, "We have to find a way." Western states are spectator democracies.

Something could be done. I have to start with economics, and especially with poverty, because although many of the problems and most of the possible answers have nothing to do with economics, people think they do. Powerful voices insist that enough money has already been spent to prove that "social welfare doesn't work," that it is not a sensible economic option. Others wrap reluctance to take measures to combat poverty in a cloak of phony concern, lest its victims get trapped in "welfare dependency." A few, still powerful, voices openly blame the victims of poverty for being and begetting the poor, and would punish them and their children with destitution.

The principal problems of rich societies that do not grant everybody the right to aspire to a home, a baby and a few beers are not economic but attitudinal, not a shortage of money but of political will. *Those* attitudes. *Our* political will.

New Approaches to Poverty
and Privilege

Poverty and debt are the major problems of the richest nations the world has ever known. While some individuals reach pinnacles of wealth, others become destitute. The rich-enough are balanced by the too-poor and growing pockets of people are hemmed in on the wrong side of opportunity. World leaders may still boast of humble origins; President Clinton makes much of his childhood in "a place called Hope," but the black baby born in today's urban ghetto has no hope of becoming tomorrow's president or prime minister, and her parents know it. That sort of knowledge is an important feature of modern poverty in post-industrial societies. Mobile and mass-communicating, bombarded with materialistic aspirations that are often difficult to disentangle from moral exhortations, every individual can see what others have, and what she or he ought to (but does not and probably never will) have.

Of course everyone has a lot. When the historian Thomas Macaulay forecast in 1875 that within a century "numerous comforts and luxuries that are now unknown or confined to a few may be within the reach of every diligent and thrifty working man," he imagined luxuries that became necessities for our grandparents, including meat at main meals and clean shirts on most days. Now, the meat is no longer regarded as essential, but comforts that even our grandparents scarcely dreamed of—central heating, telephones, cars, television sets—are realistic expectations for everyone. That does not mean that we are all richer now, though, despite the efforts of world leaders of the eighties, Margaret Thatcher in particular, to convince us. With an increase in average real disposable income of 24 percent during her terms in office, Thatcher claimed to have made everyone in Britain richer. Whenever her attention was drawn to the increasing poverty concealed within that average, she insisted that people are not poor because they grow richer more slowly than their neighbors. Semantics apart, people who grow richer more slowly certainly *feel* poorer. Subjective poverty is relative, so if societies aspire to social cohesion, only relative measures of poverty are meaningful.

The distribution of real incomes is probably the most widely accepted basis for the measurement of relative poverty and on that basis its incidence and upward trend in the post-industrial West are startling. During the Reagan years, America's rich doubled their share of the national income. Between 1979 and 1989 in Britain, the percentage of people living in households with less than half of the national average income rose from around 8 percent (4.4 million individuals) to around 19 percent (10.4 million individuals), and the rise continued through 1991. The EEC saw a comparable rise by 1987 of 4.5 million individuals (using average equivalent disposable income in each of the twelve member states separately). In 1985 the Community-wide figure was 15.9 percent, but this figure conceals vast differences between member states. By this calculation, Portugal, for example, had 69.5 percent of its population living in relative poverty and Spain 32.4 percent, while Belgium had 1.8 percent, Germany 7.1 percent, and France 12.1 percent. At 15.9 percent, the United Kingdom's rate was the fifth highest in the Community. Comparable overall figures for the United States are difficult to derive because official poverty is not defined by the income of one group relative to another, or by their shares in the nation's total income, but in terms of an income "line" developed by the federal government and including welfare payments in kind, such as food stamps. In 1990, an annual income of $13,359 marked that line for a family of four; $9,009 for a woman and one child. Using the line then operative, and bearing in mind that the figures are for individuals in "post-transfer" poverty (those whose incomes fell on or below the poverty line after they had received everything to which they might be entitled from Aid to Families with Dependent Children [AFDC], social security and unemployment insurance), about 33 million Americans, or 14 percent of the population, were poor in 1985. Just as overall figures for the EEC conceal vast differences between countries, so figures for the United States conceal vast differences between states and between—somewhat related—racial groups. That 1985 figure was made up of 11.4 percent of white Americans, 31.3 percent of black Americans and 29 percent of Hispanics. Comparable U.S. figures in 1993 were 14.5 percent overall, made up of 11.6 percent of whites, 33.3 percent of blacks and 29.3 percent of Hispanics.

How poor is poor? Transatlantic comparisons of what it means to individual people or families to be included in official poverty statistics are bedeviled by differences in the policy implications of the figures. The United States poverty line is a statement, in dollars, of the minimum income required to stay out of the classification "poor." The government of, for example, the United Kingdom makes a similar statement in pounds. But what matters to individuals is what happens when and if their incomes drop to, or below, that level. In the United Kingdom that poverty line is a safety net. People whose income falls below it become entitled to Supplementary Benefit or Income Support *to take them back up to that line*. In the United States, the poverty line is not a safety net; falling below it does not *automatically* entitle everyone to public assistance. Furthermore, even the few people who are able to claim assistance under federal programs can expect to receive only a percentage of the poverty-line figure. For the vast majority who depend on state-administered programs, that percentage may be very small indeed. Federal government sets the poverty line but it is up to individual states to set their own standard of need for means testing and *then* to decide how nearly the benefits it pays should meet that need standard. In 1987, for example, Minnesota set its need standard at $532 and its maximum benefits were 100 percent of that sum, but Illinois set its standard at $689 and paid only 49.6 percent of that, while Alabama set its standard at $384 and paid only 30.7 percent. While rates for Supplemental Security income—the only federally administered cash benefit, and available only to elderly people, blind people and people with disabilities on low incomes—are usually somewhat higher, it is Aid to Families with Dependent Children which primarily concerns us in this book.

Safety nets do not catch everyone. People can, and do, fall through them in EEC countries. Nevertheless their intention—and usual effect—is to set a bottom limit to the relative poverty any citizen will experience, and that bottom limit is substantially higher on the European side of the Atlantic than the level to which people can sink on the American side. In the United Kingdom for the years 1988–1989, for example, the line below which income support was paid, and the limit to which it was paid to a lone parent with one child, was £54 per week in addition to her necessary payments for housing. That sum, £2,808 per year, was 34 percent of average income for the United Kingdom. At the same date, average income in the United States was $19,704 so 34 percent of average income would be $6,999 per annum or $558 per month. None of those three American states mentioned above paid AFDC rates that reached that figure. Minnesota came closest, paying $532 per month; Illinois paid $342, and Alabama paid $118 per month. Given that the United Kingdom paid housing costs in addition, and that British families could count on the National Health Service for all medical costs, they were very clearly "less poor" than the American families, relative to the rest of their respective populations. Complex though comparisons are, it is clear that individuals who live below the United States poverty line, even in the more generous states, are likely to be, in European terms, not just poor but extremely cold-and-hungry poor. By 1990 that was about 34 million people, over 14 percent of the population of the United States, and the percentage is still rising.

Poverty lines are drawn by governments; every time a line is redrawn, national poverty statistics change. If the British government makes benefits payable at a higher income level, the numbers of people "in poverty" (below that line) increase—and vice versa. Less easily altered, and therefore more shocking, is the increasing gap between the richest and the poorest segments of populations. In Britain during the eighties, the real disposable income of the top 10 percent rose by 30 percent, a substantially greater increase than the national average of 24 percent. But the real disposable income of the bottom 10 percent did not only rise more slowly than that average, it actually *fell* by 5 percent. In the United States during the same period, average disposable income, adjusted for inflation, rose by 17 percent in the top 20 percent and fell by 6 percent in the bottom 20 percent. On both sides of the Atlantic, then, poor people have not only become richer more slowly than everybody else, some of them have become absolutely poorer.

While all Western governments seek to maximize their nations' GDP through the operation of market economies, the balance struck between wealth generation and wealth distribution varies widely from country to country and from time to time. Redistributive fiscal policies—such as those on which Scandinavian welfare policies have been based—can substantially reduce the differentials between rich and poor within any society. According to the dogma of the Reagan-Thatcher era, however, fiscal policies that impose controls on free enterprise and reduce the strength of the profit motive also reduce the generation of wealth and therefore the total to be distributed. In North America, the United Kingdom and—to a lesser extent—within other EEC countries, the preferred strategy has been to concentrate on facilitating economic growth, relying on a putative process known as "trickle-down" to ensure that a share of extra wealth generated at the top eventually arrives at the bottom.

The trickle-down strategy has been notably unsuccessful in preventing increase in relative poverty. It is difficult to see on what comparative or historical grounds it was expected to be otherwise. Rich empire builders have never brought their subjects up to their own levels. Wealth poured into colonies has never been equitably shared with indigenous populations. Aid to developing nations helps the richer rather than (and often at the expense of) the poorer. Wealth is sticky stuff; it does not trickle easily or far. But can increasing wealth that will not redistribute itself to reduce relative poverty prevent increases in absolute poverty—even ensure that everyone gets richer, however slowly they do it and therefore however poor they feel? Some economists still believe that if the boom growth of the early eighties had continued, there would not have been the observed increases in absolute poverty in the United Kingdom or the United States. But the optimistic assumption that this is a temporary phenomenon related to the immediate world recession and that rapid growth will return once it bottoms out seems unrealistic. Most post-industrial Western economies are growing very slowly, and long-term trends suggest that they have been doing so for at least the last thirty years, with boom rather than slump the aberration. The annual average growth rate in GDP for all OECD countries, for example, was 3.8 percent between 1965 and 1980; 3 percent between 1980 and 1989. Even those countries whose phenomenal growth rates all Western leaders sought to emulate—Germany, Japan—are now down to similar levels, and growth rates around 2 percent seem the best that can be expected as the recession bottoms out. If even saving the icing for the rich cannot keep national cakes growing, only slicing them more fairly will keep the poor eating at all.

The adoption of redistributive policies, however, has serious political, as well as economic, implications. Even under the stress of world recession and high rates of unemployment, voters in Western democracies tend to favor political parties that promise to keep their hands off profits and paychecks. In 1991, after almost a generation of equalitarian social policies, Swedish citizens voted out the party responsible for the taxation levels that made them possible. In 1992, after more than a decade of waiting in vain for boom-wealth to trickle down from the haves to the have-nots, British citizens voted the Conservative Party yet another term in office rather than risk a change that threatened slightly higher rates of personal taxation for the well-off. Americans broke that pattern by electing a Democratic president; they demanded and were promised attention to the domestic economy, and they are getting it, but whether they wanted, or will get, redistributive economic policies still remains to be seen. President Clinton's health plan, for example, would certainly increase social equity in American society, and while much of its cost would be met through increased efficiency, there is certainly an element of redistribution—of profits from large pharmaceutical companies, or from large insurance conglomerates, to new groupings, for example. But how much of the spirit of the plan, and of Clinton's plans for funding it, will survive Congress and pass into legislation?

Any Western government or political party determined on redistributive policies leading to greater social equity faces an enormous task in public education to overcome attitudes which confuse selfishness and self-sufficiency and reject socialism without wondering what it might mean. However much, or little, people have, they want to hold on to it, or at least keep control of it, and they particularly resent what is taken in taxation for the benefit of those who have less. Firms want competition that is unfair to them controlled, and do not see their competition as unfair to others, but as enterprise that should be free. Everyone wants the services she or he uses to be well financed but resents expenditure on services only others use. As populations age, many people fear dependency on the state—which others' taxes must pay for—but most still fear the dependency of others—financed out of their own taxes—even more. Such naiveté, reminiscent of the thinking of children who have not yet understood the interdependence of all members of the kindergarten, is the inevitable result of years of individualistic, enterprise culture, lent spurious but enormously influential intellectual support during the early eighties by conservative social scientists. Charles Murray, for example, whose book *Losing Ground* was once referred to as "the Reagan administration's bible," believed that poverty was largely caused by the availability of financial support from outside families, all of which was a dire mistake; if starvation was their only alternative people would work, and if a shortage of jobs meant some had to accept extraordinarily low wages, that was "the discipline of the workplace" which everyone should accept.

Now, almost a decade later, up to a quarter of all adult men, up to half of all adult women and as many as eight in ten of all those leaving school are unemployed in some parts of the United States and other Western countries, yet Murray's influence reverberates on both sides of the Atlantic. People who are poor are newly described as suffering from "behavioural dependency," but while the recommendations for dealing with "them" may be more politically acceptable for being described as "treatment" (Murray himself realizes that "to expand upon my policy prescriptions is to give large numbers of readers too easy an excuse for ignoring my analysis of the problem, on the grounds that I am obviously a nut. . . ."), they are no less punitive.

Far from being dismissed out of hand, Murray's basic thesis, and especially his focus on the increase in female-headed households, was crucial to the formation of *The New Concensus on Family and Welfare* in the United States, and to the Family Support Act of 1988, with its insistence on "workfare" and its new measures to curtail public support for single mothers and to withdraw it from claimants who set up independent households before they reached eighteen. That same thesis contributed to the thinking behind Britain's Child Support Agency and has been honed to its sharpest point so far in the United Kingdom during 1993. Murray believes that by forsaking "traditional family values," Britain's single mothers are wreaking havoc on society. He argues that the decline of the two-parent family and the absence of fathers is responsible not just for a drain on the public purse but for rising crime. He believes that government should not merely reduce the monetary and housing benefits available to single mothers but divert all such spending to adoption services and orphanages. The director of the Institute of Economic Affairs ended his foreword to Murray's *The Emerging British Underclass* with the words "Bring back stigma; all is forgiven!" and government seems to have heeded that exhortation. At the Conservative Party conference in October, ministers such as Peter Lilley, the Secretary of State for Social Security, and Michael Howard, the Home Secretary, blamed lone parents for most of the United Kingdom's social ills and floated a range of measures designed to restrict their rights and benefits. The statistical facts do not support this moral crusade. Seventy percent of British lone mothers have been married; of the 940,000 receiving some welfare benefits, only 42,000 are under nineteen. More than a quarter of lone mothers spend up to half their pay on childcare in order to work, and 90 percent of those without jobs are seeking them. Government knows all this; even members of its own party use the media to make sure that everyone knows the facts: "The true picture is one in which teenage mothers are a small minority and most single parents are women who no longer live with the father of their offspring . . . and are anxious to make their own living but are trapped in dependence on benefits by lack of jobs and the insurmountable costs of childcare." But this transatlantic attack on young single mothers is only a particularly extreme case of a general tendency to blame the victims of poverty. Many people still see the poor as recipients of undeserved largesse, taken, almost stolen, by governments from enterprising hardworking individuals and profitable concerns. The poor, furthermore, are often seen as the *only* beneficiaries of fiscal policies; without the poor, many intelligent people believe, they themselves would be able to keep everything they earn. Marian Wright Edelman rails against the "amnesia or hypocrisy that wants us to think that poor and middle-class families must fend entirely for themselves; that makes us forget how government helps us all, regardless of class; and that makes us believe that the government is simply wasting its billions supporting a wholly dependent, self-perpetuating class of poor people, while doing nothing but taxing the rest of us. Chrysler and Lee Iacocca didn't do it alone. Defense contractors don't do it alone. Welfare queens can't hold a candle to corporate kings in raiding the public purse." But although her book *The Measure of Our Success* reached the American best-seller list in 1992, its messages do not seem to have been heard by taxpayers, nor by the policy-makers, who, especially in Britain and North America, are still inclined to subsidize industry rather than its employees. High rates of unemployment, for example, have forced all post-industrial countries to reconsider the interrelationship between their wage and their welfare policies. No country can allow individuals in full-time, but low-paid, jobs to be worse off than unemployed individuals on social welfare. But is this anomaly to be prevented by raising wages—at a cost to industry—or by lowering welfare payments? The EEC proposes to approach it by establishing a legal minimum wage and social contract for the Community. The United States tries to hold down welfare payments so that minimum wages that have not kept up with inflation nevertheless are higher than state benefits. Britain resists EEC proposals—arguing that if employers are forced to increase the wages of the low-paid they may employ fewer people—but adds a benefit called "family credit" to the wages of the low-paid, ensuring that their income exceeds social welfare payments. Although family credit goes to employees, and is proving an effective benefit, their employers also benefit, having their payrolls kept artificially low by what is, effectively, an indiscriminate subsidy.

Attitudes like these are as much responsible for the increasing socio-economic inequity of the last decade as economic recession and political upheaval, and even if relative prosperity and stability return, they will continue to bedevil us. "Whole nation" policies *could* be afforded; they are not rejected because they are economically impossible but because individuals want to win rather than share. National wealth could be spread; it does not fail to produce richer nations because the theorists are wrong but because the rich take pains to keep it within the magic circle where it can create more wealth for the haves rather than new prosperity for the have-nots. But the arguments for new socio-economic policies such as those proposed here are not exclusively altruistic. If nothing is done to redistribute wealth, to broaden the base of opportunity and therefore of motivation, and to reintegrate those who have become disaffected, everyone's quality of life will continue to deteriorate. Already, rural areas are depopulated and destroyed; cities fragmented by ghettos and despoiled by the despair of the homeless; public services, overwhelmed and underfunded, unable to serve citizens with courtesy, and daily lives dominated by crime and the terror of it. Increasingly, health, education and happiness escape children; anxiety and boredom quell the creativity of the young; envy of the more fortunate and guilt over the less fortunate sap the confidence of the middle classes, and the sheer size of seriously underprivileged minorities drives the rich into increasingly separatist life-styles. It is not only those who are discriminated against who suffer from discrimination, not only the poor who suffer from poverty. If pricked consciences cannot motivate socio-economic change, self-interest may eventually compel it, but the human cost of waiting for compulsion will be fearsome. Perhaps there is a better chance that what must be done in the name of humanity will be done if consciences are differently focused—not on "the poor," whom nobody wants to have to think about, but on children, whose well-being is of concern to (almost) everybody.

Children First

From Dickens to Edelman, generations of social commentators have bemoaned the tragedies of children trapped in poverty, and the costs and losses incurred by the societies in which those children grow. Now, as overall poverty increases, public expressions of concern for children are growing. A UNICEF study of the circumstances of British children, published in 1990, concluded that "during the eighties children have borne the brunt of the changes that have occurred in economic conditions, demographic structure and social policies in the UK. . . . There is no evidence that improvements in the living standards of the better-off have 'trickled down' to low income families with children." In 1979, 11 percent of children in the United Kingdom were living in poverty. By 1989 the figure had passed 22 percent. Children have borne the brunt everywhere. According to Eurostat, "in the majority of the EC member states children became relatively worse off during the period 1980–1985 and in four member states there was an actual increase in the numbers of poor children: the Netherlands, Ireland, Germany and the UK." There has been an increase in the United States, too, especially in the numbers of very young children who are poor. In 1980 about 13 percent of all Americans lived in poverty and about 19 percent of children under six. By 1985 the figure was about the same for everybody but had risen to around 23 percent for under-sixes. In 1993, the figure was 25 percent for under-sixes, 21 percent for all under-eighteens and no less than 53 percent and 43 percent for those who were, respectively, black and Hispanic. In 1991 the National Commission on Children estimated that one in five American children was living in a family whose income was less than the federal poverty line and that nearly 5 million of those children were in desperately poor families with incomes less than half of that poverty line. Contrary to many people's assumptions, a majority (60 percent) of poor American children are white. Most live outside big cities, have only one sibling (if any) and have at least one parent who is employed. Three million British children and thirteen million American children who are not just *somewhat* poor, but officially, nobody-is-arguing poor. Howard Hiatt, former dean of Harvard's School of Public Health, believes that their plight "raises a set of issues as threatening to the national security as the arms race once was."

What do those figures actually mean? According to major mortality studies, they mean that more American children in any five-year period die from causes directly related to poverty than American soldiers during the Vietnam War. They mean one quarter of all American babies born to women who did not receive adequate prenatal care; 9 million of those children still with no health insurance as I write in the fall of 1993; only half of all preschool children receiving their full course of immunizations, and up to 500,000 without homes of any kind. The figures mean teenage children in Britain's cardboard cities, too—enough to shock Mother Teresa into a public offer of help when she visited London in 1990. And they mean a sharp increase in poverty-related diseases, such as tuberculosis, and the reappearance of conditions, such as rickets, that we associate more with starvation in sub-Saharan Africa than with malnourishment in the rich West. Those figures mean children begging in the streets of Paris as well as Bombay; children organized into pickpocketing gangs that sound like Rio de Janeiro but are found in Rome. And, in major cities in almost every Western country, those figures mean increased and earlier child labor and child prostitution, less and shorter time in school. The children behind those figures also suffer in a million less dramatic ways: mean ways. There are many who cannot expect birthday gifts and know that their mothers cry because they cannot give. There are children who cannot go out on winter Sundays because their only warm jackets have been washed on Saturday and must stay clean for school on Monday, and children who have no warm jackets and have never had any clothing that was new from a shop. There are urban children who have never seen the stars in a dark sky, an ocean or a forest or a mammal living wild; never climbed on rocks, waded a stream, swum in a lake or eaten anything they have planted or even picked or dug; rural children who have never visited a big city, a theater, museum or gallery; children for whom beauty, luxury and glamour are associated only with television, books only with school, and for whom there are no visual or performing arts. Behind these figures, children travel filthy, dangerous streets to schools besieged by dirt and violence and travel home again to projects that are gray under the rain clouds of Glasgow, the smog of Los Angeles or the blue skies of Milan, because gray is the color of dirt and depression: the color of poverty.

Poverty has no clear boundary lines. With up to one in four of all children already indisputably poor, millions more are arguably, or at least potentially, so; parents who can be confident of giving their children a good life from birth through adolescence are fortunate indeed. Almost one third of marriages currently end in divorce and although the broken pieces of one family may eventually become incorporated into two new ones, divorce usually makes everybody poorer. As many as a fifth of some populations are unemployed and the risk of layoffs in some geographical and age groups is even higher than that. Layoffs may be long-term, too, even permanent, and the longer unemployment lasts, the more all-embracing poverty becomes as savings are used up, everything saleable is sold, and household equipment, furniture and clothing fall into disrepair and cannot be replaced. And if everyone in the neighborhood is poor, nobody can help anybody with swaps, loans, cast-offs or hope. Even the security of fortunate or prudent people with property, savings, investments and pension plans is at the mercy of market forces that can be merciless. Hundreds of thousands of home-owning families, for example, have been plunged into poverty because they can no longer afford their mortgage payments but cannot escape the debt by selling houses that are now worth far less than the money borrowed to buy them. As post-industrial Western societies have become richer, poverty has become more probable in prospect and, perhaps, more painful in actuality. An acquisitive circle traps rich and poor alike, leaving little room for other values, little energy for the meeting of other needs. Materialism is simultaneously aspiration, defense and disaster.

In this context, concern over the *effects* of socio-economic policies on children can never be more than peripheral. What is needed is a child-centered focus for the *making* of those policies: an economic blueprint that has the commitment to ensure that every child is "rich enough" as its starting point and patterns all other considerations around it, rather than adding child welfare as an afterthought aspiration that throws the pattern out of balance. The proposition is that poverty in childhood has such heavy long-term costs that money spent to prevent it would yield far better returns than extant welfare policies—that any extra costs incurred, over and above current budgets, would be more apparent than real, and that focusing on children would ultimately produce more caring and creative societies.

Child-focused socio-economic policies would have their first and most obvious impact on the poor, but they would not be "welfare policies" in the usual, limited sense, but polices that, by ensuring every child's right to a fair hand, reshuffled the cards of all players. If childhood disadvantage is to be prevented, a bottom-up approach is the only one that makes sense in the light of recent international research into its nature. That body of research has gradually made it clear that attempts to evaluate particular kinds of childhood, or particular childhood events, with a view to crisis intervention are a waste of effort because they will always produce contradictory results. We can only judge "good" and "bad" childhoods by the results. Faced with an unsuccessful and unhappy young adult, or a successful and happy one, we can say that her childhood clearly was not, or clearly was, "good enough" but we cannot objectively say why. Intuitive explanations for adult outcomes are often cited, of course, but they do more to excite the media and confuse the public than to sharpen anyone's understanding. Different studies in various countries have shown, for example, that children reared by lone parents are at a serious disadvantage; that they are not necessarily at any disadvantage; that they may have advantages over children brought up in two-parent households. The conclusion to be drawn is not necessarily that some or all of the research is flawed but that "it depends." And what the results of lone-parent rearing (or any other specific factor) depend on is *other* factors.

It is the concept of cumulative risk factors in children's lives that makes research findings like these comprehensible. In post-industrial Western countries where family patterns are in flux and their reality is often at odds with the ideals of the society in which they are located, lone-parent rearing *is* a risk factor for children. But the magnitude of the risk depends on a wide range of family relationships and circumstances and may often be less than the risk that attaches to being reared amid unfavorable relationships and circumstances but with both parents. Gradually we are learning to identify some of the risk factors that, piled one upon the other, make rotten results for children cumulatively more likely. The more we learn, the clearer it becomes that, in post-industrial societies at least, poverty is the biggest risk of all. That is not to suggest, of course, that poor children cannot or do not become healthy, happy, productive adults. Rather it is to suggest that there are barriers, large or small, between every baby and the eventual realization of her full potential for contented, creative citizenship, and that whatever the nature of those barriers, poverty will make them more difficult to surmount. To be born deaf is to be faced with an enormous barrier, but who is more likely to receive all the special education she can use, the rich deaf child or the poor deaf child? Having a mother who has no choice but to return to full-time work when he is four weeks old is a risk factor, minimized by excellent alternative care and the absence of a pile of other risk factors. The poor child is far more likely than the rich one to spend his early days in substandard daycare, to experience health problems that are inadequately dealt with and to miss out on preschool education.

In study after study, conducted in country after country, family poverty has been shown to be inexorably correlated with premature delivery; postnatal, infant and childhood mortality, malnutrition and ill-health; childhood neglect; educational failure; truancy; delinquency; school-age pregnancy and the birth of babies who are victims of premature delivery, post-natal, infant and childhood mortality, malnutrition and ill-health . . . and so on. Each of these is, in itself, a risk factor. Each can and does occur, singly or in combination, where families are in privileged socio-economic circumstances. But poverty increases the statistical chances of those risk factors accumulating and the difficulty of dealing with any one of them. Cycles of deprivation *can* be broken but cannot be, and are not being, broken by nervous short-term measures to deal with specific "problem groups" of children after any of these events, let alone by measures primarily intended to reduce the numbers of parenting adults on welfare—and thus reduce benefit costs. Everyone who works with older children and adolescents in trouble or distress—be she a doctor, teacher, social worker or juvenile court judge—knows that whatever the manifest problem, poverty is usually a contributory factor, and that the very best that she can do or arrange will almost always be too little and too late. Only a new economic priority for all children, from the moment their conception is recognized, will produce a post-industrial society that instead of being notable for the richness of its knowledge and the paucity of its action, acts on its knowledge and does enough, soon enough.

Often there are chicken-and-egg difficulties in deciding when is "soon enough." Money and effort devoted to the well-being of even newborn children is expended too late if their parents are children themselves. School-age births are major risk factors for two sets of children—the parents (especially the mothers) and their infants—so effective action is needed before conception rather than after birth. It is not being taken, though. Studies in almost every Western country show that the numbers of child pregnancies are rising while their ages drop.

Adolescent births are a devastating example of the cumulative effect of risk factors and their exacerbation by poverty. Getting pregnant is a common reason for dropping out of school, accounting for more than 20 percent of girls' premature departures from American high schools. Failure to complete formal schooling, whatever the reason for it, is in itself a major risk factor. The demand for unskilled labor is diminishing; the proportion of young people within aging populations is decreasing. Youngsters who enter adulthood without qualifications or skills are increasingly likely to live in poverty and welfare dependency. When the burden of a baby is added, those grim probabilities rise steeply. In the United States, for example, girls who drop out of high school to have babies earn less than half the lifetime income of girls who drop out of high school at the same age but remain childless until later. Seventy-one percent of all mothers under thirty receiving AFDC assistance had their first babies before they reached their eighteenth birthdays. Poverty compounds those risk factors, making it less likely that the high school dropout, male or female, pregnant or not, will eventually acquire qualifications and skills.

In the same way, being born to an adolescent mother is, in itself, a major risk factor for her child, but one that is much exacerbated by poverty. The younger his mother, the greater the chances that a baby will be born prematurely, at low birthweight for the length of his gestation and with assorted handicaps such as cerebral palsy. But the poorer she is, the less chance he has of surmounting a physically poor start. Although of course there is enormous diversity in the way the infants of very young mothers turn out—many people know of at least one loving sixteen-year-old who, ably supported by her own family, eventually made a success of life and parenthood—studies comparing them with children born to mothers who match their own in every way save that they were five years older show that as a statistical group they do less well, physically, educationally, socially and emotionally. And many of those babies who are girls will, of course, repeat the pattern.

The baby who is born to an older mother is spared one major risk factor, then, but if she did not want him, he faces another. The Pro-Life lobby, aware that appearing to want to force women to produce unwanted children does its cause no good, stresses that unwelcome pregnancies often result in welcomed infants. But while this may sometimes be the case, there is evidence that babies born to mothers who asked for and were refused abortions are at definite disadvantage. A careful Swedish study, for example, compared 120 such children with a sample matched in every other respect. Followed to the age of twenty-one, the "unwanted" children had significantly less education and were significantly more likely to be dependent on public assistance. More than twice as many of the unwanted as the wanted children had histories of delinquency. What of babies whose mothers were both very young *and* reluctant?

Wanted or not, being one of several siblings may also be a risk factor—when compounded by poverty—and too many babies born too soon after each other are also at risk. A study of working-class families in London showed that the chances of juvenile delinquency were more than 50 percent higher if a boy had more than three siblings by the time he was ten years old. Michael Rutter's studies of poor families in England and on the Isle of Wight showed that children with three or more siblings were at increased risk of delinquency or of developing conduct disorders. He suggested that where a family was already poor, every successive child increased the socio-economic disadvantage and diluted the available parental attention.

Depending on the socio-political stance of the individual, such findings may be either taken to point to the need for new initiatives in family planning or for a reassertion of what insular conservatives choose to call "family values." Neither type of response will ever be more than peripheral and palliative. Of course it is important to ensure everyone free choice in planning her or his family and particularly important to motivate and educate those too young for independent parenthood to defer childbirth. Of course societies may feel it legitimate to insist that men take financial responsibility for their children even if they are unwilling to share parenting responsibilities or their partners reject them. But simplistic single-issue policies—family planning clinics, child-maintenance regulations—will never accomplish complex social ends. As Dr. David Rogers put it, during his presidency of the Robert Wood Johnson Foundation, "Human misery is generally the result of, or accompanied by, a great untidy basketful of intertwined and interconnected circumstances and happenings."

It is not poverty alone that fills those baskets, but poverty is the thread that tangles them up. The longer an individual has lived in and with poverty, the more difficult it is to disentangle their contents and tackle one risk factor at a time. Effective policies need to address themselves to *children* from the moment of each one's beginning, ensuring that, whatever barriers may exist to the fulfillment of her potential for self-sufficient citizenship, every child is rich enough, relative to her community, to enjoy the health, education and happiness that will minimize those barriers. If that were done for even a single generation there would be less to do in the next because fewer of those grown children would produce babies sooner or more often than they wanted them, or be unable to cope with the wanted babies they produced. Some still would, of course, and once there *was* a baby—even another and *another* baby—those children's well-being would still have priority and be worth whatever it would cost because, in the long-term, intervening only at crisis points costs much more. Some cost-benefit analyses from the United States even enable us to see how much more.

Premature birth is always a life-threatening crisis. Intensive medical care for a preterm baby, needed for anywhere from three to sixty days, costs approximately $3,000 per day. The rates of premature birth are reduced manyfold by adequate prenatal care; such care currently costs around $600 per pregnancy. The Institute of Medicine of the National Academy of Sciences calculates that the extra cost of increasing the availability and accessibility of prenatal care sufficiently to reduce the numbers of babies born preterm by 2 to 3 percent would lead directly to savings of at least three times its magnitude.

Schoolgirl parenthood is a personal crisis for both the mother and her child. The total price tag is so widespread and long-lasting as to be incalculable, but the immediate public assistance costs have been carefully considered. A study by the Urban Institute, financed by the National Institutes of Health, shows that a reduction of 50 percent in births to girls under eighteen in 1990 would have led directly to a reduction in expenditure of $390 million in AFDC, $160 million in Medicaid and $170 million in food stamps.

All acute illness is a crisis, and measles is a more serious one than many people realize, often necessitating hospitalization and sometimes leading to disability or even death. The Children's Defense Fund reckoned that the average cost of hospitalization for a child with measles in 1992 was $5,000; the cost of immunizing a child for life, $8. It is calculated that the first decade of America's measles immunization drive—largely concentrated on reaching elementary school children— saved the nation $1 billion. It is reasonable to assume that twice the effective effort, aimed at the 50 percent of preschool children who are currently not fully immunized, would more than double the saving at today's prices.

The ultimate crisis intervention is removing a child from home. The total costs of long-term measures to prevent abuse and neglect are difficult to compute, but even when a child's removal is imminent and otherwise inevitable, short-term intensive casework can render it un-necessary and, although expensive, it is highly cost-effective. In 1985 the Homebuilders program cost $2,600 per *family,* compared to $3,600 per annum per *child* for foster care and up to $67,000 per annum for institutional care. At the end of one year, 90 percent of the children were still with their families. The savings for that year were calculated to amount to at least three times the otherwise inevitable expenditure. As the Committee for Economic Development stated in 1987, "Improv-ing the prospects for disadvantaged children is not an expense but an excellent investment, one that can be postponed only at much greater cost to society."

Figures like these seem to speak for themselves, making it abundantly clear that child-centered socio-economic policies are not only af-fordable but economical. Policy-makers, bureaucrats and taxpayers are difficult to convince, however, because many investments in infancy are so long-term and diffuse that their payoffs are easily missed—or as-sumed to consist of soft ideals rather than hard currency. Overall bene-fits such as living in a more socially just society cannot be easily defined, let alone entered on a balance sheet. Measurement of the effectiveness of prevention programs often depends not on measuring *something,* but on measuring *nothing:* the absence of an acknowledged ill. And even when the purpose and evaluation of programs is agreed upon, their payoff is not more money in hand but less money spent than it might have been otherwise. Money used to provide prenatal care for every mother or immunizations for every baby, for example, is insur-ance against disasters that might not have happened anyway (but all too often do). Money spent on ensuring that a child reaches kindergar-ten ready and raring to learn does not make his subsequent education cost less than his peers', but ensures that he can make as good use as they of the public money spent on them all, and that he does not cost the much, *much* more he would have cost if he had developed special educational needs later on. And since not all poor children have trouble in utero, *or* build up a backlog of ill health that eventually kills or costs thousands, *or* experience learning difficulties, educational failure and welfare dependency, those who allocate scarce national or state re-sources can always choose not to cross as-yet-invisible bridges.

Even when the profit from an early investment in children is obvious to outside observers, including policy-makers, it may still not be at all obvious to bureaucracies because the department that authorizes the original expenditure is seldom the department that enjoys the long-term benefit. Public Health puts money in and, years later, Public Education saves, or spends more effectively, as a result. Public Housing sees that one of its precious units has been blocked for ten years by this troublesome family; what it does not see is that during that time many departments have *not* had to pay out to support members of a homeless family. It is a kind of accounting that is difficult to audit and difficult to justify to electorates, especially when the investing departments are under continual pressure to cut costs.

If children are to be put first, their interests will need to be recognized at national, regional and local levels and represented by people capable of foreseeing and overseeing policy impacts on children and of highlighting and communicating trade-offs. Some countries are already taking the first hesitant steps in this direction, but they do not yet go nearly far enough. Norway, for example, is the first country to have a Children's Ombudsperson. The first incumbent played an important role in providing policy-makers with child-friendly parameters and in righting wrongs, but her position was one of influence, not power, and the position of her successor seems to be similar. The role envisaged for a Children's Rights Commissioner, as proposed in the United Kingdom, includes representing children's interests at government's highest levels, but even if the post were established it is questionable whether the Commissioner could actually ensure that those interests were met. The establishment of a cabinet-level post of Minister for Children—as discussed by the British Labour party at the time of the 1992 general election—is probably an essential first step. A token post—even one with executive power at the top—would not be enough, though. We need to bring children into the very center of society's stage so that we act around them and can see—cannot avoid seeing—the effects of our actions on them. "Child impact statements"—similar to environmental impact statements—should be required with any planning or licensing application, any policy proposal, any new regulation or addition to case law. Children's interests would not always override other interests, of course, but they should always be recognized, assessed and weighed with the rest. That would require much more than an influential and child-friendly figurehead. It would mean extensive networks of staff with the power to demand statements from government departments, institutions and businesses, with the knowledge to advise on drawing them up and with the authority to insist on a proper assessment of their weight. Some clues to the American public's reaction to the idea of child impact statements may emerge from a publicity campaign that is being designed in Boston.

If it is difficult to convince policy-makers and bureaucrats that putting children first, and poor children first of all, would be economically efficient, it will probably be even more difficult to convince electorates that it would be fair. Blind to the devastating discrepancies of wealth and privilege within them, Western democracies all pay lip service to the idea that everyone has—or should have—the same opportunities and nobody should be given unearned or undeserved advantages. Poverty-relieving measures are widely regarded as both unearned and undeserved. In a 1990 survey of the European Economic Community, for example, about one sixth of the population in each country picked "laziness/lack of willpower" as the main cause of poverty. As to America: perhaps only the then-vice-president, Dan Quayle, would actually have described the poor as "those people" in a public debate, but if his words were politically incorrect, his sentiment was clearly shared by millions. Such attitudes seem especially extraordinary at a time when almost every individual in the recession-ridden West must be at least acquainted with somebody who is poor because of lack of job opportunities, layoffs or other no-fault disaster. But prejudice seldom yields to demonstration of its error and, even today, there is widespread prejudice against the poor.

Poor *children* arouse somewhat different reactions, though. Concern for children is part of the value system of all post-industrial countries, however little it may be acted upon. Furthermore, most people realize that adults who have earned advantage pass it on to their children who have not, and, conversely, that *children* who are poor are not necessarily "undeserving." Many people who are prejudiced against poor adults therefore find welfare measures that target their children acceptable. Unfortunately, though, that acceptance is usually conditional on help being targeted *exclusively* at children. Experience in several countries suggests that many taxpayers complain vociferously if measures aimed at children provide any spin-off advantage to their parents. British and German taxpayers, for example, are infuriated when priority for scarce public housing is allocated to lone-parent or immigrant families who have young children.

Some targeting of school-age children separately from their parents is possible. Various countries provide free school meals, for example, and these certainly help to ensure adequate nutrition for children in families below the poverty line. But similarly exclusive targeting of infants and very young children is neither practical nor desirable. The health, development and happiness of babies, toddlers and preschool children is so intimately meshed with that of the people who constitute their families that they gain or lose together, both ways around. Any society that is genuinely determined to ensure that all children are rich enough will have to approach childhood poverty with a startling new mind-set: children *and* their parents first.

Children and Parents First

Such a mind-set would make silk purses out of some of the smelliest sows' ears of social intervention. Take homelessness, for example, one of the fastest-growing and most shameful manifestations of modern post-industrial poverty. Almost every urban area now has its cardboard cities and terminal dwellers, its desperate drift of people who have fallen out of the bottom of society and, lacking the bureaucratic necessity of a fixed address and the social necessity of a shower and clean clothes, have little prospect of scrambling back up again. No Western country is comfortable with the idea—let alone the actuality—of small children sleeping in the streets. An American scientist at the 1992 Earth Summit, besotted with the dramatic modernity of Rio de Janeiro, could only protect her image of the city by insisting that the dozens of children dozing on Copacabana beach "must have been having a midnight picnic." But people cannot tolerate the idea of homeless adults being housed out of turn and tax dollars, either, "just because they've got kids." So what happens? Sometimes, in some places, the children are taken into "care," swapping the hell of street life with people they know for separation into the institutional or foster care that may seem more tolerable to us but may be another kind of hell to them. Sometimes, in some places, the children and their mother (not father, however "intact" the family) are taken into shelters that do more to protect our sensibilities from their existence than to protect them from its hardships. Sometimes whole families are put into hotels where bed-and-breakfast sounds but does not feel like a cheap holiday. Such "solutions" cost vast sums of public money and solve nothing. They do not buy decent living conditions for those children now, nor a realistic opportunity for their parents to do so in the future. It would be immediately cheaper to rent apartments for them in the private sector. It would be less expensive in the longer term to extend the existing provision of public housing. And in the long term it would make economic sense to build and maintain such accommodation to the very highest standards available in their communities rather than to the very lowest. The notion that this would be unfair to childless people, buying their own, less desirable homes, or already lining up for public housing, comes from the old mind-set.

It is not only people's sense of personal injustice that makes such ideas unpalatable; policy-makers and the general public alike also fear that positive discrimination for people who are parents will lead to more "irresponsible child-bearing" or even, horror of horrors, to people having babies "on purpose." When Charles Murray warned, almost a decade ago, that the availability of welfare benefits made it "rational on grounds of dollars and cents" for poor unmarried women to decide to have babies rather than work, he expressed an unfounded fear that is still deep-seated in North America and in the United Kingdom and underlies the moral crusade against young single mothers described earlier. A conviction that poor women have (or might have) child after child in order to live in idleness haunts American welfare policy discussions. At the 1992 conference of the British Conservative Party, the minister responsible for Britain's Social Services, promising a "clamp-down on the scroungers," especially singled out unmarried girls who "get themselves pregnant in order to be given a home." In the summer of 1993 another British minister proposed that any British woman who had a child and would not, could not or dared not name the father so that child-maintenance could be extracted from him should be cut off from all welfare benefits. The government was quick to state that he was not expressing official policy, but not quick enough to forestall some expressions of sympathy with his view from its own backbenches. In the event, Britain's new Child Support Act does not exclude such women entirely from the benefit system, but does impose a substantial weekly penalty.

Babies-for-gain are a myth and a myth without foundation because *there is no gain.* Even in Norway, the country that through its "transitional benefit" provides most generously for women rearing children as their sole parents, the total package of entitlements enables them to avoid poverty but cannot maintain them at a level as high as that enjoyed by two-parent families. French provision is actually intended to encourage as many women as possible to have three, rather than two, children, so entitlement rates rise steeply with each child. But although its financial support for all mothers and young children is superb compared with most other non-Scandinavian countries, much of it ends when a child reaches the age of three and lone mothers almost all work full-time thereafter. Belgium's family allowance, on the other hand, is referred to as an "indirect wage" and continues until a child reaches eighteen or graduates from full-time education. It is not means-tested and is intended to assist mothers in staying out of the labor force if they wish. But even this support, generous though it sounds and *relatively* generous though it is, does not make motherhood a profitable role. The possible benefits received by a Belgian mother amount to less than 2 percent of the average Belgian family's income. In America, even in those states with the most generous provisions, AFDC never lifts recipients out of poverty and neither does the complex package of means-tested and universal benefits a single mother may be entitled to in the United Kingdom. Much is made, in both countries, of the risk of women having more and more children because welfare or benefit payments are increased as the number of children increases. Only prejudice, ignorance or both can sustain a belief that the extra sums constitute extra "income" or "profit" for the mother. Under AFDC, for example, a second child brings an extra $30 per month in Alabama, $40 in Florida. Which of us would like to attempt the impossible task of maintaining a child on less than $10 per week? Which of us would actually plan a pregnancy to obtain such a sum? The evidence is that nobody does. A European survey in 1990 found that the levels of family allowance, or similar benefits, available were an insignificant factor in people's decisions about having babies, ranking seventh after factors such as economic prospects, partnership stability and the availability of satisfactory child care. A state-by-state comparison of American birth-rates and AFDC rates shows variation in each but no correlation between the two. And over the whole of the United States, the birthrate and total family size of women in receipt of AFDC is exactly the same as it is for the entire American population—1.9 children per woman.

Equally mythical is the related belief that increases in welfare benefits lead to earlier sexual activity and are therefore responsible for observed increases in teenage pregnancies. Statistics across different social groups within single countries show that early sexual activity is just as common among relatively privileged girls as among those for whom going on welfare is a reasonable expectation. Nowhere is there a positive correlation between birthrates to young single women and rates of benefit paid out to them. On the contrary: the United States, with minimal social welfare payments, has far higher rates of teenage births than European countries such as Belgium, France or the Scandinavian countries which provide far more generous support. Some people argue that this finding is spurious because America's teen birthrate is disproportionately inflated by higher birthrates among black adolescents. In fact the difference between American and European rates remain statistically significant even if black Americans are excluded from the comparisons. There are complex personal and societal reasons for teenage births, many of them exacerbated by poverty, but a cool calculation of financial advantage is not among them. Most result from conceptions that are accidental, at least at a conscious level, even though the resulting pregnancies may provide unique boosts to previously rock-bottom self-esteem, and culminate in beloved babies.

Ridiculous though it may be, the fear that women will use their exclusive capacity to have babies—their final irrefutable power over men—to take advantage of (predominantly male) establishments remains widespread. In 1990 a young British woman who had been found guilty of shoplifting became pregnant while awaiting sentence. In due course she returned to court, where, to everyone's astonishment, the eminent judge gave her a prison sentence. Acknowledging that non-custodial sentences are usual in such cases, he explained that since a nonpregnant woman *could* be imprisoned for such a theft, he felt that this pregnant woman *should* be, so that it would be clear to other women that getting pregnant while awaiting sentence was not a clever way to stay out of custody. Only a male, benched above reality, could possibly imagine that a woman would (or even could) get pregnant for such a reason and during a six-week remand on bail, so that particular case was a tragic absurdity. Nevertheless it raises an important point of principle. Supposing a woman *did* conceive a baby, hoping thus to avoid a prison sentence: would it not be more important to ensure that her baby was born outside prison than to ensure that she served time inside? Likewise, if a woman or a couple, desperate for a decent place to live, did start a pregnancy in order to get priority in public housing, should they and their baby therefore not have it? If the new mind-set is to put the well-being of children and their parents first, it must hold even under extreme provocation. Children's welfare is the prime social consideration, so once a baby exists, whatever the circumstances of her conception, doing justice to that baby's needs must take priority over ensuring justice between adults. Any exceptions, whatever their justification, will keep alive the concept of the "undeserving poor" and all its associated horrors.

If positive discrimination for children *and parents* contradicts people's ideals of interpersonal fairness, the idea that such positive discrimination should even be balanced against the principal of strict equality in the eyes of the law will undoubtedly appall many. Nevertheless, children's well-being demands a reconsideration of the relationship between fairness and justice because strict equality between convicted wrongdoers visits the sins of parents on their children. At the end of 1992 approximately one fifth of all women in British prisons were "mules"—women who swallow condom-wrapped drugs and thus carry them across borders. Most of those women have children. Some had children with them at the time of their arrest and lost them to relatives if they were lucky, into "care" if they were not. Such children often lose their mothers forever because sentences of five or even ten years, served in women's prisons that are few and far between, mean that "maintaining contact" is usually bureaucratese for "pipe dream." Other women had left children in the countries they came from, promised a quick, safe and profitable return trip by the wholesalers. Nobody in Britain ever knows what happens to those inadvertently deserted infants. Surely not even retribution and deterrence can weigh more heavily in the scales of justice than the needs of those children.

Far more men than women are imprisoned in Western countries, so when children lose parents into legal custody, they usually lose fathers rather than mothers. But should they, must they, lose either parent? All post-industrial countries try to avoid custodial sentences for nonviolent crimes; many have outlawed them for certain categories of offense, such as debt, and for certain categories of offender, such as the mentally ill. Is it not strange that no country has a formal policy, or even guideline, against the imprisonment of practicing fathers convicted of nonviolent offenses? Given the enormously high cost of a place in prison, and the probable cost of welfare assistance to the now-lone mother, the substitution of fines or community service would make immediate economic sense. And since having a father in prison is known to be highly correlated with juvenile delinquency, especially among boys, it would certainly make even greater sense in the longer term.

If whole societies are to benefit from policies that put children and their parents first, those policies must start by addressing poverty—known to be the most basic risk factor for children—with such energy that it no longer exacerbates other risk factors, which therefore become easier to tackle. But even that necessary bottom-up sequence will not create effective policies unless it starts from the very bottom—from sections of populations that are generally seen as being beyond society, out of contact with any social values, no-go areas for positive change as well as for police officers. The new mind-set will not face its severest challenges in relation to those whom it sees as pathetically supplicant—epitomized by a category called "the homeless"—but in relation to those whom it sees as incomprehensible and threatening and sometimes labels the underclass.

So what about people who are not good parents or good citizens, but, rejecting well-meaning attempts to "help" them to be so, produce children and grandchildren who seem locked into cycles of deprivation, disaster and despair? Has enough money not been spent to prove that there are people for whom social welfare does not work, is certainly not a sensible economic option and may do more harm than good?

Versions of those questions constantly recur, even among liberals, and while a cynical comeback is tempting—"so what do you suggest we do: deport them all to Devil's Island?"—they require answers.

It is true that most post-industrial countries have increased their overall social spending in the last twenty years (though relatively more on the old than on the young) and it is true that more people are poor despite it. More children grow up in poverty; more grow up without stable families; more fail in the educational and employment stakes, and more of these vulnerable people drop into pitfalls of addiction and mental illness, debt and crime, from which there seems no escape. But if all those are facts, the conclusions those questions suggest are manifestly untrue. It is not increased spending on social programs that has caused increases in poverty and its associated disadvantages, but economic stagnation, high unemployment, social disruption and increases in social inequity. Antipoverty programs—America's, for example—have not been ineffective: her poor would be even worse off without social security, AFDC, Medicaid and food stamps. What those programs have been is inadequate in scope and in spirit: too little, often misconceived and much, much too late. The chilling effects of budgetary deficits, especially at a time of world recession, make it difficult to argue for new or increased social spending: difficult, indeed, to combat the cuts in welfare benefits and services that are such a feature of life in post-industrial Western countries today, because those deficits lower rates of economic growth and threaten future living standards. But difficult or not, it has to be done because failure to invest in the upcoming generation, from the very bottom, has exactly those same effects. We have to do more, not less.

— 10 —

New Approaches to Human Rights for Children

The socio-economic interests of nations would be well served by giving children—and their parents—priority. Children's lives and prospects would be improved by a generous allocation of resources to their care and education. But the interests of children themselves will not be fully met, nor will continuance of that priority be assured for their children and grandchildren, as long as they are regarded principally as objects of adult concern. Children are not objects; they are not our creation. They are not ours; they are us. No society can claim to do its best for children as children unless what it does is based on acceptance of children as people. Accepting children as people does not mean treating them as if they were adults. Children are small and vulnerable so they need special consideration and services from their societies; they are apprentices in the business of growing up so they need protection, nurturance and teaching from individual adults. Nobody would wish to remove the rights to have their "childish" needs met that children have been given through laws concerning child support, child labor and education, and through innumerable exemptions from the responsibilities borne by adult citizens. But societies originally gave those special privileges to children within "the empire of the father" and by virtue of their incompetence to act outside it. Wives were once within that empire too, but the modern world that has recognized women as competent legal persons has not similarly recognized that "children are people too," and as such entitled to the same human rights as everybody else—rights that belong to them in their own right as individuals rather than as appendages of parents or guardians who have a right to own them.

Most people pay at least lip service to human rights, even universal human rights, but the phrase "children's rights" often evokes an oppositional response: "What about *my* rights, then?" or "I'll give them rights when they can show me a sense of responsibility." We are so accustomed to thinking of children as inferior others rather than junior selves that rights for children seem certain to be *extra* rights—rights that are for children only and at the expense of our rights, or of parents' rights over them. It is not so, of course. Human rights must include children, because they are human. Children's rights must therefore, by definition, be the same as everyone else's. That phrase, "children's rights," is only needed because children have been excluded. A new respect for children's rights will only upset the balance of power between the generations to the extent that it corrects accumulated inequities that arise from past disrespect and are lost in the mists of family histories that start "When I was a child . . ." and end ". . . it didn't do me any harm." The harm done has been so great that many individuals cannot even identify with the children they used to be. No wonder they cannot identify with the children they have now produced. No wonder they see children in general as an out-group.

Children as an Out-Group

Seeing children as separate from ourselves is dangerous. If they are not part of us, they are not necessarily like us. If they are not like us, we do not have to assume that they have the same senses and sensibilities as the rest of us. We may choose to be kind to children—our own and everyone else's—but without that most basic layer of shared humanity it is not axiomatic that in our dealings with children we should "do as we would be done by" (or as we wish we *had* been done by). Much of the time we do not.

Baby boys, circumcised without anesthetic, shriek. Every adult male shudders to think of such a procedure. But parents are told "it doesn't really hurt them" and they believe it. Western people have always performed nonritual infant circumcision in that way and if it did really hurt, they wouldn't—would they?

A wakeful baby's unanswered cries spiral toward panic as she hears her own helpless despair in the night quiet. Parents, who would hasten to answer any adult's call for help, assure each other that this is how she will "learn not to cry." Babies must "learn" to go to sleep at the right time and to stay asleep for a conventional and convenient number of hours, too. Even the most insomniac parent seldom wonders whether her child is any more able to sleep and wake on purpose than she is herself.

A toddler, bested by rightful adult authority, stalks, stiff-backed, from the room, followed by gales of unrighteous adult laughter. We do not laugh at each other in defeat, but infant dignity is not to be taken seriously, nor is the frustration and rage that adults' lack of respect evoke: "It's the terrible twos, you know." How terrible to be two.

The three-year-old will not be jealous of the coming baby if the news is broken carefully: "We're going to have a new baby because it'll be so nice for you to have a sister or brother to play with. . . . We love you so much that we just can't wait to have another little girl or boy. . . . I shall really need my big girl to help me look after the little baby." Humph. If a husband spoke to his wife in similar terms, would he be more likely to prevent jealousy or provoke homicide? "I'm going to get a new partner because it'll be so nice for you to have some company and help with the work. . . . I love you so much, I just can't wait to have another wife. . . . I shall really need my reliable old woman to help me look after the new one."

A four-year-old recoils in shuddery horror as the guinea pig that is like nothing he has ever seen before is forced furrily against his resisting hand. He must not be frightened because there is nothing to be frightened of. Once he discovers that it will not hurt him, he will love the dear little thing. Will he? Does Mommy love the dear little spiders that never bite her? Would she love them if we put one in her hand?

A five-year-old who seeks privacy in the bathroom meets teasing impatience: what has *she* got to be modest about? Asking why she must do something, she is told "because I say so"; how can she learn? Caught pushing her toddler brother, she is spanked ("I *will* not have you hurt your brother . . ."); what does she learn? Overwhelmed by love she throws her arms around her mother: "Go on with you," she says gruffly, pushing the child gently away. When, oh when will we learn?

Not very soon, it seems. A British woman fostered a newborn baby and eventually tried to adopt him, but lost him at the age of eighteen months to his natural mother. Everyone recognized, even assumed, the bereaved foster mother's pain: social workers, colleagues, family and friends all felt with and for her. But nobody, not even the foster mother herself, the only mother that toddler had ever known, ranked his agonized distress in the same league as that adult grief: "He's bound to cry for me, poor little mite, but he's only a baby; he'll soon forget." Children's feelings, so often missed or dismissed, regarded as temporary or disregarded as trivial, matter as much to them as our feelings matter to us—and sometimes more. That means that children's feelings merit at least equal considerations with the feelings of adults even when they are evoked or displayed in different ways. The despair of the baby who feels deserted is real despair even though the desertion is no more than a parent's routine departure for work. The frustration of the toddler who cannot manage his new toy is just as acute as that of his mother who cannot start her car. And fear of a vacuum cleaner is the same disabling emotion as fear of a hurricane. Believing that—knowing it to be true—is a necessary, though by no means sufficient, step towards meeting children's special childish needs within the context of their shared human rights, and gradual assumption of responsibility for themselves and towards others.

Children's Rights in a Political Context

"The well-being of children requires political action at the highest level. We are determined to take that action. We ourselves make a solemn commitment to give high priority to the rights of children." So said the world's leaders, including seventy-one heads of state, at the World Summit for Children held at the United Nations in 1990. That summit, together with the United Nation's Convention on the Rights of the Child, adopted in 1989 and ratified by 147 nations—although not the United States—by September 1993, raised the political profile of children's rights. Thanks to the work of UNICEF and of campaigning groups in many countries, there was already growing support for the establishment of independent public bodies to promote the interests of this large, but unenfranchised and therefore singularly powerless minority. As noted earlier, Norway led the world by establishing a *Barneombud* (Children's Ombudsperson) in 1981. Australia—whose federal constitution makes its state developments important—followed with an official Children's Interests Bureau set up by the state of South Australia in 1984 and substantially enlarged in 1988. Ratification of the United Nations' Convention has stimulated work for children's rights all over the world. Although it remains in the hands of nongovernmental organizations in many countries, including the United States and the United Kingdom, New Zealand created the post of Commissioner for Children in 1989, and several Canadian provinces have appointed advocates for various aspects of children's rights. All such developments are politically crucial. They constitute real progress now and the potential for real change in the future. Nevertheless, in the practical sense they are embryonic. Even if goodwill and good intentions do not abort, a long slow gestation must pass before they emerge as part of the realpolitik, having a real effect on the lives of all children. The preamble of the United Nations' Convention on the Rights of the Child emphasizes the "equal and inalienable rights of all members of the human family," but post-industrial nations still make most policies with no regard to their impact on children. The preamble also insists on children's rights to "special care and assistance" and insists that where policies and decisions directly concern children, nations adopt a guiding principle that "the best interests of the child" are a primary consideration. But while there is no fault to be found with the principle, there are many faults of commission and omission in its application, especially with the processes by which children's best interests are assessed.

There are no simple answers to questions such as "Who has the right to judge a child's best interests?" But while the answer clearly cannot be "the child" if she or he is four months old, it certainly ought to include any child who has comprehensible language, even if she is only three years old, and it might indeed *be* her if she is thirteen. Many legal theorists and children's rights activists stress the absurdity of treating people as legally incompetent until their sixteenth, eighteenth or twenty-first birthday and as legally competent the next day. Some advocate the construction of a calibrated scale of increasing competence to apply to all children; others think this would be impossible. Hillary Rodham Clinton has argued forcefully for a reversal of the legal presumption of children's incompetence so that all children are assumed competent until proved otherwise. In most Western countries, though, the answer to that vital question is almost invariably assumed to be "parents or legal guardians," whatever the age of the "child," and even if children are in public rather than parental care, it is still assumed that the adult world will make decisions on their behalf, often with minimal input from them. This directly contravenes Article 12 of the Convention: "States Parties shall assure to the child who is capable of forming his or her own views the right to express those views freely in all matters affecting the child, the views of the child being given due weight in accordance with the age and maturity of the child. For this purpose the child shall in particular be provided the opportunity to be heard in any judicial and administrative proceedings affecting the child, either directly or through a representative or an appropriate body, in a manner consistent with the procedural rules of national law." In Britain, since the Children Act, children who have been taken into public care do have a legal right to be consulted on all decisions affecting them and some degree of consultation almost always takes place. But how much consultation? And how effective is it? Children are often excluded from the case conferences or other professional consultations at which crucial plans are made for them. That phrase "in the best interests of the child" can, and often does, reflect a (more or less) benevolent authoritarianism. Outside personal relationships with family, teachers or grown-up friends, the best most children can expect of most adults is patronage.

Children have no votes. In many countries they can marry and have children of their own or join armies and learn how to kill other people's children before they can take part in the democratic process. Debate about the age at which young people should be enfranchised so as to take an equal part in electing the governments that will represent everyone is outside the scope of this chapter. What I am concerned with here is not children's lack of political influence on adults' lives but their lack of control over their own.

Western societies provide no institutional means by which children can influence decisions about matters that affect them, or control what happens in their own lives. Children can make their views known only by speaking through their parents, teachers or adult friends (if they will listen) or by direct participation (if it is allowed). Direct participation in planning, policymaking or administration is rarely offered, in any country, to children who have not yet reached puberty, and only occasionally to adolescents. Schools, for example, are run, theoretically at least, for the benefit of children, but children's views on schools, teachers or curricula are rarely sought. Educationists who have explored the possibilities of student reports to match school reports suggest that these might be extremely helpful to subject teachers and to those charged with pastoral care, but to most adults, the idea of being criticized by a mere child is anathema. Some schools, in some countries, do have school councils, but the executive powers of those few that exist range from nil to minimal. Even when children and young people are offered participation—whether in school, in a club setting or a youth movement—they are very rarely offered any real control. They are usually excluded, for example, from all discussions of financial matters. Adults seek to justify this on the grounds that accountancy is neither interesting to children nor within their competence, but control of the agenda ensures that adults retain effective control over the debate.

Opportunities for children to participate in discussions affecting their lives in the communities they share with adults are even rarer. Many of the early complaints received by the Norwegian Children's Ombudsperson were from children protesting decisions that had been taken without reference to them, about matters of direct concern to them such as sports facilities or pedestrian safety.

Sometimes, though, children are not merely excluded from equal participation with everyone else, but singled out for patronage, denigration and deprivation. This list of rules enforced upon a group of Norwegian children in their housing cooperative was sent to their Ombudsperson in 1989. It could be matched in most Western countries. In many there are also housing developments where children are forbidden altogether, or where adult tenants, often elderly people, have successfully requested housing authorities to house families with children at a distance from their own blocks:

CHILDREN ARE NOT ALLOWED TO SCRIBBLE ON WALLS

CHILDREN ARE NOT ALLOWED TO MAKE NOISE IN CORRIDORS

CHILDREN ARE NOT ALLOWED TO PLAY INSIDE THE BUILDING
  EXCEPT IN THEIR OWN APARTMENTS

CHILDREN ARE NOT ALLOWED TO HANG AROUND INSIDE THE
  BUILDING OUTSIDE OTHER APARTMENTS

CHILDREN ARE FORBIDDEN TO PLAY OUTSIDE OTHER
  ENTRANCES TO THE BUILDING OTHER THAN THEIR OWN

CHILDREN MUST NOT LEAVE BELONGINGS OUTSIDE; SUCH
  BELONGINGS WILL BE PLACED IN THE RUBBISH CONTAINERS

CHILDREN MUST NOT USE TRICYCLES, BICYCLES, ETC., ON THE
  PEDESTRIAN WALKS

CHILDREN MUST NOT STEP ON THE GRASS

Let me be clear what is objectionable about this list—and all other measures like it. It is not that children *should* be allowed to scribble on walls or make noise in corridors. It is that *nobody* should be allowed to do so and therefore that notices—and enforcement of regulations—should either address all age groups or none. The admonitions to children alone are rudely discriminatory. But the actual rules further discriminate against children. Why are children forbidden to hang around inside or outside when nobody would dream of breaking up a group of adults, discussing last night's game? How can it be just to forbid the use of wheeled toys on walkways when space for adults' "wheeled toys" is taken for granted? How can the arbitrary disposal of children's lost and found property possibly be justifiable when such disposal of adult property is against the law?

Discrimination against children in communities is so commonplace that such examples may seem merely rude. Even notices in shop windows that state "only two unaccompanied children permitted at a time" are sometimes shrugged off as "unfortunately realistic." We have to ask ourselves how we would react to identical discrimination against any other minority group. If a small shopkeeper in a particular city could show that black people were responsible for more thefts from his shop than white people, would it be acceptable for him to put up a notice reading "only two blacks at a time"? Could residents who preferred not to associate with gay people ask for them to be housed at a distance, or pass regulations specifically addressed to them? Such behavior would be unthinkable (outside Colorado); in most post-industrial countries antidiscrimination legislation ensures that it would also be illegal.

Children and the Law

Equality under the law is basic to all other constitutional or civil rights in Western societies, but even this does not cover children as it does adults. Every Western country moderates legal penalties in deference to children's immaturity—specifying minimum ages of criminal responsibility, minimum ages for custodial sentences, a minimum age for capital punishment and so forth—but they also moderate children's legal *protection* in deference to the adults who are responsible for them. Take the principle of *habeas corpus* for example. No adult citizen in any post-industrial Western country may be deprived of his liberty by anyone without due process under the law, and, with the exception of the tightly controlled possibility of compulsory admission to the hospital when an individual is considered a danger to himself or others, the law allows that deprivation of liberty only when a person is suspected of a crime that is being actively investigated, or after conviction. In most countries, however, children may be deprived of their liberty without recourse to law. Parents—and sometimes teachers or other caretakers—can imprison children, extending a time-out to hours spent locked in a bedroom or worse, or "grounding" to days of house arrest, with virtual impunity, because the only laws that restrain them are those against cruelty to children and such behavior is rarely categorized as such. Britain's forward-looking Children Act, although silent about parents and private schools, strictly regulates the imprisonment of children by public schools and both public and private health facilities. But if children are considered a danger to themselves or others, they can still be locked up for seventy-two hours before a court's permission must be sought, and this is longer than the period for which police can detain adult suspects without charging them with an offense.

In most countries, including the United Kingdom and the United States, social workers and police can take children forcibly from their homes and deprive them of their liberty without even a suspicion that they are dangerous or have committed a legal offense. A court order is usually required, but in most places the only justification required for such an order is that the child is coming, or would otherwise come, to harm. The British Children Act is explicitly intended to keep such compulsory removals from home to a minimum and therefore strictly defines the concept of "significant harm" and strictly limits the length of time a child can be kept from his home before he and his parents can appeal in court. Looser definitions and weeks of delay are common elsewhere, especially in some parts of North America. Getting out of compulsory care can also be a great deal more difficult than getting in, and children's own views of how best they should be "disposed of" are not always even sought, let alone taken into account, by the courts. The Children Act ensures British children levels of direct participation that are unique in Western care proceedings outside Scandinavian children's courts. The child may be represented by a lawyer, separately from his parents, as well as by a guardian ad litem.

Being "in care" is not intended to be imprisonment, of course. Yet although the conditions under which he is kept may be far more comfortable, the loss of liberty suffered by a child who is prevented from returning home and is compelled to remain in a children's home or foster home is not dissimilar to that suffered by an adult in custody. Furthermore, once "in care" a child does not have to assault anyone or try to harm himself in order to be actually locked up. All he has to do is keep running away. In much of the United States and in some European countries "children's homes" may routinely be locked at night or provide some locked accommodation for runaways. In Britain this is no longer legal. Such children may only be locked up in special "secure accommodation" and only after a court has given permission at a hearing where the child is represented both directly and by a guardian ad litem. Nevertheless, even in the United Kingdom, a child who has done no legal wrong and is not thought likely to harm anyone may still end up behind bars if "he has a history of absconding and is likely to abscond from any other description of accommodation and if he absconds he is likely to suffer significant harm." Any child who is on the run is likely to suffer significant harm, but should that mean that if he will not remain voluntarily in any accommodation that can be found for him, imprisonment is the only other option? If children's civil liberties were taken as seriously as adults', our concern for absconders' welfare would be manifest in new efforts to provide care that they could accept without compulsion.

Other aspects of bodily integrity—people's right to autonomous control over their own bodies—that are important to our civil liberties are often denied to children; indeed it often seems that children's bodies do not belong to them but to their parents or to any adult with parental responsibility for them. Of course young children are not capable of caring for their own bodies or even of recognizing their own need for care that must be given by adults. But adults' rights over children's bodies are so completely taken for granted that the importance of seeking children's cooperation in matters of bodily care, and passing over control and responsibility at a developmentally appropriate pace, is seldom stressed. It would be absurd not to change a toddler's diaper, wipe her nose or shampoo her hair because she happened to be in a "no" mood, but is it not equally absurd not to *ask*? And what about the bodily indignities routinely imposed on older children, such as compulsory haircuts, or school-based and public weighing and measuring, or mass examinations for parasites? Everything adults do to children's bodies without permission is potentially disrespectful; everything they do against children's will is at least deserving of careful thought: Must this be done? Must it be done *now*, under these circumstances?

Children will not always recognize or accept the need for physical interventions that are necessary for their health or well-being. Clearly it *is* in the best interests of a five-year-old to have his head wound sutured, or a nine-year-old with juvenile diabetes to receive regular insulin injections. While everything possible should be done to explain the need to him and to help him assent, assenting for him if he cannot is clearly a proper part of parental responsibility. But "children" are not a definitive group. They grow, and as they grow up they mature in judgment. Almost every child becomes competent to make medical decisions on her own behalf long before she is legally adult. Once she is competent to decide for herself, she surely has the right to do so. The Family Law Reform Act of 1969 gave English and Welsh children their first statutory right to consent to medical treatment, but only from the age of sixteen. A landmark case softened that age barrier. A mother took a health authority to court in an attempt to force through a legal prohibition on doctors prescribing contraceptives for girls under sixteen without notifying their parents. The case failed and established what is known in Britain as the Gillick Principle: that a child of any age who is judged to have "sufficient understanding" can exercise this right. Where contraception is concerned, most non-Catholic Western countries, including North America and Australia, accept the pragmatic necessity of allowing under-age girls to seek confidential medical help, but that does not mean that the spirit of the Gillick Principle is widely endorsed. Even in Britain, where its wide applicability was confirmed by the Code of Practice on the Mental Health Act of 1983, children's self-determination in such matters sometimes proves so hard for adults to tolerate that they do all they can to prevent it being exercised.

Rights to bodily integrity remain tenuous for children long after they have outgrown the need for physical care by adults. The principle of informed consent to medical care, for example, rightly regarded as so crucial to the practice of adult medicine that even urgent public interest is not permitted to override it, is often overridden in pediatrics. Amid mounting fears of an AIDS pandemic, the compulsory HIV testing that many authorities believe would contribute to public health and safety has been resisted. And despite the anxiety of legal authorities to prosecute sexual offenders, rape victims cannot anywhere be compelled to undergo the examinations that might provide physical evidence. But look at children in comparable situations: amid rising concern about child sexual abuse, medical examinations and photography are often carried out without the consent of the child (sometimes directly against her will) and, since the adult with parental responsibility for that child may be the perpetrator or a confederate, her consent may also be dispensed with. In the United Kingdom, the Children Act does give those with "sufficient understanding" the right to refuse, but a child who is very young or very upset can readily be judged to lack that understanding. How can these humiliating medical procedures—often indistinguishable, in the child's view, from indecent assault and the taking of pornographic pictures—be in the best interests of a child who is not physically injured and insists that "nothing happened"? The real interests, in such cases, are not those of the victimized children but of those who wish to prosecute or avoid prosecution—a public health matter, then.

Children's Bodily Autonomy and Social Awareness of Child Abuse

Increasing international concern about the extent of child sexual abuse has made people aware of the importance of allowing children a sense of their own bodily autonomy and integrity. There are self-help programs in most Western countries designed to give children the self-esteem and assertiveness to protect themselves from potentially abusive contacts, by "saying no." Given children's dependence on adults, and their unremitting experience of adult power and their own powerlessness, some of these programs are simplistic, even unrealistic. But what sabotages even the best of them, in most countries, is the hypocrisy of their social context. The autonomy over their bodies that these programs offer to children is not genuine and unconditional. On the contrary, children are being exhorted to refuse bodily contacts of which adult society disapproves, while still being expected to accept those that adults approve. As one Australian mother, bent on spanking, put it, "I'm not against what they're teaching these kids in school, but she'd sure as hell better not try 'saying no' to me!"

Only in the Scandinavian countries and Austria does respect for children's bodily integrity extend to a complete ban on hitting them, though legislation is imminent in Germany, and in July 1993 Canada's federal ministry of justice announced its intention to remove the parental right to spank children from the law and to mount a public information campaign against all physical punishment. In all other Western countries, spanking or smacking, whipping or beating children is so much taken for granted that the act of hitting a child is not regarded as assault nor, in itself, as violent, as long as the intention is punitive and any damage done is limited. Of course certain kinds or degrees of corporal punishment are classified as cruel, and therefore unacceptable. But even in the context of public concern over physical child abuse, the concept of "acceptable" levels of violence towards children remains, and public opinion and laws draw protective circles around punishing adults rather than around punished children.

It is different for adults. Although laws concerning physical assault vary in detail and application from country to country, all adults in the post-industrial West enjoy legal protection against being hit by anyone else, whether or not actual injury is caused. Apart from self-defense, even the most excellent motive is not a legal justification for interpersonal violence and neither a family relationship nor one of legitimated authority undermines the adult victim's right to protection. Army sergeants may not hit recruits, even in the interests of discipline and training for the defense of the country. The police may not strike suspects, even those suspected of heinous crimes. And if family members resort to blows during a quarrel in the privacy of their own homes, there is legal recourse for the victim if she or he wants to invoke it, unless, of course, she or he is a child.

The United Nations Convention on the Rights of the Child makes it clear that children's right to physical integrity is absolute, irrespective of adults' disciplinary motives and irrespective of culture, religion or tradition. During the last decade, many countries have passed new legislation limiting the circumstances in which corporal punishment may be used. The United Kingdom banned it in all state-supported education in 1987 (it was the last Western European country to do so) and, under the Children Act of 1989, effectively banned it in all institutional settings, including daycare and foster care; parents' legal right to beat children is still protected. In America, the number of states that forbid "paddling" in public schools has crept gradually up to twenty-four—though suggestions that it be reintroduced have been made in several. Corporal punishment remains widespread in schools in other states, in some institutions (including those for variously disabled children) and in homes.

The nature and extent of corporal punishment is also being debated within the child abuse context. Although it is widely recognized that psychological and emotional abuse is potentially as damaging, the issues it raises are different, because psychological and emotional abuse is never overtly permitted in law. Physical abuse stands at the opposite end of a continuum that starts with the right of parents to "chastise" children. Child protection agencies in many countries find themselves at variance with the courts in drawing the line between "reasonable" punishment and cruel assault. In Scotland in 1989, for example, Lord Elmslie, the most senior judge, defended a mother's violent belting of her ten-year-old daughter as richly deserved punishment; and in an

English Crown Court in 1991, a mother who beat her eleven-year-old with a garden cane and an electrical cord was acquitted of assault and cruelty. In contrast, in 1990 the president of the High Court Family Division upheld the decision of the local authority to place two children on their child protection register because their mother had hit one of them three times with a wooden spoon, causing slight bruising. A 1992 report by a highly influential governmental body, the Scottish Law Commission, recommended making it illegal to punish a child with any implement—strap or belt, cane or stick, slipper or miscellaneous object—or in any way likely to cause more than minor pain or discomfort.

Of course all reforms of laws that permit children to be deliberately hurt and humiliated in the name of discipline are to be welcomed. If fewer adults and institutions have the right to beat children, there will be fewer beatings. If new limits are put on the violence that parents may legally use, children will be hurt less. Listening to Oprah Winfrey sharing memories of childhood "whuppings" with participants in a show on "discipline" made any measure that means children will no longer be sent to pick switches from the backyard and be beaten with them until they bleed seem worthwhile. But however desirable it may be in itself, this kind of legal reform is irrelevant to the burning question of children's human rights, which does not ask "Where, by whom and how much should children be hit?" but "Why is it legal, permissible, acceptable, for anyone to hit children at all?"

The Interface Between Human Rights and Childish Needs

Since it is not acceptable for adults to hit each other, it cannot be acceptable for them to hit children. Children are people, first and foremost, and negative discrimination among people is unacceptable. But children are not yet adults. As young, vulnerable, developing people, they have special needs for nurturance and care, protection and education, and it is the meeting of these needs which serves as motivation, explanation or excuse for many discriminatory practices. It is from the crucial interface between children's universal and lifelong humanity and their special and temporary childishness that most social injustice to children arises. Post-industrial Western countries make parents almost solely responsible for meeting the childish needs of their own offspring and in return they give parents almost total control over children's lives, vesting in them, by proxy, human rights that should belong to the children themselves. The absence of those rights is not always obvious to children or adults. Young children's security and happiness are founded on relationships with parents (or the people to whom they are attached as parents), so as long as their families are viable working units, the enforced delegation of their rights is not necessarily irksome and may not even be noticed before adolescence. But it is a different matter if there is no such unit, or it ceases to function, or it functions in ways that clearly, to the child himself or others, are not in his best interests. When childish needs become the responsibility of adults who are not linked to children by affectional ties, it is their lack of human rights that renders them both vulnerable and helpless.

Children have no rights to be with the people they regard as their parents. In this respect even the United Nations Convention on the Rights of the Child fails: article 9 says that states "shall ensure that a child shall not be separated from his or her parents against *their* will" (my italics). It says nothing about separations from parents that are against the child's will. In most Western countries, biological parenthood gives adults a claim to a child, irrespective of the care given to him or the personal relationship formed with him. Biological parents are often referred to as "natural" parents, as if genes were, indeed, the heart of the matter, and such parents are often regarded as having greater claims to a child than the foster mother who may have cared for him for years, or the grandmother he may always have known as his mother. Such adults may dispute their claim to a child as if he were, indeed, an object, or perhaps a pet. Media headlines will call him a "tug-of-love child" even if there is no tug at all in *his* love. An adult may eventually be "awarded" him: a prized possession. If a child is regarded as "old enough"—and this usually means having achieved an age of at least five or six years, rather than having achieved, much earlier, the verbal facility necessary to expressing a view—he may be consulted. Under Britain's relatively child-centered Children Act, he certainly will be. But what he says will not necessarily be very influential, and if he is too young to express himself in words, decisions about his best interests will be made without reference to his observed or probable feelings. Even when biological mothers are not in dispute with other caregivers, but plan to give up their infants for adoption, their rights to their babies are often protected over a period that jeopardizes the infants' well-being. Many countries insist that such an infant be cared for by a third party—in either a foster home or an institution—for a period of several months before he may go to his adoptive parents, in order to give the mother every chance to change her mind and reclaim him without a tug of love. The fact that after six weeks, let alone three months, with one mother figure, the move to another *will* tug at that baby's first attachment is disregarded.

Authorities seldom remove children from their homes lightly, or carelessly. Britain's Children Act is notable for its emphasis on avoiding doing so. But there is heavy evidence, in all Western countries, of physical, sexual and emotional child abuse and of the varying mixtures of poverty and illness, addiction and criminality, relationship breakdown and extended family disintegration that can compound into deadly neglect. Media accounts of children whose parents or parent substitutes have beaten them to death, raped them, tortured them, used them for pornographic profit or satanic rituals increase its burden. Faced with such horrific possibilities, and the reality of relationships and environments that bear little resemblance to conventional images of loving families and homes, it sometimes seems urgent to remove children from their families—so urgent that the most difficult of decisions on what constitutes children's best interests is made without any reference to them. Did any of the brave relief workers who struggled to get children out of Bosnia even *ask* themselves if it would have been better to take each with a parent or known adult caregiver, even if that meant rescuing fewer children in total? A dawn raid by police and social workers on several households in Scotland snatched children who were suspected victims of satanic abuse, to spend many weeks incommunicado. American parents who went on vacation, leaving their two small children alone in the house, were taken straight into custody on their return and may have permanently lost all parental rights and access. Those, and similarly dreadful incidents, may satisfy public opinion but they cannot be in the best interests of the children.

If due respect is given to both human rights and childish needs, it is arguable that the abrupt removal of an unwilling child from the people to whom he relates as parents can never be justified. Whatever traumas those Scottish children had already suffered, being dragged from their homes without preparation can only have exacerbated them. However lonely and vulnerable those deserted American children had been, they wanted their parents to come back, not go out of their lives forever. If children are thought to be at immediate risk of injury, if they are starving, in need of urgent medical treatment, or suffering from a compound of neglect, they may have to be taken to a hospital or some other place where specialist help can be given, but what valid reason can there ever be for preventing a parent or familiar caregiver—even one who is not trusted alone with the child—from going too? Where children are literally snatched from home, even from parents' arms, or where parents are forbidden any contact with them, it is often the evidence for a future prosecution that is being protected, not the children's best interests.

Social workers in child protection roles have a most unenviable task and, since doing too little may result in abuse, or even the death of a child, it is inevitable that once a child "at risk" comes to their attention, it will often seem that removal into the care of a foster mother or childcare institution is in his best interests. But is it? The doubt arises less from the possibility that the parental home is better than it appears (it often is, but the stakes are too high to gamble on) than from the evidence that those alternative forms of care are worse than they appear. Wherever statistical evidence has been collected—and it is available in one form or another for most Western countries—the long-term prospects for children who are taken "into care" are so grim that the fact of being thus removed from home is a major risk factor for almost any negative development, from school failure to adolescent pregnancy, delinquency or adult mental illness. The immediate prospects for such children are dismal, too. Stable placements are very difficult to achieve and repeated rejections by foster caregivers or staff are extraordinarily damaging. Furthermore, as scandal after scandal unfolds in different countries, it is becoming clear that "places of safety" are sometimes as dangerous as the worst of homes, and "care" a tragic misnomer. If children's human rights are to be respected and their childish needs met, they themselves must decide when, and if, it is in their best interests to be removed from their home and/or parents, and their care and protection must then be provided for accordingly. If a child *asks* to be removed from her home, she certainly should be, even if the parenting adult objects and abuse is not apparent and is denied. The particular story the child tells may or may not be literally true—and must, of course, be carefully investigated for the accused adult's sake—but whether it is factually true or not, it is an appeal for rescue that is, in itself, an emotional truth for the child. It should not be ignored in favor of "parental rights" but acknowledged, explored and, hopefully, resolved for all the individuals concerned.

If a child does not want to leave her home and/or parents, she should not be compelled. Instead, the resources needed to deal with the current emergency or chronic situation should be taken to her. Even if an abused child has been terrorized into rejecting offered rescue, or is too withdrawn to ask for help, twenty-four-hour supervision will ensure her safety and quickly reveal the true situation. There may be no happy resolution to it, but there is more hope for the future of a child who can be given time to see that different arrangements are needed, and who can share, however sadly, in making them, than for the child who is treated as a pawn in adults' games.

The breakdown of relationships between parents separates far more children from people who are important to them than bureaucratic interference. Efforts to make divorce proceedings more child-centered are being made in many countries—an easier task for European countries whose legal systems are designed to seek the truth than for the United Kingdom and North America, whose systems are confrontational. The recent British Children Act has "once a parent, always a parent" as one of its fundamental principles and holds divorcing parents jointly and equally responsible for arrangements concerning the children, and for taking account of the children's views. It has also made it possible for children to make representations to courts, on their own behalf and with their own lawyers, rather than only through the Official Solicitor or a court-appointed *guardian ad litem* or "next friend." A new right to independent litigation by children is being explored in the United States, where the case of Gregory Kingsley is regarded as a landmark. Furthermore, codification of American child support rates at the state level may reduce the amount and bitterness of litigation in straightforward divorces. Yet in most Western countries, most divorces still constitute a struggle between adults. The issues are adult issues such as property and pride but if those adults are parents, the children get involved, usually in arguments about maintenance and visitation. Even when a child is mature enough and brave enough clearly to state what living arrangements or plans for parental access she or he would prefer, the struggle is between the two adults and their advisers, and the one who wins will not necessarily be the one whose suggestions most closely approximate the child's preferences, but the one whose personal circumstances best approximate the social workers' and court officials' views of that child's best interests. There are some real changes being made. In Norway, for example, visitation rights after divorce belong to the children themselves rather than to parents. Instead of the absent parent having a right of access to the child—which the child may not want and an ex-wife or ex-husband may sometimes take pleasure in blocking—the child has a right to see the absent father or mother, and parents share the responsibility for seeing to it that she can do so if, but only if, she wishes. Norway and Britain have also given welcome recognition to other relationships that may be important to children and at risk following parental divorce. Formal access or visitation rights with grandparents and stepparents, for example, can be assured and, in theory at least, even the most unconventional relationships are treated as family if that is how the child perceives them. But how much children manage to say, and how much notice adults take of what they do say in any type of legal case, remain open questions. Most European countries have family courts that pride themselves on being informal and welcoming to children—but few children find them so. British and North American "next friends" work tirelessly to ascertain, and advise courts on, children's best interests, but unless they really know the children, are truly their friends, they cannot really know what those interests are. Most have only a month or two and a handful of meetings in which to build a relationship with the small people whose happiness rests in their hands.

Better communication between children and adults is making small stepping-stones through the swampy area between childish needs and human rights, but nobody is yet engineering real bridges. As long as it is assumed that children are less likely to know for themselves where their best interests lie than adults are to know for them, just finding adults who will listen to children is not enough. How, for example, can children talk freely, even to people who will take the trouble to tune in to them, if those people will not grant them the confidentiality—and therefore the control of the results of their own confidences—that is the right of every adult? The moment abused, neglected, bullied or otherwise distressed children confide in parents, teachers, doctors, church or community workers or older friends, what they say passes into adult ownership and the children lose all autonomy. The determination of child protection people that children's concerns and allegations should not be ignored, derided or turned against them is admirable. But the kind of taking notice that does not just offer help to children but insists on acting for them, even when that or any action is directly against their expressed wishes, often constitutes a further betrayal.

If children want adult help but do not want matters taken out of their hands, their only currently available option is a telephone hotline. There is no doubt that such telephone services help children so we must be glad that there are new ones opening up all the time. Britain's ChildLine, certainly one of the best, receives more confidences concerning physical and sexual abuse than are reported by all other British confidants put together: a clear indication that, like the rest of us, children in trouble are more likely to confide if they know they can control the consequences. But control-by-anonymity limits the help that can be given to verbal support and advice. Is that really the best we can do?

It is probably the best we *shall* do until something more respectful than benevolent authoritarianism dominates our adult dealings with children. Confidentiality, after all, is a difficult and disputatious issue even when it relates to adults, and never more so than when the secrets being told are relevant to issues of immediate social concern. There are those in Northern Ireland and in Sicily who would see the secrets of the confessional breached if it would bring terrorists to justice. Journalistic privilege is never more likely to be challenged in the courts than when the information concerns a major case, while AIDS has brought pressure on medical confidentiality in many countries because people believe that the duty to protect the public (or the insurance company's purse) may, or should, outweigh the practitioner's duty to protect his patient's privacy. Child abuse, especially sexual abuse, is an issue of prime social concern—and one that arouses so much guilt and projected anger that the mass desire for prosecution and vengeance is very strong. But there is a radical difference between the priest who receives a confession of terrorist activity or the doctor whose HIV-positive patient confides his promiscuous and unprotected sexual adventures, and the teacher whose student tells of being abused: the first two not only need not but *must not* breach professional confidentiality; the third not only may but in many countries *must*. The balance that should be maintained between individual human rights and society's well-being is infinitely complex and delicate, but it cannot be right that the individual end should weigh more lightly when it carries a child than when it carries an adult. Children may be smaller than we are, but their rights must weigh as heavily as our own.

— 11 —

New Approaches to
Working and Caring

Poverty is the principal risk factor in children's development because its global effects undermine the possibilities, restrict the choices and overpower the practices of good parenting, however that may be defined. A new economic priority for children and the people who matter to them, coupled with a new recognition of children's human rights, is therefore absolutely necessary and long overdue. The inequities and deprivations suffered by children in post-industrial societies are not our misfortune but our shame. We cannot continue to distance ourselves from them with talk of "cycles of deprivation" or an "underclass" that sounds as if these misfortunes had a will and an existence beyond our understanding or control. Child poverty and the abuse of children's human rights are integral parts of our socio-economic systems. We know how to change them; we can change them and we must. But when we have done that we shall only have stopped doing the worst that Western societies do to some children; that is still a long way from meeting our moral obligation to do the best we can for them all.

We cannot meet that moral obligation with socio-economic policies alone, or with any collection of policies aimed solely at children. Real change for children means changes all through society, and especially changes in society's attitudes towards parenthood and towards people who are parenting. Nations, states, cities, institutions and communities impinge on young children through their families. Social policies affect their lives through the actions and reactions of parents and caregivers. Even the outside influences that reach children directly—TV and advertising, schools and peer groups—are mediated in the microcosm of home. So no matter how good the institutional arrangements made on their behalf, children will get the benefit only to the extent that parents feel able and willing to give it to them. If children's well-being is to have priority, parents' *feelings* matter. A new policy may entitle parents to time off work to care for sick children, but what use is that policy to this child if her father does not feel secure enough in his employment and in his fathering role to stay at home when she has the flu? A new curriculum of parent education may teach that it is right to breast-feed babies and refrain from hitting toddlers, but does that mother feel confident enough to nurse her baby despite disapproving glares? And does this one feel sufficiently supported by other adults to muster a consistently grown-up response to her toddler's rage? There will be no real and self-perpetuating changes for children until the importance of parenthood becomes basic to the way we think and therefore to what we do.

Western nations rarely acknowledge the importance of positive parenting because they do not acknowledge the importance of the people on the receiving end, seeing children as parents' privilege rather than society's most precious resource. The privilege can be withdrawn from anyone whose caring falls beneath the standards of the place or time, but little is done to optimize that caring or the lives of the cared-for. Society takes for granted adults' desire to have children and parents' sole responsibility for any children they have, leaving the personal costs unremarked, the personal efforts unrewarded.

Most adults do want children, although the unthinking assumption that they will go on having them, no matter what the cost or difficulty, may yet prove unfounded. A reduction in birthrates accompanies industrialization wherever it occurs and is always mondially, and usually nationally, welcomed. But in the last twenty years, post-industrial nations have seen their birthrates drop fast to below the total period fertility rate of 2.1 children per woman that is required for stable populations. Rates in Britain and America are now around 1.8, in Germany around 1.6 and in Spain and Italy as low as 1.3. Low birthrates combined with longer lives mean aging populations that may effectively restrict socioeconomic choices. Priority for children and a better deal for parents

may one day be recommended by economists as part of urgent prona-
talist policies.

There is no evidence to suggest that people in the post-industrial
West find their relationships with the few offspring they do have any
less rewarding than people anywhere or anytime. There is abundant
evidence, though, that the business of looking after children 365 days
a year—the job aspect of parenting—is far more demanding and difficult than most people expect. Expectations may be unrealistic—many
Western parents come from such small and scattered families that their
own first baby is often also their first experience of living closely with
any small child—but the difficulties are real. People often thrive on
difficult tasks; indeed every worthwhile, creative, challenging endeavor
is alloyed with stress, effort and frustration, and successful outcomes
are often stronger as a result. But thankless tasks are a different matter:
only saints and sociopaths thrive on those. Daily—and nightly—life
with babies and small children will never be unalloyed joy, but it could
be a great deal more joyous. If society considered childrearing at least
as creative and worthwhile as building a car or a company, and parental
efforts brought even the rewards and status that accrue to an innovative
engineer or patient manager, the torment of those broken nights and
the lovely landmarks on children's road to maturity could meld to
bridge the yawning gulf between personal and public life, between
social and self-esteem.

Direct parallels between parenting for love and working for money
can be dangerously misleading, though. Media-speak often presents
them not only as direct competitors for people's time—which they often are—but also as equal choices in their lives. The two things are not
equal and only half of them are choices. However dedicated an individual may be to her career, or to the job that keeps her out of poverty,
she is always conscious, on some level, that she and it are separate.
However much she would hate to do so, she knows that she could stop
being a lawyer, even stop being self-supporting and become poor, yet
still be herself. Parenthood is different. Our children are part of ourselves. People cannot choose to stop being mothers or fathers even if
they stop parenting; they cannot abandon, or lose, a child without
themselves being diminished. So although comparisons with work are

often intended to flatter parenting, they actually denigrate it. Relationships between people and their children have incomparably greater salience than relationships between people and their jobs.

The comparison is particularly unfortunate because it implies that people who are parents have less to offer the world of work than people who are not. That suggestion is more than unfounded: it is wrongheaded because it confuses relationships with roles. People cannot ever stop being parents, but what they do about those relationships, how they fill the parenting role, is a different matter. Nobody is *only* a parent, any more than he or she is only a son or daughter, friend or lover, husband or wife. Of course there can be conflict between parenting (or any other relationship) and work (or any other activity) at the level of time-and-motion study, because all activities take time and energy and individuals have limited supplies of both. But, given the will, those conflicts can be resolved *at* time-and-motion level. Having no time left over from caring for a baby—no time to take a shower let alone take a job— does not make a woman "only a mother": it makes her someone who is currently spending all her time mothering. She will *be* a mother forever but she will not *mother* at that intensity for long, and when the mothering role contracts, time for other things will expand.

The tendency to compound people's relationships with their roles is widespread, but it is uniquely damaging to women-who-are-mothers and subtly responsible for many of their unique problems. Ask a full-time father what he does and he will not answer "I'm only a father, I'm afraid"; he will tell you something like "I'm at home looking after our daughter at the moment." As long as we do not differentiate between what mothers *are* in relation to their children, and what they *do*, motherhood will continue to be presented as an either-or choice and an all-or-nothing package. To suggest that a woman choose between her relationship with her child and her individual adult identity, largely vested in her salary- or wage-earning role, is as idiotic as asking her to choose between food and drink. It is not only that both are essential to her, it is also that they are inseparable because they are both part of her. But to suggest that she cannot fulfill the role of mother (or worker) unless she is with her child (or at her desk) seven (or five) days a week is equally idiotic. A musician is not less a musician because he is a civil servant all week, nor less valuable as a civil servant because he spends his weekends in concert halls. A daughter is not less a daughter because she marries nor less a wife because she is also a teacher. Only flexible integration and sequencing of people's various roles can defuse the conflict between parenthood and paid work.

There is time and space in most people's lives for doing a bit of everything all at the same time or several things in sequence. There does not seem to be time because the concept of "full-time" is etched into our social consciousness, even though there is no social consensus as to its definition. To many people "a good mother" is still a "full-time mother," though, curiously, a woman can spend all day at a tennis club without losing that title, but loses it if she spends half the day at work. To almost everyone a "good job" is still full-time permanent employment, stretching unbroken from the end of full-time education to the beginning of full-time retirement: "48 hours for 48 weeks for 48 years." On that basis, not many people are going to have either good mothers or good jobs. Women work as well as men, making up almost half the work force in some countries, and more than half in some areas of very high male unemployment. Furthermore it is rare for the employment history of either sex to approximate that conventional male pattern of work in a single firm, organization, trade or skill, climbing one ladder of advancement from apprenticeship to retirement. Almost all modern workers have to train, retrain and redeploy to follow the shifting demands of developing technology and changing markets; many will have periods of part-time work, self-employment or work at home, and even so, only a minority can expect to be employed without breaks. The post-industrial world cycles between boom and slump; voluntary and involuntary layoffs, and early retirements that sometimes turn out to be temporary, will remain common experiences.

Looked at more dispassionately than current world recession or local mortgage costs easily allow, this long-term pattern of recurrently interrupted and changing work suggests important but unrecognized possibilities of personal space and personal choice. If we could accept that post-industrial economies do not demand, and cannot ensure, consistent full-time employment for every adult, then planned periods without paid work, or with part-time work, or even with relatively less responsible and demanding work could be a positive feature of modern adult life and especially of modern parenting. As the first discussion document of Britain's Independent Commission on Social Justice puts it: "The problems of employment and the unmet needs for care require us to confront the issue of how *paid and unpaid work is distributed between men and women, and across people's lives*" (my italics). Previous positive approaches to the probability of less than full employment—especially *au courant* in Britain during the eighties—earned little credence because they usually suggested that people should be educated and conditioned to expect and enjoy leisure. Only individuals with exceptional inner resources, and the few for whom a hobby becomes a consuming passion, are ever going to find leisure activities a purposeful replacement for productive work. Rearing children is both productive and purposeful. We have to make it feel so.

Integrating Parenting and Paid Work

Making time and space for parenting—and other activities that are outside the marketplace—would be very much easier if perceptions of employers and employees, management and workers were dominated by their shared characteristics and concerns rather than their different roles. Despite "democratic" pretensions and the polite veneer of modern management techniques, relationships of unequal power, and sometimes confrontation, are still part of the industrial tradition of modern Western countries. As a result, real cooperation between the boss and his subordinates at work is not always striven for, let alone achieved, even though their children all attend the same school and have measles the same month. Let us hope evidence will be forthcoming to suggest that women who achieve authority wield it with a greater awareness of their after-hours humanity than men. Are gray suits respecters of gender, or can women *and* men abandon them?

The cooperation we need most is not only the already sought-after kind that would humanize workplaces, but a new and more radical kind that would reorganize work itself. Industry still insists on the economic necessity of controlling labor. It lays workers off or cuts their working hours whenever demand for their product or service falls, and although unions and individuals may object with passion, they do not do so with conviction. Management must manage, and executives execute. They could meet the same industrial goals by a different route, though, if they planned labor with employees instead of controlling it and them. But industry does not think about the social desirability—and therefore does not even look seriously at the economic feasibility—of allowing people to lay themselves off for a period, or reduce their hours, when their other roles require extra time. Parental leave is an obvious example. Currently ranging from eighteen months in Sweden on almost full pay, to a minimum of fourteen weeks on partial pay throughout the European Economic Community, to no *paid* time at all in the United States, even under its new family leave bill, it is a contentious issue between employers and employees because everybody assumes that it must be prohibitively expensive. But is it? Various large firms of management consultants in North America have shown that recruiting and training replacements for all the employees who quit when they become pregnant currently costs some businesses more than they would have to spend to allow those employees a six-month paid leave and employ cover for them. And, of course, wherever an employee is on low wages that are being topped up by welfare benefits, the extra cost of parental leave is reduced; if those benefits included publicly funded daycare for the baby, it might vanish altogether. Direct costs apart, the prospect of providing temporary cover for absent workers daunts many managers but the benefits might nevertheless outweigh the organizational difficulties and, in some places, they already do. In Sweden, for example, parental vacancies are found to provide useful opportunities to broaden the experience of other workers and offer trial periods in preparation for eventual promotion. In Britain's public education system, most of the substitute teachers who cover maternity leaves and sickness would otherwise be lost to the profession, taking their expensive training and invaluable experience with them, and this certainly happens within the nursing profession in America. Many trained people who are themselves mothers feel unable to accept long-term commitments but are happy to fill occasional short-term contracts.

Not all parents would wish to absent themselves from the work force altogether for more than a short period after a baby's birth, but, as we saw in Chapter 4 (Daycare), wherever surveys have been carried out, almost all mothers—and many fathers as well, if they are also asked—express a preference for part-time or more flexible working hours "if

only it were possible." Why is it not possible? The knee-jerk response
is that post-industrial economies depend on every adult working a full
week, that individual firms depend on employees being on the job during working hours and that few workers can afford to swap any money
for time. Substitute thought for reflex and it becomes clear that all that
is nonsense. The standard working week in Europe—though not in
North America—is no more standard than the ordinary nuclear family
is ordinary: neither includes much more than half of the population.
Furthermore that standard week varies in different post-industrial
countries, and in different businesses within each, by almost ten hours
and by far more than that when different arrangements for compulsory,
expected and voluntary overtime, including work taken home, are ac-
counted for. Britain works longer hours than any other EEC country
but it still has engineering shift workers, such as those at Rolls-Royce,
on a 37-hour, 4 1/2-day week. Although agreements for shorter working
hours are, of course, sometimes pressed by unions with a view to increasing potential overtime for their members, more time to spend with
their families is often equally important. In her book *About Time: The
Revolution in Work and Family Life,* Patricia Hewitt describes a campaign by the Confederation of Shipbuilding and Engineering Unions
for a thirty-five-hour week "to give our members more time to spend
with their families and to have more time for leisure." So what is a full
week? When it suits their fiscal policies, as in assessing insurance status,
countries such as the United Kingdom and the Netherlands actually
define as full-time employment the twenty hours per week that many
parents would welcome as part-timers. Furthermore, widely varying
working patterns—night shifts, split shifts, weekend working with time
off in lieu—are demanded by employers when it suits them, though
dismissed as impossible when it does not.

Abandon preconceptions and prejudices in favor of international research findings, and it becomes clear that no imaginable working plan
or pattern is impossible and that many unimaginable ones are not only
possible but actually in place and working: "flexitime, four day weeks
or nine day fortnights, weekend-only jobs, term-time working, new
shift arrangements that combine shorter individual working hours with
longer operating hours, 'week on, week off' contracts, annual hours
contracts, voluntary shorter hours working, a wide variety of part-time

arrangements, individual choice of working hours and so on." None of them would be operational if they reduced either productivity or earnings to an unacceptable degree. In many cases *neither employer nor employee loses out.* A simplified account of one of the most unlikely-seeming choices that is already offered by several European and United Kingdom companies, weekend-only working, illustrates the point. My imaginary workplace is a hi-tech production line that must, for economic reasons, run seven days a week. For simple math, my workers are paid £200 for a standard five-day week of forty hours—£40 per day. If they work on Saturdays and Sundays their overtime is at double-time: £80 per day. Instead of paying workers weekend overtime, the firm offers weekend-only employment comprising ten hours on Saturday and ten on Sunday (instead of the usual eight hours). It pays £80 for each of those two days as before, so it has gained four hours' work per employee per weekend. In addition the weekend workers work either Friday afternoon or Monday morning, for which they are still paid at the weekend rate—a further £40. The firm can afford to pay £40 instead of £20 for those four hours because of the extra four hours worked on the other two days. The result? Keeping the production line running through the weekend has cost the firm exactly what it would have paid in overtime and the scheme has additionally ensured that extra workers are available to cover long-weekend absenteeism. As for the weekend workers: they make exactly the same money for two and a half weekend days as the rest of the work force makes for five weekdays.

Do employers really depend on having employees physically present in the workplace during stated hours? Some clearly do, but many do not and are beginning to realize it. There are around six million American "telecommuters" currently using computer modems, fax machines and cellular phones installed for them by their firms at home instead of in an office downtown. That is up 20 percent from 1991. The number is growing, and it includes an increasing proportion of senior employees in highly paid positions. A survey of 250 leading businesses in the United Kingdom—including Rank Xerox—suggests that this way of working can increase productivity by an average of 45 percent and that if 15 percent of the work force operated in this way, five billion pounds would be wiped off the nation's office rental bill and almost two billion would be saved in fuel. One adult cannot usually work *while* caring for small children at home, and some firms specifically forbid the attempt, but work can often be organized around children's hours at nursery or school, and parents can undertake an evening shift without disrupting family life. Some find it lonely, though, and count on spending at least a couple of half-days each week at headquarters. Even where a job does demand full-time physical attendance, it can often be done better by two people than by one. Job sharing brings substantial advantages to the (still dismally few) employers who will countenance it. Sharers usually give extra hours to briefing each other at changeover points. Routine jobs benefit from having a fresh worker take over from one whose energy and concentration are waning. Creative and executive jobs—in teaching, broadcasting, management—have been shown to benefit from the different but discussed input of two equally qualified people. Even America's newsrooms have begun to allow, even offer, job-sharing options to reporters. In 1993, for example, the Washington *Post* had three married couples sharing foreign bureau posts and a "maternity conversion" scheme allowing full-time posts to be shared among part-timers, while the Boston *Globe* and the Chicago *Sun-Times* both had posts shared by unrelated individuals, including one supervisory editing position. Of the twenty largest newspapers, thirteen had formalized part-time policies available to parents.

The real reason that part-time and a range of flexible work, including job sharing, is not possible for all, or almost all, of those who would prefer it is that employers' expectations and employees' eligibility for promotion and benefits are still based on those traditional—and largely outdated—male patterns. In 1974 Barbara Castle, then a cabinet minister, described British part-time women workers as 'second-class citizens entitled to third-class benefits.' Almost twenty years later, the House of Lords report on part-time and temporary work found it necessary to state that " 'non-standard' employees are not 'sub-standard' employees," yet in Britain and in the United States, many of them still are, and even in other EEC countries they are not always treated equitably. A very high proportion of part-time workers in all Western countries are women—65 percent in the United States, 76 to 90 percent in the European Community—but contrary to many people's assumptions, this is not principally because childcare responsibilities keep women from full-time work, but because they are not offered it. The huge increase in female employment that has taken place in the last ten years or so has been largely in the service sector and has mostly consisted of low-status, insecure, ill-paid jobs, many of them deliberately kept on a part-time (or even short-term or temporary) basis so that employers can avoid offering the benefits that apply to full-time employees. Most of those part-time female employees are not women currently committed to childcare. The highest proportion in the United States and in the European Community is women over the age of fifty. Over the whole of the EEC, 36 percent of those older women who work do so part-time, compared with 29 percent of women in the twenty-five to forty-nine years age bracket, the peak years of childcare.

The presence of children in the home does make it more likely that an employed woman will be a part-timer, but not much more likely, especially in the United States. If American mothers take outside employment at all, they tend to take full-time employment, even while children are very young. Just over 53 percent of all women are in the labor market (employed or seeking work) and almost 26 percent of those are part-time. Of the sixteen million women with children under six, an identical 53 percent are employed and 30 percent of them work part-time. Figures for the nine million women with children under three are little different: 49 percent are employed, 32 percent of them part-time.

In the European Community the difference children make to the likelihood of women who are in the labor force working part-time varies widely from country to country. In the Netherlands, for example, 63 percent of all women aged twenty-five to forty-nine worked part-time in 1991—85 percent of those who had children. In the United Kingdom those same figures were 45 percent and 65 percent, respectively, and they were very similar in Germany. In other countries, such as Italy and Spain, however, children made only 1 to 2 percent difference, while in Denmark, Portugal and Greece the proportion of working married women with children who worked part-time was actually lower than the proportion of working married women without children.

Although many parents would like to work part-time while their children are young, it is clear that large female part-time work forces do not consist mainly of mothers making that choice but of women who, mothers or not, *have* no choice. In the United Kingdom, many of them are disqualified from rights to unemployment, health and maternity benefits and cannot expect a lifetime of working to protect them from poverty if their partnerships break down or to provide them with an adequate pension when they reach retirement age. They are disqualified because they fail contribution tests that are unquestioningly accepted as part of the National Insurance system. But why are they not questioned? House insurance becomes effective from day one and it is up to actuaries to work out premiums for all that will cover the few that burn down on that very day. Furthermore, the two other European countries—Denmark and the Netherlands—with equivalent numbers of part-time workers and similar National Insurance systems to that in Britain operate them without contribution tests. An employee, part-time or full-time, is insured from the day she joins the work force. In the Netherlands, even casual workers with irregular and minimal hours are treated as fully insured for any week in which they have done even one hour's paid work or been covered by a contract of employment. There is no just economic argument against paying wages and benefits pro rata whatever the hours worked.

If good part-time jobs were available or, better still, almost all available jobs could be held on a part-time basis and rewarded pro rata in every sense, could parents afford to take them? The answer must be yes for many, because where those conditions are met they do. In 1989 Britain's Civil Service stated, "Regardless of the pattern of working, all staff should have fair and open opportunities for career development, including promotion and training, and be able to move between patterns at different stages in their career." Women can and do move from full-time to part-time work, or accept part-time posts. They are guaranteed pro-rata pay, holidays and other benefits, and the Treasury still reckons that there are considerable benefits to management. By 1991 the proportion of female civil servants working part-time had tripled from under 5 percent to over 14 percent. Most of those women are not working part-time because they cannot find or afford childcare to cover longer working hours but because they want more time with their children. The ideal for most women is shown by surveys in many countries to be twenty hours or fewer until children go to school and then employment during school hours and terms only. As Hewitt points out, "The rapid growth in dual-income families does not necessarily require two *full-time* workers." But neither need it be structured in such a way that the father works full-time and the mother half-time: "the same one-and-a-half-times income could in theory be produced by two three-quarter workers—a man and a woman both working shorter than full time hours." Of all the parents who want and need to work, but to work short hours that fit with children's lives, lone parents have the greatest need to do so. Similar working patterns should therefore be made available to them by, for example, matching their part-time earnings with benefits. The cost to society would be far less than the all-too-usual alternative of reluctant unemployment and inadequate social security.

Available research shows that all the accepted economic arguments against paid parental leave, against part-time work and against flexibility in working hours and practices are flawed. But available research does not include full cost-benefit studies of the many possible options, including all the personal gains to parents and children and all the resulting long-term savings in benefits and services. *That* kind of research might well turn many of those arguments upside down. If Western societies truly wanted to facilitate the flexible integration of working and parenting roles, and were held back only by concern about the effect on GDP of parents contributing less to the labor market, economic scenarios and research models could quickly clarify ranges of more and less sustainable policies. The fact that large-scale studies have never been rigorously carried out strongly suggests that political will is lacking: that a desire to find viable ways of making life easier for parents (and therefore better for children) is not high on Western agendas. In 1989 the city of Fremont, California, held America's first-ever city election on the question of whether or not a tax should be levied to pay for childcare. The answer was a resounding 3.5-to-1 "no." The principal reason was that voters felt childcare was a private matter rather than a public good: parents, and only parents, should pay.

Parents do not get the policies they need because parenting per se does not command sufficient social status to merit them. In contrast, other roles that may be filled, at different stages in their lives, by the same people who parent *do* command that respect and are granted equivalents to the flexibility parents need. The academic world is a case in point. Although financial stringencies have reduced their privileges, almost every Western country still gives some financial support (and continuing access to student concessions) to graduate students who qualify for postgraduate work. Nobody gets rich on what is usually available but because a graduate student is an honorable, even admirable, thing to be, the recipients feel the struggle is worthwhile. Is a Ph.D. really of more value to society than a well-launched child? Later in life academic institutions all over the Western world give some staff sabbatical leaves: opportunities to improve their professional status, make contacts, prepare for promotion and produce books and papers. How many produce anything as lastingly valuable as a baby who was allowed to nurse until she weaned herself? If a parent was regarded as an especially important and honorable thing to be, and parenting a job so important to society that the individuals doing it merited all possible social support, similar justifications and arrangements could apply to people producing children. And if that is too much to ask, what about helping future parents to finance "sabbaticals" for themselves, just as we are all helped to finance retirement pensions? For every week's pay you save you can have a week's paid leave later—and you get tax relief on your contributions and a share in the fund's profits in the meantime.

If we really tried we could think of ways to provide not only a year or more of parental leave, but an open option for adults to spend three or five years giving one or two children a good start by combining infant care with a training period, with the slower pace of part-time work, with unpaid but relevant work in the community, with a job that balanced lesser pay with greater logistical convenience or with a new venture in self-employment or artistic self-expression. Whatever outside work either or both parents chose to undertake at the same time, the particular demands of this first phase of their parenting would be recognized as their immediate priority and, crucially, as the most socially desirable occupation they could have. Termed a "mommy track," such proposals, made by a female senior executive in America and widely publicized in 1989, aroused understandable anger. The proposition that women-who-are-mothers should place themselves in a permanent professional slow lane relative to all men (including their partners) and to all nonmothering women is clearly discriminatory. But that does not mean that the notion of all individuals tailoring and altering levels of paid work according to the changing demands of other aspects of chosen life-styles should be dismissed out of hand. It is time to consider working to live rather than living to work. People who have relatively little to go home to may choose to make paid work their lives and contribute and earn a great deal by doing so. But people who have more currently invested outside the workplace may prefer a different balance. If bringing up children were recognized as a particularly high-status contribution to society, so that anything lost in earnings was gained in kudos, a "parent track" might look attractive to many people, women and men.

— 12 —

New Approaches to Practical Parenting

Recognizing the prime social value of parenting and determinedly making space for it among other adult roles are necessary but not sufficient moves towards meeting children's needs. There is much more that needs to be done.

Bringing up children is probably the most difficult life task people undertake, yet society offers less preparation for it than for any other. Even indisputably vital sex education deals more with preventing than with preparing for this still-common result of sexual relationships. Why? When I ask, many people say that child rearing is, and should remain, in the private domain, but surely even those who wish to keep child-rearing (and sexual) *practices* free of public regulation must accept that education concerning them is a public responsibility. Private domains (families) are now too limited and fragmented to be relied upon as sole conduits for information; even in cultures with intact and influential extended families, some parenthood education is usually institutionalized, often by incorporating it within puberty rites. Some people maintain, rather wildly, that no preparation for parenthood is necessary because the whole process of bearing and rearing children is natural or instinctive. It is difficult to see how it can be considered more so than the sexual processes that necessarily precede it, or to attach meaning to those terms in post-industrial societies that take such pride in having improved on nature. I have more sympathy with the people who say that whether preparation is desirable or not, it is actually impossible because parenting is unimaginable. There is truth in that: just telling people how they may feel one day (about a sexual partner or a child) does not fully prepare them for what they do feel. But that does not mean that telling—or, rather, talking—is not worthwhile. Nobody, after all, would want a young person to meet either sexual intercourse or childbirth without prior discussion. Most crucially, though, preparation for parenthood is needed as much for the children who will be born as for the parents who will give them birth: to tell people about their future children rather than to tell them about their future selves. When a modern Western parent first holds his or her first baby, that is often the first newborn she or he has ever met. With no prior knowledge of all babies' developing capacities, communications and needs, a parent often has idealized expectations of *this* baby culled largely from advertising. Who would embark on breeding horses or rearing dogs in such ignorance?

Preparing for Parenthood

Now that developing children are so scarce in most people's lives, child development should be part of everyone's education and it can begin with young children's experience of themselves. Even in early childhood, children observe their own and peers' feelings and reactions to events, and are aware of various group phenomena, such as scapegoating. Given the chance, most are passionately interested in exploring these observations, through role play, art, drama and discussion. Evidence from value-oriented programs—such as those targeted against bullying—suggests that such prosocial teaching can be highly effective in preschool and kindergarten. Personal-social education programs, in groups that truly esteem children, could be equally effective in bolstering their self-esteem and thus helping them to care for and protect themselves in the present, and their children in the distant future.

Throughout early and middle childhood, children need to take their parents for granted; critical thinking about their own upbringing is not developmentally appropriate and insofar as they consider personal relationships at all, it is usually relationships with peers that are most interesting to them. At ten or eleven, though, children are still young enough to perceive themselves as children being parented but are old enough to observe their parents parenting, and to be interested in the differences between their own families and others. At this stage there can be direct observation and discussion of infant development but it need not be presented in terms that relate it directly to imminent personal experience—as sex education or parenthood preparation. Grade-school children commonly undertake projects about animals: why not projects about the human kind? Bringing the realities of children's dependency and adult responsibility, and the crucial importance of adult nurturance to society, into open discussion would provide a sensible context for the direct discussions of sexual relationships that become appropriate a year or two later.

By mid-adolescence, the syllabus should incorporate discussion of parenthood as a major adult-life decision, along with more direct preparation for parenting roles and relationships. There are few available courses to serve as models. Parent-craft classes, often taught as an option only for less-academic students and sometimes, by default if not by design, primarily to girls, tend to concentrate on teaching practical skills. Bathing a borrowed baby may give young people a useful opportunity to meet, handle and be smiled at by an infant, but it teaches them nothing they will not learn from personal necessity when the time comes. Furthermore, the implication that it is practical skills that really matter in relation to babies does nothing to raise the status of children or parenthood. And yet that is the prime purpose of the program. Whatever the exact content of a parent-education curriculum, what matters is that at school, at home, and outside both, adolescents should be made aware of children as real people with needs and feelings as powerful and legitimate as their own, and as society's most important asset. Only thus will we produce a first generation of young adults who can see parenthood as an honorable option rather than an assumption or an accident, and an option not to be exercised lightly, or too soon.

Ideally, people would not decide to become parents until, or unless, they were ready, willing and able to make each child the principal factor in their life-style decisions for at least three years and a major factor forever. Those who made that commitment would know that it was supported by public opinion, by social institutions and, if necessary, by public funds. Instead of omitting children from job or housing applications for fear of being passed over in favor of somebody childless, people would write those children in knowing that their very existence guaranteed any privileges necessary to their well-being. It sounds strange because we are accustomed to thinking about parenting (if we think about it at all) as an extra to be fitted into already full and fulfilling lives—a universal hobby that is awkward because it cannot be shelved during the working week, interrupts important adult business and is hard on soft furnishings. But if parenthood were thoughtfully and positively chosen by some people rather than taken for granted by almost all, those attitudes could change. There is a precedent in parenting by adoption. Prospective adopters do not expect, and their counselors will not accept, a casual approach. They consciously want and wait for a child, try to think through the emotional and practical implications of having one and see nothing strange in advance discussion of his or her likely needs and their own capacities and plans to meet them.

Positive Parenting

Rights and responsibilities should always be packaged together; the extra level of responsibility expected of people who choose to become parents should bring them new rights as parents—not rights over their children, though, as that phrase so often suggests, but rights to society's help and support in parenting them. Once a given couple had chosen to produce a child, or another child, it should be assumed that they, linked to those children by atavism and attachment, would almost always be the best people to care for them. The more social resources we devote to assisting those in difficulty within their parenting, the fewer resources will need to be devoted to helping, or forcing, them out of it. That is important because current attitudes and practices sometimes produce vicious circles. If a single mother is clinging to a social safety net by her fingertips, a nursery place for her baby so that she can take a job may be the most life-enhancing offer that can be made to her— or it may not. The offer may seem to her to mean that nobody considers her personal mothering really important—that everybody thinks that if she cannot manage on whatever benefits she can claim, her baby will be better off cared for by "professionals" while she earns money to pay them to do so. Sadly, such unintended messages are often received with resigned agreement that bodes ill for the future: "She's better off in the nursery really; I'm not much good at being a mom. . . ." Every time a child is added to an "at risk" register, parents hear their personal relationships with that child denigrated, their kind of parenting classified as dangerous. Although children's safety must, of course, be the first concern, we need to be aware that trampling on parents' self-esteem does nothing to help them become "better parents." Sometimes it may even do something to make our grim prophecies self-fulfilling and their child's need for a "place of safety" urgent.

Of course, there will always be some parents who, by the standards of any particular place or time, are neglectful, or some mixture of disorganized, incompetent and unfortunate. They need help, but it will be better for their children as well as for them if that help is on their own terms. Is a nursery place for the baby and a job for her what this mother chooses or the only solution she is offered? There should be other solutions she can be offered. More financial help, perhaps. A place where she can go with the baby while she gets herself together. Someone to befriend and support her for a while. There will always be a few parents who are abusive, too, whether physically, sexually, emotionally or in any combination of these. But our best hope of reducing the number and keeping it down probably lies in making "acceptable parenting" easier for most parents and respectful help readily available to all. Very few children with epileptic disorders are hidden away in attics or cellars today, as many used to be in Victorian times. Changing public attitudes rid those illnesses of their shameful or devil-ridden connotations, so that parents became able to acknowledge such children in the expectation of acceptance and assistance. If that is what made a common practice of yesterday into a rare horror of today, it may also be the way to reverse today's abuse statistics for tomorrow.

If society is to do its best for children, changing social attitudes towards parenting is the primary task because once that has been done, everything else will follow. A social context that gives real priority to children's needs, and real respect to parents' roles in meeting them, will release a flow of fresh approaches to facilitating both. And once there is the political will to do so, translating new approaches into practical policies will be relatively easy and rewarding to everybody. Policies that address the basic conflict between children's need for parents' presence and companionship, and parents' need to be elsewhere and with other people, for example, can transform the life-styles not only of individual parents and children but also of whole communities and, eventually, societies.

Fresh Approaches to Childcare

If crucial attachment and dependency needs are to be generously met, parents have to enjoy being with their children. New financial and work arrangements are important, but they are not enough. They have to be integrated into a supportive and companionable adult life-style. There are still individuals who choose and manage to arrange to live in extended families or close communities that provide shared care and companionship. But for most people in post-industrial societies, being at home full-time when almost all other adults are in workplaces full-time soon means isolation, loneliness and that uncomfortable combination of overwork and boredom that comes from being constantly confronted with unremittingly repetitive, trivial chores. It is the impoverishment of life at home, as much as the enrichment of paid work, that has so dramatically reduced the ages at which many infants enter daycare, and the numbers of caregivers available in domestic settings.

Home base—or a place of similar scale and warm familiarity—is probably most crucial in infancy, but it remains important as children grow. The toddler can, and the preschool child should, spend part of the day with a larger range of children and adults than most modern families provide, and peer-group life becomes increasingly important to schoolchildren. But although the ideal balance between time spent at home and time spent outside it changes, the quality of life at home and especially of relationships with the adults who constitute the family within it remain crucial. Attempts to prescribe home life for small children at the expense of women-who-are-mothers—such as those made by "family values" lobbies in various countries—inevitably fail because home life (and "mothering"), as such lobbyists perceive it, is a thing of the past. But daycare for all, as it is evolving, is neither the only alternative nor satisfactory for children or their parents.

The public image of daycare is an unrealistically positive one: preschool children playing and learning together in the playgroups and nursery schools that should indeed be freely available to them all. Less positive and less looked-at are images of those same children, seven hours later: past playing, past learning and still with two hours before they are collected. And then there are the images that are seldom seen: images of babies, a few weeks or a few months old, with nothing to gain from being with other children and much to lose in being left to the care of adults whom they must share. Workplace nurseries are often presented as a means of softening and shortening the separation between working parent and child. Campaigns for them talk of "going to work with Mommy," as if employers truly made space for children to share employed parents' lives. Perhaps some do and more could. But if workplace daycare is to be an important aspect of industry's potentially vital role in helping people to integrate their working and parenting roles, most firms will have to rethink their physical relationship to communities. Right now, those campaigns do not often reflect the realities of life for parents or for children. Reality is usually a mother taking a baby or toddler twice daily on a packed commuter train and then a bus to a daycare center that is indeed sponsored by her company but is probably housed in a lower-rental back street. If it is close enough for lunch-break visits, reality is forgoing lunch-hour shopping for the evening meal and facing saying goodbye an extra time. Most existing workplace nurseries get no daytime visits from parents unless staff summon them in an emergency. They can still be excellent daycare and early childhood education facilities, of course, and some of them are. But however happy a child may be there, being there may present problems when kindergarten or first grade looms. Unless the firm and its daycare center happen to be placed within the school district used by most employees, children will lose all their preschool friends and may have to enter their new peer group without a single familiar face.

There is a seldom spoken political reality that has to be faced, too. A workplace nursery means that a child's daycare place depends on a parent's employment. While that dependence certainly contributes to what management pamphlets call "work-force loyalty," it could act—as company housing notoriously does—to reduce parental choice and job mobility and even to contribute to exploitation. While every effort firms make to assist parents trapped in the working-caring dilemma is to be welcomed, the provision of funds for daycare in parents' home communities may be a better option than the provision of daycare at work.

Popular images of daycare, and the possible use of workplace nurseries, end abruptly when children go to school, but the problems posed by childcare remain. School hours do not fill full-time work hours, especially with a commute at either end. Furthermore, schools have regular vacations and midsemester breaks and often close for Election Day and teachers' in-service training. And schoolchildren get sick. In most families an unbroken run of five or even four school weeks' attendance is exceptional.

The present care young schoolchildren—especially the under-eights—receive in many Western countries ranges from scanty to scandalous. In the United Kingdom, for example, the Kids Club Network estimates that one in five children between the ages of five and ten years is left alone at home during school holidays and one in six comes home at the end of each school day to an empty house. After-school clubs do vital work, but are available to only a fraction of the children who need them. A police-schools liaison officer in a privileged part of southeast England once told me: "Anyone who is buying a house in this area needs two incomes to meet the house prices so every day I see dozens of five- and six-year-olds finding their own way home. A lot of them are scared to let themselves into dark houses in winter, though they wouldn't tell their mums that. I'm scared for every single one of them: scared of the traffic, scared of the bullies who take their sweet-money and scared of the adults who might harm them."

The difficulty is widely recognized, but the possibility—necessity— of adapting adult lives to children's needs is seldom taken seriously. Instead, attempts are made to adapt children's school lives to adult work patterns, often to the detriment of teachers as well as students. In most European countries, the school day is starting earlier and finishing later even though, for the younger children at least, the conventional day was often already too long. For teachers, a working day that approximates that of most of the work force means that they must actually work much longer hours, with lesson preparation and marking going on long into most evenings. Many of them also have children of their own, of course. In some countries, especially in the United States, the teachers' day in school is being left untouched, but children's after-school programs and vacation care are being provided as an extension of theirs. As long as teachers are replaced by less highly trained and expensive "care personnel," making fuller use of school buildings is sound economics. It is doubtful that it is sound childcare, though. Most small children already find the school day stressful; many find the buildings, and the groups within them, uncomfortably large. To those who are only just coping with a short day supported by their familiar teachers, a longer day finishing with a different adult must be intolerable. And even somewhat older children who can cope with these programs often do not want to. As a group of seven-year-olds in Massachusetts told me: "We like to play with our friends after school. We want to go home." Holidays at school are surely a dismal prospect, too, whatever the program of play activities. Few adults would wish to spend much nonworking time in their factories and offices. We all need to escape the tensions of group life, institutional buildings and the identities we have assumed within them. We all need to come home, relax and be a more private version of ourselves.

Whatever the arrangements made for children who are well, children who are unwell upset them all because schools and care groups will not accept them. Like the rest of us, sick children need to stay home but, unlike the rest of us, they cannot do so alone. The problem is being addressed with astonishingly antichild solutions. In some American cities, Boston for example, children too feverish or rash-covered to go to school can spend their days on special "lollipop wards" in hospitals—if their parents are rich enough. I thought the battle for sick children's right to have familiar caregivers with them, rather than being abandoned to strange hospital personnel, had been finally won at least twenty-five years ago.

So: schoolchildren need to come home; preschool children need short hours away from home; toddlers and babies need to be based at home and with home or homelike people. How are all those needs to be integrated with the realities of adult life-styles? Softening the edges of those realities with gender equality, with supportive social attitudes and with the flexible working practices that would follow is a *sine qua non,* but it is not enough. Whatever arrangements a parent can make, a life that is dependent on making arrangements and a life-style that falls apart when arrangements go wrong is not conducive to the adult enjoyment on which children's well-being depends. We have to find secure and companionable frameworks within which all families, whatever their current composition, personal priorities or failing fortunes, can be sure of meeting changing childish needs. How could that be done?

The issues that are important to all families, albeit to different and probably changing degrees, are home, work and childcare. Any workable solution to the early years of parenting has to knit these three together into a blanket that warms all family members and smothers none. Small changes in the emphasis placed on each of the three change the knitting pattern; so many fine gradations are possible that everyone's blanket would be individual.

Putting the Emphasis on Homes

If being at home with young children did not isolate parents or parent figures from other adults, some would be happy to leave the workplace altogether for a while and others would be able to make reciprocal arrangements so that all adults worked and all children were cared for.

There are many existing examples of communal living, ranging from the well-known kibbutzim in Israel or the Mormon groups in the United States, through "drop out" communities in every Western country to personal arrangements made by small groups of individuals. Many communes float successfully on the enthusiasm of their founders but disintegrate under the weight of subsequent generations. The reasons are various but they often share an obvious basis: adolescent children do not usually want to live exactly the life their parents chose. The more different a parental life-style from that of the majority of a society, and the greater its relative hardship, the more likely it is that those adolescents will reject it and seek the mainstream if they have a choice.

When communal living reflects religious or cultural conviction, its longevity over generations is a measure of its success. But if it is simply set up to fulfill the particular needs of a group of people at a particular stage in their lives, it can disband when that phase is over without being a failure. Everybody accepts that college dormitories are often the best possible background to student life but generally inappropriate thereafter. Perhaps we should approach the idea of communal living during the early years of parenting in the same spirit.

Who would live with whom, and how would it be arranged and financed? The possibilities are infinitely various and there are many models we could call on. Three-generation living, for example, has much to recommend it, including the value to both the old and the young of spending time together and the possibilities of shared childcare inherent in that. Extended families by blood and marriage may have dwindled and departed, but there is no reason why individuals should not choose a version of their own. Lone parents of both sexes, and their children, could obviously gain a great deal from living in shared households. Apart from the possibilities of practical cooperation, children would gain adult models of the sex opposite from their parent's, and parents would gain cross-gender support and companionship, separated from the stresses of sexual relationships that may, or may not, turn into step-parenting. But any couple with a child or children might have much to gain from finding others with whom to share housing, practical arrangements including childcare and companionship. We welcome the versions that happen by chance—because we move to an apartment in a building where three other compatible families also live, or buy a house where "the neighborhood" really means something—so why do we not arrange it on purpose and in ways that ensure more benefit?

Financing communal living can be complicated, and, of course, shared expenditure always means the possibility of disputes. But in general there are large economies of scale to be enjoyed at every level. The experience of british housing associations during the last ten years, for example, shows that properly organized communal financing enables groups of people to purchase or convert accommodations of a standard none of them could afford as individuals. Once converted for communal living, with whatever separation between families a particular group might decide upon, those accommodations can also be equipped to a higher standard, because many of the facilities people need and the luxuries they long for are sharable and therefore affordable.

Putting the Emphasis on Childcare

If children are to be cared for outside their homes while parents work, daycare needs to be organized so that it better meets the needs of all age groups. A central child-place in each community might serve, and integrate, all the disparate people presently involved: children of all ages, parents at all stages, caregivers of every kind.

The existence of a local child-place would, hopefully, prolong the period for which some mothers felt able to be with and breast-feed babies, because its most basic function—on which all the rest are built—would be to serve as a drop-in center or informal club for them, and for anyone else caring for a baby—father or grandparent, nanny or au pair, daycare mother or babysitter. Such a center serves both adults and children. It takes the isolation and boredom out of being home-based with a baby and thus facilitates a period of close togetherness, and it provides a range of intimate friends of all ages and thus facilitates gradual separation and eventually stress-free daycare. Using the center from the beginning of a baby's life, adults of both sexes would get to know each other, each others' children and the center's health, education and welfare professionals—hopefully local residents and often parents themselves. Babies and toddlers would get to know them too, and each other. Ideally, each center and loose-knit group of people would serve both adults and children rather as large extended families and small, close communities still serve a fortunate few. A pleasant place to go for a change and company, for extra facilities and different playthings, for the exchange of worries and reassurance—a place and people so familiar that they can be trusted to backstop parenting. Accustomed to spending time there with a parent or known caregiver, even babies could be left at the center for a couple of hours occasionally, without distress. And there would always be familiar adults available to serve as life rafts to any child whose parent figures were embroiled in an emergency.

Daycare groups, flexibly constituted to serve parents working any combination of hours, would be in the same setting, so every child's introduction to managing regularly without a parent or permanent caretaker of her own could be gradual and individually planned and paced. Familiar with the place and many of the people since their first weeks, many one-year-olds could calmly let their mothers go for a while if they were given into the special charge of another mother who was not yet planning outside work, for example. A new form of caregiving reminiscent of the oldest form of all: leaving your child with your sister who wants to stay home with her own. Children might then graduate into part-time hours in the professionally run toddler group, building their confidence and independence towards readiness for the (already familiar) preschool education group, with full-time care for those who needed it.

Children in those preschool care groups would not be the oldest who used the place because the groups would also serve as focal points for older children's out-of-school and vacation care. Children who could not go "home" at 3 p.m. could nevertheless be brought to a "home base" in the community, and share leisure time with younger brothers and sisters and with local friends attending different schools. This aspect of the child-place's work would provide extra part-time work for some adults in and for their local communities, and a place for others—especially, perhaps, elderly people and adolescents—to share skills and interests with the children on a voluntary basis. Having both or all their children gathered in the same safe and friendly place, on the home side of the commute, until they could pick them up would be an incomparable relief not only to parents working full-time but also to those facing the disruption of divorce, the stresses of lone parenthood or the uncertainties of establishing new partnerships.

There are places something like these already working in several countries. The superb "young family centers" run by various children's charities in the United Kingdom and those set up as part of various projects for underprivileged families in the United States serve as partial models. There is one crucial difference, though. Existing centers are not part of the everyday life of their communities, but extra to it—expensive, therefore, and only open to selected families whose children are at special risk of neglect or abuse. It is the very essence of the kind of child-place proposed here that it should be available to everyone and answerable to all. Child-places could serve as focal points for wider and wider networks in different communities: the obvious place for the local toy library, for children's book exhibitions and children's theater; a source of hands-on experience for adolescent parents-to-be taking child development courses in school, for students in childcare courses, future play-group leaders and teachers; even a sensible place for a prenatal and child health clinic. Serving the local area and employing local people, such places could do a great deal to give communities back some sense of themselves as places where people live together and relate to one another—places where children grow up.

Would such a child-place inevitably become institutional and therefore off-putting? Would many parents, perhaps especially more privileged ones, prefer too much isolation with their children to too little privacy? Not necessarily. The experience of community playgroups in many Western countries suggests that a facility provided for children and run partly by parents easily becomes central to the lives of young families. American day camps for very young children sometimes build a sense of close and caring community that parents and children both miss when summer ends. Britain's drop-in play-centers for children under five accompanied by a parent or caregiver (known as "One-O-Clock clubs") are an important social focus for many adults and children, and the rather similar facilities provided especially for daycare mothers and their charges are said to halve the work and double the satisfaction. There is always a danger, though, that any community-based facility will be least used by those who need it most. The social as well as the economic aspects of putting children and their parents first have to start from the bottom.

In setting up these child-places, or anything similar, we should have to apply research findings showing that neither equal access nor equal services produce equity between different populations. A facility in the middle of a residential area is not equally accessible to those with and without cars, money for public transportation, homes at ground or fifteen-story level, suitable clothes, adequate time or energy. The assurance of instant help in response to a phone call is not helpful if the nearest telephone is down the road and vandalized, and dropping in is only an easy-access option for those who are sure of their language skills—and of themselves. As to the services provided: if severely disadvantaged populations are to benefit equally with the better-off, services need to be enriched, not only beyond what is usually offered to the poor but beyond what is usually available to the well-to-do. If people are actually hungry, that courtesy cup of coffee needs more than a cookie in its saucer. If the landlord and the public utilities are about to foreclose, even the most sensitive advice about a baby's crying or a child's problems in kindergarten will seem crass. It is not that those issues do not concern this mother, but rather that getting hold of some money has to take priority.

A program developed in the late sixties by Dr. Sally Provence under the auspices of Yale University's Child Study Center still serves as a useful sketch of what would have to be done to get parents to places like these and ensure that they found what they needed there. It also indicates the long-term benefits that could be anticipated. Women living in a depressed inner-city area, at or below the poverty line, were recruited to the study while they were attending a prenatal clinic during their first pregnancies. More than half were unmarried; more than half the children were black or of mixed racial origin. A center was provided, offering friendship, support, advice and opportunities to offer all those to others; professional medical and educational services for the infants; flexible daycare. But it offered two vital additions: outreach and professional flexibility. Staff did not sit in the center waiting for parents to come and use it; they went out to them. And they did not act only within the rigid limits of their own specialty, or pass people who presented with particular issues among each other, in an endless series of referrals: each reacted immediately to parents' immediate concerns. The pediatrician, for example, met all the mothers while they were in the hospital having their babies, phoned each of them at least weekly during the next month and made home visits if one was sick. If he visited a baby and found it needed to be in the hospital, he did not just arrange admission but drove mother and baby there and stayed as friend and interpreter until he was sure the mother understood what was going on. The monthly examinations he offered to every baby at the center were never missed. Other professionals behaved similarly, and the social worker—defined as particularly the "parents' person"—was as ready to help mothers obtain washing machines and food stamps as contraceptives or education.

These families and their matched control group were followed up after five and ten years. The program had diverted most of the rotten results predicted for these babies who had so many risk factors stacked against them. After ten years, for example, half of the control parents but none of the program parents were on welfare, and program mothers had achieved extra years of education and waited longer before having another child. As for the children: 67 percent of the control group had serious school adjustment problems compared with only 28 percent—close to the local average—of the intervention group.

A first pregnancy or birth is probably the optimum time to introduce effective social interventions because parents are conscious of needing help with this vast change in role, responsibility and life-style and are unlikely to feel patronized or singled out by being offered it. Child-places could not operate a bias towards families with new babies, though, even at the beginning. Taking in an age-cohort means excluding all those outside it. That would not only be socially divisive but would also distort the experience and potential of the place for those included. Involving families with older children, especially those with multiple problems and long experience of unsatisfactory contacts with social agencies, would be a major challenge, but it could be met. Another American program, Homebuilders—started in Washington in the seventies and extended to the Bronx—suggests that genuinely un-limited support and skilled but undemarcated, nonbureaucratic case-work over a period as short as six weeks can enable even the most disaffected and disorganized parents to make use of continuing oppor-tunities. The families were all on the point of losing their children into care. They received round-the-clock services from highly trained work-ers who were never responsible for more than three families each. The professionals, always resisting the temptation to routinize their work, offered stable continuous relationships and as much time as each family member needed *to feel she or he was being heard.* Their wide-ranging, flexible services included very practical assistance: parents did not just get help with planning to clean their homes; they got help with the cleaning. Those six-week periods had dramatic and lasting results, of which the most objective must be the fact that six years later, 90 percent of the children were still in their homes.

If these programs of a generation ago were so effective, why have they not lasted, not spread all over America, all over the Western world? That Homebuilders program *has* lasted, not in the sense of having doz-ens of identical *projects* started up in different places, but in the sense of having its family-preservation *approach* spread far and wide by a foundation willing to lay the groundwork for systems change. The Edna McConnell Clark Foundation has supported new kinds of train-ing, funded reform in child welfare financing and helped states cope with crucial matters like public accountability and changes in work contracts. As a result, in 1993 there were "at least twenty-five states and several cities [that were] incorporating the principles of family pres-ervation in their reform of child welfare, juvenile justice, mental health, and family support." So can we learn enough from the short lifespan of other programs of proven effectiveness to ensure that a new one could last?

It is not enough for a program to be effective in facilitating individual lives and the best possible use of public money; those who control it from the outside have to understand and believe in its aims, so that they see its effectiveness and its economy within its own context. Good programs can work within tight purse strings, but when those strings are tightened further, because people believe it could produce more for less, they strangle. Cynical or naive policy-makers and bureaucrats often demand that complex programs refine themselves into "magic bullets": simple formulas that will produce clearly defined success wherever they are aimed. They do not realize that in order to achieve that, the program will have to duck the most difficult targets that were their original raison d'être, and leave some other agency to cope with them. The British education system in the early nineties, for example, encourages schools to take control of their own budgets direct from central government, shedding the control of local education authorities and competing directly with each other to produce the best (examination) results for the available money. To achieve that kind of success, schools need easy-to-educate students, so many are beginning to avoid or exclude children with language or behavioral difficulties. The magic bullet is producing some high-flying schools, but can a school that excludes rather than works with troublesome students be truly educational?

Even when they do not demand magic bullets aimed at sure success, those who control the funding often demand quantitative justification for expenditure on programs designed to produce qualitative change. Revelations of the low standards of dentistry offered to Norwegian children led to generous government funding of a program to improve them. The program started by distributing to all dentists literature designed to interest them in working with child patients—and in taking the proposed new courses in child dentistry. As soon as the number of dentists who expressed willingness to work with child patients reached an adequate level for the child population, funding—and the program—was terminated. Enough dentists is not synonymous with *good* dentistry, but the researchers' real purposes had never been appreciated by the responsible bureaucracy.

Even when qualitative objectives are understood, the time scales needed to achieve them are often underestimated. Financial support is made dependent on program evaluation; programs are evaluated on a rigid, often annual, schedule and any that are not running right are aborted. The doyen of evaluation, Professor Donald Campbell, advises, "Evaluate no program until it is proud," and certainly evaluation by those with the power to cut the purse strings should wait until those running the program believe that they are doing what they were contracted to do. In the meantime, though, earlier informal evaluation, by knowledgeable people who are sympathetic to a program's aims, can actually help to ensure its survival and healthy development.

But perhaps the most important and most difficult lesson we have to learn is that even the programs that are most positively evaluated do not always survive the procedure. The change from demonstration project to publicly funded service often turns success into failure. Again and again, in every country in the West, the process of tailoring demonstration projects to fit into existing services has cut budgets and staff discretion and increased case loads and bureaucracy. Inevitably, subsequent evaluation of the service produces less positive results and, sooner or later, it withers or is dropped.

Child-places, or any similar initiative, can only be effective if they are effective for all families. Since that includes the most disorganized and disrupted—those whose energy level and frustration tolerance have already been sapped, and all those whose prior experiences of looking for help have left them feeling more helpless—child-places will have to provide, at least at the beginning, intensive, comprehensive, individualized services, with aggressive attention to outreach and to maintaining personal relationships over time. To achieve that they will need teams of professional staff, ancillary workers and volunteers, with the flexibility, support and self-confidence to ignore or sidestep many of the limitations normally imposed by bureaucratic job descriptions and even some of those traditionally imposed by professional status consciousness. Such centers would require serious investment, have high initial running costs and depend on protection from premature evaluation linked to annual national debt–cutting exercises and quadrennial election fevers.

If they got what they required, though, such places would immediately serve individual happiness and the public good, by minimizing the cumulative effect of whatever risk factors families brought with them. The adolescent mother's baby might have many problems, but the place would make sure that they were recognized and dealt with, not compounded further while she struggled in an isolated poverty trap. The preschool child of divorcing parents might be extremely distressed by two years of family conflict, but by providing secure care for him and a nonjudgmental environment for them, the child-place might enable the mother to earn both the living and the self-respect she otherwise stood to lose, and enable the father to spend time with his son so the two of them did not have to lose each other.

If they got what they required, child-places, in the long term, would not only prevent risk factors in children's development from exacerbating each other, but also prevent many from forming in the first place. Children reared in greater security and with higher self-esteem will be at lesser risk of teenage pregnancy. Men and women whose personal and work lives are more easily integrated will be less vulnerable to conflict in marriage and more able to end it, if they must, without the animosity that so damages their children. Families that are defined by their value to children, and equally supported whatever their shape and structure, will less often be found dysfunctional.

Putting the Emphasis on Work

Parents have less time to spend with their children because they are spending more time at work. Recent research suggests that the total amount of time parents and children spend together—whether or not they are paying each other any direct attention—has dropped by 40 percent in a single generation. That decrease is not primarily because parents spend longer hours in the workplace and in commuting, of course, but because increasing numbers of mothers work as much as fathers, and increasing numbers of children have only one parent with whom to spend regular time. Hallmark, the greeting card company, now markets hellos and goodnights: "Have a super day at school" reads one; "I wish I were there to tuck you in" reads another.

Time conflicts between working and caring have been extensively discussed earlier in this book and many ways of shaving down working
time during children's earliest years and of refitting the worlds of work
and home together were reviewed in the last chapter. But while all those
measures together would certainly dramatically relieve the pain of time
pressure, they could not eliminate the basic conflict of needing to be in
two places at once.

It is time to seriously consider joining up those two places parents
need to be, by taking work back home. Until very recently that would
have sounded like nostalgia for an agrarian past or like a call for all
parents to drop out and grow broccoli while they grew babies. *Real*
work had to take place in factories and offices. But soon most work
will not have to be done in any particular place. We have already seen
a start to telecommuting, but there is far more to come from communications technology and an enormous and as yet unexplored potential
for using it to reshape work.

Taking work back home does not have to mean taking it right into
individual homes so that people work alone. The economic arguments
that support individual telecommuting will also support any kind of
workplace and work group individuals want to set up, because vast
office buildings and centralized working practices are becoming relatively more and more expensive. Several people with babies could set
up a workroom in one of their homes, take the babies to work with
them and share their care, maybe paying for one extra adult pair of
hands for extra-busy moments. No, that is not workplace daycare—it
is day-place work-care.

Taking work back home does not have to mean that anyone works
in a home at all. Working in the home *area* so that there is no commute,
no rush hour, no tense-making time that must elapse between a call
from the school and getting there would make a big difference to parents, and differences in real estate values downtown and in the suburbs
would often make it economical for large employers. Mini-offices could
be established in suburbs so everyone could walk to work; close to
schools so parents and children could go to work together on the same
transportation, or next to child-places. Larger subsidiaries could be
sited in local towns so people who worked at home could meet there a
couple of times a week for planning, checking, brainstorming and

lunch. There could even be mobile headquarters that spent one day each week in each of five locations, troubleshooting and stroking egos. The first few companies to try it would face rezoning problems, but only while everyone got used to the idea that once work data is carried in mobile modems, it has little more impact on residential districts than the data people already carry in their briefcases.

The possibilities of generating work from home base have also begun to reveal themselves in the last decade. Small—often very small—businesses have burgeoned in all Western countries as a spin-off from recession. People who have been laid off or forced into early retirement have used golden parachutes and/or loans to set up on their own. Many have gone bust, but enough have survived that such businesses have made a real economic contribution in most countries and have been a main source of re-employment in some hard-hit areas.

The service sector is expanding in all Western countries and it is the increasing demand for local and personalized services that offers the most opportunities to one-person businesses, partnerships and small cooperatives. Busy people will pay a bit extra to have the drycleaning or the take-out meals delivered; to get the lawn cut, the dog walked or the house maintenance carried out by someone they can trust with a key to the garage door; to have the school-run done by a driver they can trust with a child. And as mass production and mass outlets spread sameness everywhere, many individuals will also pay for the relief of a unique product or place—the locally designed knitwear, individually made birthday cake or restaurant-without-a-logo. Personal services do not have to be domestic, though. The same technologies that make it feasible to bring professional work to home bases also make it feasible to generate and conduct it there. Why travel to the city to seek the services of a lawyer or an architect? Their high-profile offices add much to the price of their work and little that is irreplaceable to its quality. Even their libraries will soon be accessible at home on CD-ROMs and conferences with colleagues available via videophones.

The potential for this way of working is enormous and scarcely tapped. Small enterprises today commonly measure their success by their growth, always aiming to expand into "real businesses" with big offices and payrolls. If they do that they lose the very qualities of small scale and easy accessibility that make them uniquely valuable to those who work in them and to their customers. More could be done to help people explore the potential demand in their own localities. Far more could be done to cut the red tape of regulations that bars them from starting. And far, *far* more could be done to ease their financing, by regulating the terms of startup loans and the foreclosure powers of banks, and by offering tax breaks.

Living on the job has always reduced parents' conflict between working and caring, but it has not been widely regarded as a solution that should be sought out because until recently that life-style has not been available to many people or often desirable in other ways. Few people want to be farmers, for example, and outside the protectionism of France, even long-established farming families often fail to make a living from the land. Only a minority of doctors can practice from the front room, and the profitability of those who used to do so commonly depended on the unpaid work of wives, which is no longer desirable or affordable. Past patterns of working at home must not blind us to present realities and future possibilities, though. A high proportion of existing jobs are now tied to particular places and environments mainly by convention and habit. People can do them as productively and economically in any setting that suits them. And those home settings that suit families particularly suit a potentially enormous number of new, entrepreneurial opportunities. Everybody has to work, but in the twenty-first century by no means everybody has to go out to work.

Children will only come first in society if parents can start them as first in their own lives without condemning themselves to coming last. Both mothers and fathers have to be able to find ways to be simultaneously solvent, self-respecting citizens and caring parents—their own individual ways, knitted from multistranded solutions offered and supported, but not prescribed, by their societies. The skeins offered here are no more than a beginning, but they are a sensible beginning, because a tangle of practical conflicts about home and childcare and work are inherent in *being* a parent in the post-industrial West.

The three approaches are very different. Putting the emphasis on home imposes no extra economic burden on society and leaves the business world untouched, but it burdens parents with making a lot of difficult decisions and acting on them for themselves. Putting the emphasis on childcare commits society to heavy immediate expenditure on a new and long-term investment in local services. It would probably seek to recoup a share from business, but there would be no cost to parents, whose lives would be immediately eased. Putting the emphasis on work imposes no direct cost on society, business or parents, but demands that all three invest energy and imagination in working together.

But if the three approaches are different, they all point to resolutions to the conflict between working and caring that are small in scale and local, and in this they reflect an important subtext of this book. Small children need to grow with small, knowable numbers of adults in small, encompassable environments. Putting them—and their parents—first may take big ideas, but the successful ideas will always be those that break down the big, centralized units that characterize modern Western societies and reassemble the pieces in small human scale. Children's needs are better met in small local playgroups and small classes in neighborhood schools than in big centers at the end of a bus ride. Parents will be better able to meet those needs as well as their own if they, too, can be big fish in local ponds rather than insignificant ones in an ocean at the end of a commute.

Looking Forward

If the principle of positive discrimination for children and parents together is to mean anything, it has to be converted into real policies. If those policies stabilize stressed-out societies on a new community base with a real stake in the future, life-enhancing changes will spin off them—for everyone.

People attract people. The more parents and parent figures spend time at home, the less isolating and lonely being "at home" will become and the more inclined other parents will be to follow suit. The more cheerful adults there are around home bases, the more attractive home-based work of every kind will become, so the more their numbers will swell. It is not only children and parents who will gain from each others' presence, but everyone in the locality, including retired individuals, the old, the sick and those who care for them.

People attract businesses that attract more people. If there are many adults around residential neighborhoods in the daytime, it will be worthwhile to reinstate the commercial enterprises and leisure facilities—shops, cafes, swimming pools—currently concentrated in business districts. They will enliven suburbia while doing business seven days each week rather than five.

Those local businesses will create local employment. Since it is children, above all, who need adult time, parents should have priority for jobs in the neighborhood while these are scarce. But once communities come commercially alive it is to be hoped that working close to home will become a choice for more and more people. Commuting is uncomfortable, expensive and environmentally destructive, whoever does it.

Communities that are to be given new life by having children as their focus will have to give parents priority in local housing, too, and that means priority for the right housing in the right place. The United Kingdom makes much of the fact that it does not leave homeless people on the streets if they have young children, but little of the fact that if a local authority houses them out of turn, it puts them in the very worst accommodations there are—often into apartments so nearly derelict that people on the waiting list have refused them. Any home is better than none, but if anyone has to move far away from family members in order to find one, or to live in damp decrepitude, it cannot be children, because they come first. That priority will mean different things in different places: new public building programs, new mortgage schemes, new tax breaks. More than any other group in any community, children need homes with yards so there is space for messy play, water play, pets, growing seeds. Homes that are reasonably quiet so they can learn to listen and to concentrate, undisturbed by the roar from that flight path and the TV turned higher and higher to get above it. Homes that do not only meet minimal local standards concerning overcrowding, but allow each child his or her own bed, and growing families the decent privacy of separate bedrooms.

Children need other outside spaces to play in, too, and those are scarce commodities, especially in our car-choked, dog-loving cities. Where there is a park or gardens in a square, there are prohibitions: "Keep off the grass" and "No ball games." They must be addressed to parents and children since dogs do not read and there is smelly evidence that dogs do not keep off that grass and that toddlers had better. No cycling, of course. Bikes might bother more important people, such as employees on their lunch breaks. We could take the notices down and keep the dogs on leashes, but it would be better to make those notices positive for children and parents: "Children under twelve and accompanying adults only" and "No adult admitted unless accompanied by a child." And what about under-fives enclosures in every open space, so a mother or father, a caregiver or a grandfather who does not move very fast anymore can relax without fear of losing a child, and children can run without fear of getting knocked over?

Children are apprentices to the adult world, so the more they go about with people on grown-up business, the better. Streets are dangerous and polluted places, especially for people who breathe at exhaust-pipe height. Cars and small people do not, and should not, mix. Parking on sidewalks, speeding down residential streets and blowing impatient horns at short legs on pedestrian crossings should be as shameful—and expensive—as drunk driving. Even streets could be a lot more fun than they are, though. Every railway bridge and building site needs viewing slots three feet off the ground because every child needs to see the trains and the bulldozers. Every toddler enjoys mailing things, so every letter box needs a low slot too. Postal authorities say children would "mail trash," but it is bigger "children" who mail used condoms and fireworks. And where are the slotted litter baskets for their candy wrappers and drink cans, so they get the habit of keeping public places tidy, and learn about recycling, while the actual depositing is fun?

Communities need parent people and children on every public or service committee because going out and about with small children poses a lot of demeaning problems that empathy could solve at little cost. In most Western cities we still have to ask, "Where *is* a man supposed to take his little girl to pee?" And whoever takes her, why are there so few child-sized toilets or sinks? And why no dispensers for disposable diapers when they are everywhere for sanitary napkins and tampons? Even when they do not need to pee, children find it much more difficult than older people to wait their turn. They have to learn, of course, but they do that with their peers at kindergarten age when they can see the point. In the meantime, waiting in line with a toddler is a major stress for him, for his adult companion and for everybody within earshot, and it is almost completely avoidable. We have special supermarket check-outs for people with fewer than nine items, or for people paying cash. Why don't we have them for people with under-fives, and make sure no candies are displayed there? Parents with small children should go first at the doctor's. Why not? Somebody has to and the waiting room will be more peaceful for everyone if that feverish three-year-old does not have to wait. And what about that line at the post office? And at the bus stop? Airlines let adults with babies and small children board first, and sometimes give them the seats with extra legroom; why not all public transportation? Some European intercity trains have special children's play cars; why not every Western train?

Why not indeed? The Manhattan cab driver who told me, "Kids—I hate 'em" was surely in a barefaced minority. Most people love children—don't they? It is not really *our* fault that society sees them more as hobbies for parents than as people in their own right—is it?

Loving children is not enough. Children grow up and have more children. By ignoring the moral obligation to do their rich best for children, post-industrial Western societies are failing everybody now, and failing their own future. Of course the answer to "Why not children (and their parents) first?" is "social attitudes." Of course it is only changes in theoretical-sounding attitudes that will make hard, practical economic, political and social changes possible, as well as ensuring that the waitress mops up a child's spill as politely as an adult's, and that his mother does not feel like slapping him. But neither "society" nor "social attitudes" can ultimately let individuals off their own moral obligations, because there is no society that is separate from us. The whole complicated, conservative, consumerist collective is nothing but the children we were, the children we have had, the children we have now and those they will have in the future. The people who work, care and are cared for are the same people. There is nobody else to turn the social tide.

NOTES

Introduction

xvi • "for pleasure and for fun": This, and other insights into parents' own feelings and ideas about parenting, in various cultures, can be found in Jacqueline J. Goodnow and W. Andrew Collins, *Development According to Parents: The Nature, Sources and Consequences of Parents' Ideas* (Hillsdale, N.J.: Lawrence Erlbaum Assocs., 1990).

• post-industrial Western: This cumbersome phrase is the most accurate description I could find of the countries and cultures this book deals with. "Post-industrial nations" are often defined as those which derive 60 percent or more of GNP from the service sector. It therefore includes all OECD nations with the marginal exceptions of Greece, Portugal and Turkey. I add "Western" to make it clear that post-industrial nations with very different cultural traditions, such as Japan and Taiwan, are excluded.

xv • many fail to thrive and some die: See R. A. Spitz, "Anaclitic Depression," *Psychoanalytic Study of the Child* (vol. 2, 1946), 313–42. See also Public Health Paper No. 14, "Deprivation of Maternal Care: A Reassessment of Its Effects" (Geneva: World Health Organization, 1962).

• Children under seven: For a readable account of the consistencies in developmental stages of childhood across cultures, see Melvin Konner, *Childhood* (Boston: Little, Brown, 1991).

• child-friendly choices: Amid a vast literature, I would especially recommend Lee N. Robins and Michael Rutter, eds., *Straight and Devious Pathways from Childhood to Adulthood* (Cambridge: Cambridge University Press, 1990).

1. People, Profits and Parenting

4 • C. P. Snow: "The Two Cultures and the Scientific Revolution," 1959 Rede Lecture (Cambridge: Cambridge University Press, 1959).

• pure and applied forms of [science and art]: Britain's 1993 White Paper on Science—hailed as the nation's first coherent science policy in twenty years—has nevertheless been nicknamed "Waldegrave's White Paper for Wealth"

(William Bown, *New Scientist* [May 29, 1993], 4.) It recommends the annual publication of a national strategy for science, focused on wealth creation and industry's needs. It recommends disbanding the Advisory Boards of Research Councils in favor of a director general within the Office of Science and Technology, and the appointment of industrialists as part-time chairmen of each council. It suggests that all government-funded research laboratories and agencies be considered for privatization. .

6   • its expenditure on the young: See Edward Ng, "Children and Elderly People Sharing Public Income Resources," Canadian Social Trends, *Statistics Canada* (Summer 1992), 15.

• the Nordic nations: Although the policies of the Nordic nations in this, as in other respects, vary, and it is Sweden's child-and-family policies that are most widely cited and known, there is more similarity among the policies of these countries than between any one of them and any other OECD country.

9   • divorces granted for every 1,000 people: See S. A. Hewlett, *Child Neglect in Rich Nations* (New York: UNICEF, 1993), 11.

• until their youngest child leaves school: There is, of course, some between-country and within-country variation around this figure. The central importance of a dynamic approach to the study of families, as well as relevant figures for an American sample, are given in Brian C. Martinson and Lawrence L. Wu, "Parent Histories: Patterns of Change in Early Life," *Journal of Family Issues* (vol. 13, no. 3, 1992), 351–77. European statistics are to be found in *Eurostat: Demographic Statistics* (Luxembourg: Office for Official Publications of the European Communities, 1988). See also J. Roll, *Lone Parents in the European Community* (London: Family Policy Studies Centre, 1989).

• define modern Western families: See S. Bould, "Familial Caretaking: A Middle-Range Definition of Family in the Context of Social Policy," *Journal of Family Issues* (vol. 14, no. 1, March 1993), 133–51.

11   • the lifetime income a woman can expect to earn: See, for example, H. Joshi, "Sex and Motherhood as Handicaps in the Labour Market," in M. Maclean and D. Groves, eds., *Women's Issues in Social Policy* (London: Routledge, 1990); and H. Joshi, "The Cash Opportunity Costs of Childbearing: An Approach to Estimation Using British Data," *Population Studies* (vol. 44, 1990). See also S. Korenman and D. Neumark, "Marriage, Motherhood and Wages," *Journal of Human Resources* (Spring 1992).

• costs of raising a child: There are useful estimates in H. Joshi, "The Cost of Caring," in C. Glendenning and J. Miller (eds.), *Women and Poverty in Britain in the 1990's* (London: Wheatsheaf, 1992), and in Hewlett, *Child Neglect in Rich Nations*, 52.

• Detailed budgets: See N. Oldfield and A.C.S. Yu, *The Cost of a Child* (London: CPAG Ltd., 1993). Less detailed, estimated figures for the United States are given in Andrea Rock, "Can You Afford Your Kids?" *Money* (July 1990), 88–99.

14   • "family values"; "full-time, exclusive motherhood": I use these here as catchphrases from a current American lobby whose viewpoint is well represented by a recent article by Barbara Dafoe Whitehead: "Dan Quayle Was Right," *The Atlantic* (April 1993).

15   • many humanitarian professionals: The leading figure was Dr. John Bowlby, whose seminal work *Maternal Care and Mental Health* was published by the

World Health Organization in 1951. As always, though, it is interesting to compare what he actually said with what a generation of people grew up believing he had said. Even in the early fifties he did not suggest maternal chains; here are the final words in his pamphlet for mothers, commissioned and published by the National Association for Mental Health: "It is better to leave a child (under three) at home in familiar surroundings than in a strange place. It is better to leave him with someone he knows and likes than with a stranger. It is essential to leave him in the care of one person, who will be a mother-figure to him while you are away." The first two volumes of John Bowlby's mighty trilogy, *Attachment and Loss* (vol. 1, *Attachment*; vol. 2, *Separation*. London: Hogarth Press and the Institute of Psycho-analysis, 1969, 1973), do more than any other single work to establish the importance of parental relationships to human development and mental health.

• many women resented their summary ejection from the labor force: My own mother was one of them. Her job with Britain's Special Operations Executive was concerned with selecting agents who would be dropped into Occupied Europe so, in her words, "mine naturally ended when the war ended. But for most women there was a real sense of rejection by the country, of unfairness by the male, military world, of being just helplessly disregarded—everything that powered the women's movement afterwards. While the men were at the Front there was nobody to do anything *but* the women and they did everything: jobs most of them wouldn't have dreamed they were capable of five years earlier. They made armaments and clothes and vehicles, drove ambulances and staunched blood, dug cabbage fields and drains. They found that they could, and that they liked working and being *paid* their own money. But then it was over and the male ranks closed along with the nurseries. Suddenly, if you were a woman you not only didn't *have* to work, you got sacked."

• "the new familism": See M. Robson-Scott, "Back to the Future," *The Guardian* (August 31, 1993), 19. See also C. Tolliver, *At-Home Motherhood—Making It Work for You* (San Jose: Resource Publications, forthcoming).

16 • average weekly working hours: See Rhys Williams, "Office Slaves Miss Out on the Leisure Revolution," *The Independent on Sunday* (July 4, 1993), Home/5.

• a recent survey suggests: The survey is described by Hewlett in *Child Neglect in Rich Nations,* 7.

17 • "Leisure time is what people crave": Zelda West-Meade is quoted in Rhys Williams, "Office Slaves Miss Out on the Leisure Revolution."

• people who do combine productive activities with personal caring: Present trends and future possibilities in working patterns are discussed in Chapter 11, pages 229–39, and Chapter 12, pages 247–62.

18 • workers who "telecommute": see R. Calem, "Working at Home for Better or Worse," *New York Times* (April 18, 1993), 6F.

• Workplace nurseries: This topic is addressed more fully in Chapter 12, pages 246–47.

• With national unemployment rates between 5 and 10 percent in most countries: See, for example, "Employment/Unemployment Study," Interim Report by the Secretary-General (Organization for Economic Cooperation and Development, PCDE/GD [93], 102, Paris, 1993).

19 • full employment of that kind may be a permanently unrealistic aspiration: See Patricia Hewitt, *About Time: The Revolution in Work and Family Life* (London: Rivers Oram Press, 1993). This issue is explored in Chapter 11, pages 229–39.

• freeloading on welfare payments is generally rare and unemployment abhorred: See Marian Wright Edelman, *Families in Peril: An Agenda for Social Change* (Cambridge, Mass.: Harvard University Press, 1987). This issue is explored in Chapter 9, pages 181–84.

20 • delegated to one elderly woman as her suitably lighter share of the work: In rural West Africa, for example, where cultivation may be carried out at considerable distances from rural villages, a farm hut is often constructed in the fields. At certain seasons families may live in it, to save the long walk to and fro, and all will eat and rest in it at midday. But these huts also often serve as informal "nurseries" where the young children of all women working in those fields are cared for by one. These nurseries differ from any Western equivalent in two important ways: the childcare job is definitely a privilege and given, usually, to elderly women not because they are less capable than the others by reason of their age, but because they are more honored by reason of it. Secondly, the care group is not so much for the purpose of keeping children out of their laboring mothers' way as for the purpose of keeping them out of danger and boredom. When any infant wants his mother or is distressed, caregivers take him to her, or summon her to him.

2. Mother, Father or Parent?

32 • [British] legislation that also ensures parental responsibility *for* a child always outweighs parental rights over him or her: Children Act, 1989 (implemented in October 1991); see *Working Together under the Children Act 1989* (London: HMSO, 1991).

35 • new games of egalitarian diversity: New game plans need input from both genders. Institutional power is certainly still biased towards men, but there are many male individuals who would like to see it rebalanced. The potential for their political cooperation with women is no doubt lessened by "male-bashing" and the profitable pleasure taken by media in reporting it. A recent essay by Neil Lyndon in the *Sunday Times,* for example ("Bad Mouthing: Why the Way Women Talk about Men Is Still Hurting All of Us"), is illustrated with photographs of women who are household names, captioned with inflammatory quotes—for example, Jane Fonda ("I still believe that women are the superior sex"), Julie Burchill ("A good part—and most definitely the most fun part—of being a feminist is about frightening men"), Yoko Ono ("Humour is probably something the male of the species discovered through his own anatomy").

36 • "the paradox of masculinity": D. H. Bell, *Being a Man: The Paradox of Masculinity* (New York: Harcourt Brace Jovanovich, 1984).

• an adult desire for children is common to both sexes: The most illuminating discussion of gender issues in parenting is that in T. Berry Brazelton and Bertrand G. Cramer, *The Earliest Relationship: Parents, Infants and the Drama of Attachment* (Reading, Mass.: Addison-Wesley, 1990).

39 • the birth of a first child puts relationships between women and men under

tremendous stress and, with hindsight, is often seen as the beginning of their ending: For a detailed study of new marriages and the changes brought about by the births of first children, see P. Mansfield and J. Collard, *The Beginning of the Rest of Your Life,* and the sequel, *Person, Partner, Parents* (London: Macmillan, 1988, 1994). See also D. J. Dormer, *The Relationship Revolution: Cohabitation, Marriage and Divorce in Contemporary Europe* (London: One Plus One, 1990).

• One couple tried very hard to understand each other: Personal communication.

42 • from babies' point of view, measurably wrong: Breast-feeding as a political and economic as well as biological and personal issue is discussed in Chapter 3.

46 • everything [father] does is different and he may do different things, too: The leading figures in studies of fathers are Michael Lamb, at the University of Utah, and Charles Lewis, at Lancaster University in the United Kingdom. See M. Lamb and D. Oppenheim, "Fatherhood and Father-Child Relationships: Five Years of Research," in S. Cath, A. Gurwitt, and L. Gunsberg, eds., *Fathers and Their Families* (Hillsdale, N.J.: Analytic Press, 1989) and C. Lewis and M. O'Brien, eds., *Reassessing Fatherhood: New Observations on Fathers and the Modern Family* (London: Sage, 1987).

47 • clarification of their dawning sense of sexual identity: It used to be assumed that fathers contributed more to the development of sons than of daughters, but recent research strongly suggests that both sexes need a male parent to an equal extent, thought not in identical ways. The complementary roles played by fathers in the development of girls and boys is well described in a document from the European Commission Childcare Network, *Men as Carers for Children* (EC document DGV/B/4, 1990). There are some interesting clinical case studies of fathers and daughters in C. Olivier, *Jocasta's Children* (New York: Routledge, 1989).

3. Getting Started

50 • puzzled West African response: Personal communication.

• "bonding": See T. B. Brazelton, *Touchpoints* (Reading, Mass.: Addison-Wesley, 1992), and T. B. Brazelton and B. G. Cramer, *The Earliest Relationship.* See also P. Leach, *The First Six Months: Getting Together with Your Baby* (New York: Knopf, 1987).

51 • Swedish research: Conducted at Malmo General Hospital in Sweden and reported in *The Lancet* (November 1, 1990).

• obstetricians' fears of litigation: Many members of the American medical establishment acknowledge fear of litigation as a factor in decisions to carry out Caesarean sections. According to the American College of Obstetricians and Gynecologists, 77 percent of all obstetrician-gynecologists have been sued at least once, while 23 percent have been sued more than three times.

The charge of operating for profit is, of course, disputed, but it seems to be supported by a range of results from individual states and cities—and not to be contradicted by any. In 1989, for example, Blue Cross/Blue Shield of Illinois began to reimburse physicians the same sums for Caesarean and vaginal deliveries, thus removing any incentive to conduct one rather than the other. A 1 percent reduction in Caesareans in Illinois was noted in the subsequent year.

51 • one in four of them is delivered by Caesarean section: Overall American C-section rates come from the National Institutes of Health. In 1980 an institute task force showed that the numbers of women being delivered by C-section had risen to 16.5 percent from 5.5 percent in 1970. By 1988 one million of the four million babies born in the United States—25 percent—were delivered by this method. The rate is not thought to be increasing further.

• Increasing use of epidural anesthesia in the United Kingdom: Overall maternity figures for England and Wales used in this chapter are derived from the annual volume *Birth Statistics*; detailed figures for the whole of the United Kingdom are taken from the *Hospital In-Patient Enquiry Surveys* (HIPE) published in 1988. Even more detailed—and sometimes more recent—figures are derived from special studies that are carried out regularly, such as the *Confidential Enquiry into Maternal Deaths* (published triennially).

Statistics such as these should, as always, be interpreted with caution. Data used in producing them vary not only from country to country but from survey to survey and publication to publication within countries. Trends, in particular, are often not as clear as they seem. A record of 400 Caesareans in one year and 450 in the next suggests that Caesareans have increased; 500 in the next year suggests that they are increasing. But those apparent increases may reflect an increasing number of deliveries rather than of operative interventions. If 3,000 deliveries took place in the 400-Caesarean year and 4,000 in the 450-Caesarean year, the Caesarean *rate* has actually fallen from 13.3 percent to 11.2 percent. Definitions of terms also vary dramatically. In some countries medical records classify births as "normal" if they have no lasting morbid aftereffects for mothers or children; in other countries only a spontaneous vaginal birth is "normal."

52 • "Don't just do something, stand there": Attributed to Dr. Stephen Myers, director of maternal and fetal medicine at Mt. Sinai Hospital in Chicago. He is said to have given this instruction to his ob-gyn residents during a two-year program between 1987 and 1989 that reduced the hospital's C-section rate from 17 percent to 11 percent, largely by redefining "abnormal labor" and therefore the cues for intervention.

53 • American firms such as MotherCare Services, Inc.: The work of Mother-Care Services, Inc., and of others, is reported in the *Newsletters of the National Association of Postpartum Care Services*.

54 • have no resident male partner: See notes to page 9.

• expect fathers to participate in the birth drama: There is some evidence to suggest that the presence of a partner alone throughout labor and delivery is not as measurably helpful as the presence of a partner *and* a Doula (trained female birth attendant). Statistics from studies carried out in Houston, Texas, and in Florida show that women who had a Doula present throughout labor, in addition to her partner, had significantly shorter labors, lower rates of C-section delivery or epidural anesthesia and a lower incidence of babies requiring more than thirty-six hours in intensive care. (Marshall Klaus, "The Doula's Role," lecture given at a childbirth conference in Zurich, Switzerland, September 1990.) Some obstetricians, midwives, researchers and even parents are now suggesting that men's presence may be actually unhelpful to laboring women, blocking them from the female support they really need. There are calls for a "refeminization of birth." See, for example, Adam Nicolson, "A Father's Labor of Love: Being There at the Birth," *The Sunday Telegraph* (July 25, 1993), 19.

55 • when the infant's physiology has matured and steadied so that he is a settled baby: The concept and process of "settling" into extra-uterine life is detailed in P. Leach, *Babyhood: Infant Development from Birth to Two Years* (New York: Knopf, 1983), and P. Leach, *The First Six Months: Getting Together with Your Baby.*

57 • via the World Health Organization: WHO guidelines are intended to encourage breast-feeding by reducing the attractions and visibility of commercially produced breast-milk substitutes. They suggest, for example, that maternity hospitals should not accept donations of free or low-cost supplies of such products and that advertisements for them should not be run in magazines marketed to the general public. Although the guidelines are accepted in most Western countries, they are not always acted upon. Furthermore they are under continual threat from the multi-million-dollar infant-formula conglomerates. The European Community's dietetic foods subgroup, for example, is currently discussing a new directive that would lift bans that currently control donation and advertising in the United Kingdom, Denmark, Ireland and Belgium, and advertising alone in France and Portugal. In the United States, the 45,000-member-strong American Academy of Pediatrics has conducted a campaign for a ban on advertising since 1982. Evidence given during a 1993 court case suggests, however, that the academy does nothing to hamper the activities of formula companies that promote their products through doctors and hospitals (see also note to page 11).

• Breast-feeding is not the ordinary, taken-for-granted way for a baby to be fed: Breast-feeding statistics are just as complex as birth statistics, and for similar reasons. Some reported national rates are based on the numbers of mothers who *ever* put their infants to the breast; others recognize the pressures mothers may be under while in the hospital, and therefore count only those who breast-feed after they return home. Some studies count babies as breast-fed if they receive *any* breast milk; others count only babies who receive no additional formula milk. And studies vary in their measures of the duration of breast-feeding, however defined. "Up to six weeks," for example, may include the very different experiences of babies nursed until they were anything from one week to six weeks old. Even allowing for all these complexities, though, breast-feeding clearly is not "ordinary" in the West. Figures for the United States, for example, suggest that only 52 percent of mothers ever breast-feed at home, and that that figure is much skewed towards high school and college graduates. The latest British figures, published by the Office of Population Censuses and Surveys in 1992, show that 63 percent of all babies, and 69 percent of first babies, born in 1990, were put to the breast, but 15 percent of these received no breast milk by the end of the first week. Only 50 percent of mothers were still breast-feeding at six weeks and 25 percent at four months; 39 percent of all those mothers were giving bottles of formula in addition. (Amanda White, Stephanie Freeth, and Maureen O'Brien, *Infant Feeding, 1990* [OPCS, 1992].)

• In a 1990 British survey: The survey was commissioned by the Joint Breast-feeding Initiative. One thousand restaurant owners throughout the United Kingdom were also questioned. One quarter were "against mothers breast-feeding on the premises"; almost half "would not tolerate breastfeeding at table." More than a third provided no alternative private area; three quarters of those who said they did provide such an area proved to be referring to a restroom.

58 • over the whole Western world, fewer than a quarter are fully breast-fed for as much as six weeks: This is no more than an estimate, for reasons discussed above. But if "fully breast-fed" means that the baby receives no manufactured baby foods at all, the estimate is certainly conservative.

• The related deaths of millions of babies: See G. Palmer, *The Politics of Breast Feeding,* rev. ed. (London: Pandora Press, 1993).

Formula feeding in the West is seldom held responsible for anything more serious than gastrointestinal disturbances and allergies, but serious morbidity directly attributable to manufactured milks may be more common than has been realized. For example, according to a group of Canadian and Finnish researchers, a cow's milk protein that is present in almost all infant milks has been identified as a major causative factor in childhood diabetes. A trial is now under way, involving four thousand newborns at known risk of this serious and incurable disease.

Deprivation of mothers' milk—because formula feeding is available or preferred—may also be leading to unnecessary deaths, especially among premature babies. Necrotizing enterocolitis—the most common serious gastrointestinal disease seen in neonatal intensive care units—has been shown to be six to ten times more common in babies fed exclusively on formula milk than in those fed exclusively on breast milk, and three times more common in those fed on a combination of the two. Exclusive feeding on manufactured milk could account for five hundred extra babies suffering this disease each year, of which about one hundred would die. See A. Lucas and T. J. Cole, "Breastmilk and Neonatal Necrotising Enterocolitis," *The Lancet* (vol. 336, 1990), 1519–23; and A. F. Williams, "Human Milk and the Pre-term Baby," *British Medical Journal* (vol. 306, 1993), 1628–29.

• ecological folly: see S. Huffman et al., *Breastfeeding: A Natural Resource for Food Security* (Washington, D.C.: Wellstart, 1992).

• Everyone knows that breast-feeding is a demand-and-supply system: Many people envisage that system as working rather like a ball valve; as a baby empties the breast so it will refill. But the system that links woman and nursling is not mechanical but hormonal. Birth itself stimulates the mother to start producing prolactin, the hormone that initiates lactation. Suckling then plugs the baby directly into the mother's brain and central nervous system via her hormonal reactions to that stimulation of nerves in the nipple. By nursing, the baby stimulates his mother's brain to produce oxytocin, which initiates the let-down reflex to release milk already made, and more prolactin, which stimulates the breasts to produce more. This means that breast-fed babies are literally in control of the production and supply of their own food. Any interference with a baby's feeding behavior must inevitably upset the system.

62 • Other social factors put extra pressure on health professionals: A 1993 court case brought against the American Academy of Pediatrics by law en-

forcement officers and Nestlé, and concerned with charges of unfair competition rather than ethics, has led to the publication of details of money and services given to medical professionals and establishments by manufacturers of infant formula. According to *The New York Times* (June 15, 1993, D1) the pediatric group received more than $8.3 million in donations from major manufacturers between 1983 and 1991, including $1.3 million for the construction of its Elk Grove headquarters in Illinois: "The group also received indirect funds from manufacturers for parties, and from advertising in its journals, according to court documents. Formula producers have also spent millions designing hospital pediatric units."

63 • new Norwegian law: The law referred to was passed in 1992. Women may take the time off in any way that assists them to continue breast-feeding their babies. They may reduce the length of their working days, or take breaks within them, up to the limit of one hour for private employees and two hours for those employed by the state. Employers may not reduce their wages or limit their advancement.

• "milk banks": While the sale of milk to milk banks that are run for profit is an unattractive possibility, milk banks from which donated milk can be drawn for babies with special needs their own mothers cannot meet are exceedingly valuable. Sadly, such banks are expensive to run and measures to combat the possibility of HIV infection have made them more so. In the United Kingdom, for example, most of the seventy banks in operation in the late 1980s have closed.

65 • a complete "sleeping environment": See the editorial "Who's Making a Difference?" in *Pre and Peri-Natal Psychology News* (vol. 4, no. 11, Spring 1991) describing the work of Dr. James Gatts and what he calls "Nature's Cradle." In a personal communication (August 9, 1991) he explained: "Our survey (informal) shows that most infants in our culture are isolated 75–80% of the day, that is the time I wish to address. . . . I believe (as my data indicates) that I can create an inexpensive, dependable, alternative environment for the Western World mother who is *not going* to transition (handle, hold) her infant more than 4 to 6 hours/day and offer that baby a more stable transition environment."

4. Daycare

69 • Daycare does not give women-who-are-mothers equality at home: These and many of the other statistics for daycare within the European Community referred to in this chapter are taken from the report of the European Childcare Network to the European Commission entitled *Who Cares for Europe's Children?* (Public document CB-55-89-738-EN-C, 1989). See also Arlie Hochschild, *The Second Shift: Working Parents and the Revolution at Home* (New York: Viking, 1989).

70 • Recent American analyses: Beth Anne Shelton and Daphne John, "Does Marital Status Make a Difference? Housework among Married and Cohabiting Men and Women," and B. S. Oropesa, "Using the Service Economy to Relieve the Double Burden," both in *Journal of Family Issues* (vol. 14, no. 3, September 1993), 401–20 and 438–73 respectively.

70 • A recent Italian survey: Italy, like each member-state of the EEC, carried out its own survey for the European Childcare Network. It reported that: "Men spent 6.3 hours a week [on domestic or childcare tasks] where their wife had a job, and 6.1 where she was not employed." According to other reports of member nations to the European Childcare Network, only Danish fathers show "a high degree of joint responsibility towards the children" when mothers undertake paid work outside the home.

• In the Western world as a whole, more children under five (and an even larger majority of children under three) are cared for by mothers (and a few fathers) at home than in any form of daycare: See Thomas Coram Research Unit, *Under Fives Services, Provision and Usage* (OPCS Monitor, PP1/89/1, 1990); Commission of the European Communities, "Women of Europe: 10 Years" (no. 27, June 1988); K. Young and E. Zigler, "Infant and Toddler Day Care: Regulation and Policy Implications," in E. Zigler and M. Frank, eds., *The Parental Leave Crisis* (New Haven: Yale University Press, 1988).

• A 1992 survey of six thousand (mainly middle-class) American parents: This was a survey carried out by *Parenting* magazine. Results are reported by C. Rubinstein, "The Way We Worry," *Parenting* (September 1992), 114–19.

71 • Data from the National Longitudinal Survey: reported by J. Greenstein, "Maternal Employment and Child Behavioural Outcomes," *Journal of Family Issues* (vol. 14, no. 3, September 1993), 323–54.

• A 1993 report from Population Trends and Public Policy: Martin O'Connell, "Where's Papa? Father's Role in Child Care," *Population Trends and Public Policy* (no. 20, September 1993).

• In the United States in 1991: Department of Labor, Bureau of Labor Statistics, *Marital and Family Characteristics of the Labor Force from the March 1993 Current Population Survey* (October 3, 1993).

72 • Some [women] . . . remain poor whatever they choose: See Chapter 9. There has been a 50 percent increase in the number of Americans who work full-time all the year round yet remain in poverty (Sar A. Levitan and Isaac Shapiro, *Working but Poor: America's Contradiction* [Baltimore: Johns Hopkins University Press, 1987], 3). In the United Kingdom, an estimated 2.5 million people in full employment earn incomes below the poverty line that qualifies them for means-tested benefits. Since women's average pay is only 78 percent of men's (despite equal pay legislation) most of the employed poor are women. (See Commission on Social Justice, *The Justice Gap* [London: IPPR, 1993].) See also *Poverty in the United States: 1992*, Current Population Reports: Consumer Income Series P60-185 (U.S. Department of Commerce, Economics and Statistics Administration, Bureau of the Census).

• 1990 report by Social Community Planning Research: The report referred to is *British Social Attitudes: The 7th Report*, ed. R. Jowell et al., 1990.

• a 1992 Gallup poll: Results are discussed in an editorial, "Feminists' History of Housework Challenged," in *The Independent* (July 22, 1992).

• almost 80 percent of American women: See C. Russell, "On the Baby-Boom Bandwagon," *American Demographics* (May 1991), 25–30. E. Farber et al., "Managing Work and Family: Hopes and Realities," in Zigler and Frank, *The Parental Leave Crisis*, and D. Sanders and M. Bullen, *Staying Home* (Boston: Little, Brown, 1992).

• See also T. Berry Brazelton's "Issues for Working Parents," in Zigler and Frank, *The Parental Leave Crisis*.

73 • 1987 Labour Force Survey by Statistics Canada: See also the 1986–87 edition of its *Women in the Labour Force*.

74 • A recent American report on fathers' role: O'Connell, "Where's Papa? Father's Role in Child Care."

• European Childcare Network: These quotations come from *Who Cares for Europe's Children?*

75 • figures for the whole of the European Community in 1991: These figures are taken from *Employment in Europe*, produced by the Directorate-General, Employment, Industrial Relations and Social Affairs, and published by the Office for Official Publications of the European Communities (1993), 145–70. Quotation from p. 162.

77 • "Lack of child care facilities prevents women, as opposed to men, from pursuing their careers": *Guardian,* Education section (March 26, 1991), 2.

• an important American study: Jerome Kagan, Richard Kearsley and Philip Zelazo, *Infancy: Its Place in Human Development* (Cambridge, Mass.: Harvard University Press, 1978).

• serious concerns about the effects of daycare on very young children: See, for example, M. Ainsworth et al., *Patterns of Attachment: A Psychological Study of the Strange Situation* (Hillsdale, N.J.: Lawrence Erlbaum Associates, 1978); Jay Belsky, "A Reassessment of Infant Daycare," in Zigler and Frank, *The Parental Leave Crisis*, 100–19; T. Gamble and E. Zigler, "Effects of Infant Daycare: Another Look at the Evidence," in Zigler and Frank, *The Parental Leave Crisis,* 77–99; and L. B. Silverstein, "Transforming the Debate About Childcare and Maternal Employment," *American Psychologist* (vol. 46, 1991), 1025–32.

• neither a pro-daycare nor an anti-daycare stance is tenable: See, for example, T. Berry Brazelton, "Issues for Working Parents," in Zigler and Frank, *The Parental Leave Crisis,* 37–51; and T. N. Greenstein, "Maternal Employment and Child Behavioural Outcomes," *Journal of Family Issues* (vol. 14, no. 3, September 1993), 323–54.

79 • Benjamin Spock, *Baby and Child Care* (New York: Pocket Books, 1968).

80 • in the United States, for example, catering to at least three times as many children as regulated caregivers, according to 1991 estimates: For some recent American figures and an interesting discussion of emergent patterns, see Grace-Ann Caruso, "Patterns of Maternal Employment and Child Care for a Sample of Two Year-Olds," *Journal of Family Issues* (vol. 13, no. 3, September 1992), 297–311.

81 • An expert estimate from the United States said that they *ought* to cost as much as $150 per child per week in 1988: T. Gamble and E. Zigler, "Effects of Infant Daycare."

84 • Many of those babies failed to thrive; some died for reasons nobody could quite understand: The researchers of the day concluded that those babies were suffering from "maternal deprivation." See notes to page xv.

88 • eighteen British nurseries: P. Moss and E. Melhuish, *Current Issues in Day Care for Young Children* (London: HMSO, 1991).

• comparative licensing study of American states: This survey, carried out in

1982, is the subject of an interesting study of issues of quality in daycare centers. See K. Young and E. Zigler, "Infant and Toddler Day Care: Regulation and Policy Implications."

88 • a recent report: *Who Cares for Europe's Children?*, 25.

90 • the autonomy of the toddler is as much an illusion as his toughness: See P. Leach, *Your Baby and Child* (New York: Knopf, 1989), 285–90. For a fascinating study of toddlers and their relationships with their mothers, see E. Furman, *Toddlers and Their Mothers: A Study in Early Personality Development* (Madison, Conn.: International Universities Press, 1992).

92 • A major British study: Barbara Tizard and Martin Hughes, *Young Children Learning: Talking and Thinking at Home and at School* (London: Fontana, 1984).

• early daycare may foster: T. Gamble and E. Zigler, "Effects of Infant Day Care," 89.

• "men who were rated as dependent": A. Caspig, G. H. Elder, Jr., and E. S. Herbener, "Predicting Life Course Patterns," in Lee Robbins and Michael Rutter, eds., *Straight and Devious Pathways from Childhood to Adulthood* (Cambridge: Cambridge University Press, 1990).

93 • there are more than 100,000: Charlotte Breese and Hilaire Gomer, *The Good Nanny Guide* (London: Century Hutchinson, 1988), 6.

• 6 percent of American under-fives: D. Fallows, *A Mother's Work* (Boston: Houghton Mifflin, 1985).

5. Growing Up Takes Time

105 • We all have children for ourselves and our pleasure: See L. W. Hoffman, "Cross Cultural Differences in Child-Rearing Goals," in R. A. Levine, P. M. Miller and M. M. West, eds., *Parental Behavior in Diverse Societies* (San Francisco: Jossey-Bass, 1988).

108 • Bayley Mental Development Index: See N. Bayley, *Bayley Scales of Infant Development* (New York: Psychological Corp., 1969).

• infants tested by the Gesell Institute: Dr. Arnold Gesell's tests for infants and preschool children first appeared in 1928 in *Infancy and Human Growth* (New York: Macmillan). With the staff of the Yale Clinic of Child Development, Gesell studied a large population of children through the 1930s, leading to the publication of A. Gesell et al., *The First Five Years of Life* (New York: Harper, 1940). In 1950 the Gesell Institute of Child Development was founded. The book that specifically compares the performance of that generation of children with the next, on a range of developmental measures, is L. Bates et al., *The Gesell Institute's Child from One to Six* (London: Hamish Hamilton, 1980).

• "the infant with superior equipment": A. Gesell, *The First Five Years of Life*, p. 12.

6. Discipline, Self-Discipline and Learning How to Behave

115 • every generation considers the one that follows it worse behaved than itself: Furthermore, every generation accounts for the "deterioration in standards" in the same ways: there are impassioned essays about fragmenting families, declining moral standards and materialism dating from each of the past five

centuries—and earlier. "Children now love luxury. They have bad manners and contempt for authority. Children are now tyrants." That is not a quote from a present-day schoolteacher, nor from one, two or three generations ago, but from Socrates.

117 • Up to 90 percent of British, North American, Australian and Caribbean populations "believe in spanking": The literature on the physical punishment of children, especially in Europe, is excellently reviewed by Peter Newell in *Children Are People Too: The Case Against Physical Punishment* (London: Bedford Square Press, 1989). The issue is further discussed in Chapter 10.

The physical punishment of children is both more common and more commonly severe than most people realize. In the United States, for example, many people believe that corporal punishment is banned in the public school system. In fact only twenty-four of the fifty states had banned it by the end of 1992. An international survey was carried out by EPOCH (End Physical Punishment Of Children) WORLDWIDE, with Radda Barnen (Swedish Save the Children) during 1992. It reports, for example, that in 1985 more than 60 percent of U.K. mothers admitted to disciplining babies under one year old by hitting them and that three quarters of U.K. seven-year-olds were hit or threatened with an implement; in the same year, 89 percent of a representative sample of 3,232 American parents had hit their three-year-olds during the previous year and about one third had hit their adolescents. In Barbados a 1987 survey found that 76 percent of parents endorsed beating children with belts or straps, while a 1987 survey of Australian primary school children showed that 81 percent of the boys and 74 percent of the girls were hit by their mothers. A survey of Indian university students, reported in 1991, showed that 91 percent of males and 86 percent of females had been physically punished during childhood. In Romania, a 1992 survey found that 84 percent of parents regarded spanking or beating as a normal method of child rearing.

118 • Negative discipline is built on the assumption that babies are born full of original sin: The religious roots and psychological effects of physical punishment, especially in the United States, are fully explored by Philip Greven in *Spare the Child: The Religious Roots of Punishment and the Psychological Impact of Physical Abuse* (New York: Knopf, 1990).

119 • Most people believe that punishment is [so] basic to discipline: Public misapprehensions about the value or necessity of punishment are largely based on psychological research findings that have been highly selected and poorly presented. A summary of relevant psychological research findings and references is in P. Leach, "Should Parents Hit Their Children?" *The Psychologist* (vol. 6, no. 5, May 1993), 216–20.

7. The Preschool Years

134 • play therapy: E. Erikson, *Childhood and Society* (New York: Norton, 1963), 32.

137 • Schools and teachers do not only enjoy higher status: National policies concerning the transfer of young children from the care system to the education system differ from country to country; correlations between policy and provision differ within countries, and what is actually provided for children in individual institutions differs most of all. The transfer is everywhere complicated, however, by the fact that even a full school day of six or seven hours is not as long as the adult working day plus travel time that care centers are designed to cover. Furthermore, schools have holidays. In some places, such as northern Italy, solutions are being found in centers that integrate all-day care with part-time education; in others, notably Denmark, children are promoted from care centers to kindergartens at three, but bussed back again for the after-school hours. In France there is enormous pressure to extend the school day to match full daycare but there is also strong resistance to committing professional teachers to caretaking. Some French three-year-olds spend two or three hours at the end of the day being supervised in an empty classroom, or even a corridor. In much of the United States and Britain, however, there is almost no provision for the after-school and holiday care of these much younger children, so their "promotion" from daycare to school may be extremely problematical for parents. Nevertheless most parents still reckon that their struggle to make individual arrangements is a worthwhile price for that precious pre-school education.

138 • Early school entry means different things to different proportions of children in different countries: In Ireland and the Netherlands, and for some children in the United Kingdom, "early primary schooling" means that four-year-olds spend a full school day in the entry class of a primary school building—with often twenty or more of them to one teacher.

In other EEC countries public policy interposes "pre-primary education" as a bridge between daycare and primary school for three- to five-year-olds but while this may mean specially designed and staffed facilities, such as Denmark's separate kindergartens with a staff-to-child ratio of 1:7 through the age of five, it may not. The average European class has about twenty to twenty-five children to two adults and is often part of a primary school establishment. In France and Belgium—the former noted for its excellent provision for young families—the pre-primary schooling policy has resulted in some children who are scarcely capable of going to the toilet alone being "educated" as if they were six years old. Before they are three years old some such children may be admitted to full-day classes of twenty-five to thirty with one teacher and no special facilities.

In the United States (and in parts of the United Kingdom), a nursery class or kindergarten in primary schools may take children by four, but the teacher can usually expect help from a care assistant and attendance is likely to be for half-days rather than full-time.

143 • for fear of provoking rejection by all those who lost: Reissland and Harris, *British Journal of Developmental Psychology* (vol. 9, 1991), 431–35.

145 • Early childhood education can help them to do all that: Head Start and other early childhood intervention programs were primarily intended to assist children in developing their cognitive skills and thus prepare them for elementary school. Assessments consistently showed the value of the programs, especially to disadvantaged children, but many also showed that initial gains, as assessed by measures of general ability, quickly disappeared after a program was terminated. (See, for example, Westinghouse Learning Corporation/Ohio University, "The Impact of Head Start: An Evaluation of the Effects of Head

Start on Children's Cognitive and Affective Development" [Washington, D.C.: Office of Economic Opportunity, 1969].) The findings of a Dublin study undertaken between 1969 and 1975 and followed up when the subjects reached the age of sixteen suggests that while the effect of this kind of intervention on young children's cognitive abilities is indeed marked but also short-term, there are important long-term gains, which may have more to do with children's overall development and the use they can make of whatever opportunities are available to them than with their measurable school performance (T. Kellaghan and B. J. Greaney, "The Education and Development of Students Following Participation in a Pre-school Programme in a Disadvantaged Area in Dublin" [Bernard Van Leer Foundation, Studies and Evaluation Paper 12, 1993]).

8. 7-Up

146 • Freud's latency period: See S. Freud, "Psycho-analysis," in J. Strachey, ed., *Sigmund Freud: Collected Papers,* vol. 5 (New York: Basic Books, 1959), 107–30.
• Piaget's concrete operations: See J. Piaget, "Development and Learning," in R. Ripple and V. Rockcastle, eds., *Piaget Rediscovered* (Ithaca, N.Y.: Cornell University Press, 1964).
• Kohlberg's conventional morality: See L. Kohlberg, "Moral Stages and Moralization: The Cognitive-Developmental Approach," in T. Lickona, ed., *Moral Development and Behavior: Theory, Research and Social Issues* (New York: Holt, 1976).
• All over the world: The cross-cultural stability of the five-to-seven shift is interestingly discussed by Melvin Konner, *Childhood* (Boston: Little, Brown, 1991), 239–90.

149 • Children learn about the issues that are important to adults (like employment and money): See, for example, Martin Glachan and Judy Ney, "Children's Understanding of Employment, Unemployment and Pay," *Children and Society* (vol. 6, no. 1, 1992), 12–24.

152 • The jury is still out on the direct effects of violent entertainment on children's behavior: Few topics have evoked more sets of convincing and contradictory research findings than the effects of TV violence on child viewers. The latest comes from Holland: the result of a three-year study of almost five hundred children between the ages of six and ten. In this, as in most such studies, first results suggested a positive link between the amount and degree of violence that is viewed and aggression in behavior, but the association vanished once all other variables had been partialed out. Interestingly, in this and in very similar collaborative studies carried out in the United States, Finland, Poland, Israel and Australia, children's general intelligence, and perhaps moral development, seemed to be positively correlated with limited viewing of violent programs and with less aggressive behavior (O. Wiegman, M. Kuttschreuter and B. Baarda, "A Longitudinal Study of the Effects of Television Viewing on Aggressive and Prosocial Behaviors," *British Journal of Social Psychology* [vol. 31, 1992], 147–64. A useful summary of the most important studies in this field, and a balanced assessment of their results, is given by

Jerome Burne in "When the Medium's Message Is Violent," *New Scientists* (May 29, 1993).

153 • Most of today's parents believe that sex education, for example, is a good thing: While this statement is true as far as it goes, it does not go nearly far enough. In most Western countries the content of sex education, and especially its secular starting point, is highly contentious. For an interesting overview and useful recent references, see the background paper by Kaushika Amin, "Values Conflicts in a Plural Society: The Case of Sex Education in Schools," *The Runnymede Bulletin* (July/August 1992), 6–8.

154 • Statements by Carlene Davis and Rasheda Ashanti: Taken from an article in Britain's *Guardian* newspaper (June 25, 1992). Similar sentiments, in a more generalized context, are expressed by Michael Medved in *Hollywood Vs America* (New York: HarperCollins, 1993).

• fathers and father substitutes all over the West: See, for example, D. E. H. Russell, "The Prevalence and Seriousness of Incestuous Abuse: Stepfathers vs. Biological Fathers," *Child Abuse and Neglect* (vol. 8, 1984) 15–22; and A. Gledhill et al., *Who Cares?* (Centre for Policy Studies: Policy Study no. 111, 1989).

157 • under the United Nations Convention on the Rights of the Child: See Chapter 10, pages 206–208, and second note to page 206.

• objects to be taught: I owe this concept, and other valuable ideas for this chapter, to Rachel Hodgkin, Policy Officer at the U.K.'s National Children's Bureau.

159 • one in five children in this age group will suffer from bullying and about one in eight will bully: See E. Roland and E. Munthe, eds., *Bullying: An International Perspective* (London: David Fulton, 1989) and K. Rubin and D. Kopler, eds., *The Development and Treatment of Childhood Aggression* (Hillsdale, N.J.: Lawrence Erlbaum Associates, 1989). A useful summary of current thinking and research results is in Peter Smith, "The Silent Nightmare: Bullying and Victimization in School Peer Groups," *The Psychologist* (June 1991), 243–48.

160 • playtime program for the first four grades: Described by Julia Hagedorn in "Simon Says: Play Nicely, Children," *The Independent* (October 14, 1993), Education/31.

162 • "with most new jobs demanding more education": W. B. Johnston and A. Packer, *Workforce 2000: Work and Workers for the 21st Century* (Indianapolis: Hudson Institute, 1987), 102.

• many educationalists are concerned: See, for example, "And Then There Were Three" (comments on a British education discussion document—produced by a group that has been nicknamed "the three wise men"—entitled "Curriculum Organisation and Classroom Practice"), *Child Education* (April 1, 1992), 26–27.

• the International Assessment of Math and Science: See E. Erlich, "America's Schools Still Aren't Making the Grade," *Business Week* (September 19, 1988), 132.

163 • comparing the school performance of American: The study is described and its results and implications are discussed in Konner, *Childhood*, 264–70.

• professor of education: Professor Phillip Gamage, Dean of Education at the University of Nottingham; quotes are in "And Then There Were Three."

164 • "I've got sixty kids, from eight to eighteen . . .": Volunteer teacher of math and physics, sponsored by Voluntary Service Overseas, in Guinea. Personal communication.

• Teachers cannot do that alone: At a conference on educational achievement held at Harvard University in November 1993, James Coleman, a Chicago sociologist with the U.S. Department of Health and Human Services, National Institute of Education, presented a paper called "Effects of School on Learning: The IEA Findings." After comparing the effects of school and home on a wide range of children's performances, Coleman has concluded that "the total effect of home background is considerably greater than the total effect of school variables."

165 • Research studies and governmental inquiries in many countries: See, for example, R. McKey et al., *The Impact of Head Start on Families and Communities,* Final Report of the Head Start Evaluation, Synthesis and Utilization Project (Washington, D.C.: CSR, 1985); J. Tobin et al., *Preschool in Three Cultures* (New Haven: Yale University Press, 1989); R. Davie et al., *From Birth to Seven: A Report of the National Child Development Study* (London: Longman, 1972).

167 • "I don't approve of it, but it works": Personal communication.

Introduction to Part Three

172 • could afford practical measures that would revolutionize all children's lives: United Nations Children's Fund, *The State of the World's Children 1992* (Oxford: Oxford University Press), 1–2.

173 • 300,000 homeless children: These figures are taken from Hewlett, *Child Neglect in Rich Nations,* 17–18.

• "We have to find a way": See P. Hewitt and P. Leach, *Social Justice, Children and Families* (London: Institute for Public Policy Research, 1993).

9. New Approaches to Poverty and Privilege

175 • Thomas Macaulay: In his *History of England,* 1875.

176 • relative measures of poverty: The classic account of poverty as a relative concept is Peter Townsend, *Poverty in the United Kingdom: A Survey of Household Resources and Standards of Living* (Berkeley: University of California Press, 1979). In a subsequent debate (with David Pinchaud in *New Society* [September 1981]), Townsend wrote, "Individuals . . . can be said to be in poverty when they lack the resources to obtain the types of diet, participate in the activities and have the living conditions and amenities which are customary, or at least widely encouraged or approved, in the societies to which they belong." The message of Ruth Lister's Charter for Social Citizenship a decade later is very similar: "The Wages, social security and tax system should, together, ensure that all members of society have sufficient income to enable them to meet their public and private obligations as citizens and exercise effectively their legal, political and social rights as citizens " (*Citizenship and the Poor* [London: CPAG Ltd., 1990]).

For an up-to-date account of the concept as it applies in the United Kingdom, see Carey Oppenheim, *Poverty: The Facts* (London: CPAG Ltd., 1993), especially the preface by Fran Bennett, vii–ix; for the EEC, see Graham Room, "A Time for Change," in Saul Becker, ed., *Windows of Opportunity* (London: CPAG Ltd., 1991); for North America, see Michael Katz, *The Undeserving Poor: From the War on Poverty to the War on Welfare* (New York: Pantheon Books, 1989).

176 • America's rich doubled their share: Statistics for the United States are taken from the Bureau of the Census, Current Population Reports, series P60-185, *Poverty in the U.S. 1992* (Washington, D.C.: U.S. Government Printing Office, 1993), tables 4 and 5.

• Between 1979 and 1989 in Britain: These statistics are taken from Carey Oppenheim, *Poverty,* 46. Although Oppenheim prefers to use figures for income after housing costs, I have elected to use his alternative figures for income before housing costs, as this results in statistics that are more nearly comparable with those from other countries. It should be noted, though, that Oppenheim's preferred method corrects the figures given in the text to: 1979, 9 percent (5 million); 1989, 22 percent (12 million).

• the rise continued through 1991, according to figures published by the government in 1993 (*Households Below Average Income: A Statistical Analysis 1979–1990/91* [London: HMSO, 1993]), showing 13.5 million people—24 percent of the population—living in poverty. Almost 4 million were children—about 31 percent of all children in the United Kingdom.

• The EEC saw a comparable rise: M. O'Higgins and S. Jenkins, "Poverty in Europe: Estimates for the Numbers in Poverty in 1975, 1980, 1985." Paper presented at European Communities seminar on Poverty Statistics, 1989.

178 • Minnesota, Illinois and Alabama: See T. Munby and M. Noble, "Benefits in the USA," *Poverty* (vol. 77, 1993), 15–17.

• In Britain during the eighties: "How the Other Tenth Lives," *The Economist* (September 12, 1992), 63.

• In the United States during the same period: These calculations, and many useful ideas, are derived from Michael Katz, *The Undeserving Poor.*

179 • long-term trends [in the economic growth of Western economies]: With due awareness of the complexities, these figures are taken from the World Bank, *World Tables 1991* (Baltimore: Johns Hopkins University Press, 1991).

181 • Charles Murray: See his *Losing Ground: American Social Policy, 1950–1980* (New York: Basic Books, 1984).

Charles Murray's *Losing Ground* was referred to as "the Reagan administration's bible" by Robert Greenstein in "Losing Faith in Losing Ground," *New Republic* (March 25, 1985), 14.

• "to expand upon my policy prescriptions": See Charles Murray, *The Emerging British Underclass* (London: Institute of Economic Affairs, 1990), 73.

• *The New Consensus on Family and Welfare:* Washington, D.C.: American Enterprise Institute, 1987.

• honed to its sharpest point so far in the United Kingdom: In May 1992 the Institute of Economic Affairs organized a seminar to discuss the American-born "new consensus." An article by one of the seminar participants gives an interesting account of the ways this body of American thought is being brought to bear on British affairs: A. Deacon, "Moral Dilemmas in an Age of Consent," *Poverty* (vol. 76, 1992), 7–10.

182 • "Bring back stigma; all is forgiven!": D. Green, in *The Emerging British Underclass,* ix.

• "The true picture": A. Howarth, "Pulling Single Parents from the Pit of Poverty," *The Guardian* (October 5, 1993), 20.

• Marian Wright Edelman: *The Measure of Our Success* (Boston: Beacon Press, 1992), 90–91.

183 • The EEC proposes: See Commission of the European Communities, "Employment in Europe," 1990.

Some details of European policies are taken from *Social Europe,* a triennial review issued, with many supplements, by the Directorate General for Employment, Social Affairs and Education. See especially "The Fight Against Poverty" (CE-NC-89-002-EN-C, 1989). See also "The Social Policy of the European Community: Looking Ahead to 1992" (European File No. 13/88 CC-AD-87-004-EN-C). An interesting account of current facts and current thinking in the United Kingdom is: Anna Coote, Harriet Harman and Patricia Hewitt, *The Family Way: A New Approach to Policy-making* (London: Institute for Public Policy Research, 1990).

184 • public expressions of concern for children: See, for example, Hewlett, *Child Neglect in Rich Nations;* Jonathan Freedman, *From Cradle to Grave: The Human Face of Poverty in America* (New York: Atheneum, 1993); and A. Hughes, *Family Lifestyles 1993* (London: Mintel, 1993).

• UNICEF study: J. Bradshaw, "Child Poverty and Deprivation in the UK," National Children's Bureau (1990).

• Eurostat: Commission of the European Communities, "Inequality and Poverty in Europe (1980–1985)," Eurostat rapid reports. (Statistical Office, 1990).

185 • American figures from the National Center for Children in Poverty: Cited by G. Cowley in *Newsweek,* "How Kids Grow," Summer 1991 (Special Issue 3), 18–21. 1993 breakdown from *Poverty in the United States 1992.*

• the National Commission on Children: See R. Kelly and S. Ramsay, "Poverty, Children and Public Policies," *Journal of Family Issues* (vol. 12, no. 4, December 1991), 388–403.

• a majority (60 percent) of poor American children: See United Nations Children's Fund, *The State of the World's Children 1992* (Oxford: Oxford University Press).

• Howard Hiatt: Quoted in John de Cuevas, "Our Children Are in Trouble," *Harvard Magazine* (September–October 1992), 46.

• increase in poverty-related diseases: See J. Bradshaw, "Child Poverty and Deprivation in the UK" (National Children's Bureau, 1990).

187 • Different studies in various countries: Coote, Harman, and Hewitt, *The Family Way,* 25–32. See also M. Thomas, "Children with Absent Fathers," *Journal of Marriage and the Family* (vol. 30, no. 1, 1982), 89; and L. White and A. Booth, "The Quality and Stability of Remarriages: The Role of Stepchildren," *American Sociological Review* (vol. 50, no. 5, 1985).

188 • the concept of cumulative risk factors in children's lives: This is best explained and extensively exemplified by Lisbeth Schorr and Daniel Schorr, *Within Our Reach: Breaking the Cycle of Disadvantage* (New York: Doubleday, 1988).

See also David Hamburg, *Today's Children: Creating a Future for a Generation in Crisis* (New York: Times Books, 1992); Fred Hechinger, *Fateful Choices: Healthy Youth for the 21st Century* (New York: Hill & Wang, 1992).

189 • Cycles of deprivation *can* be broken: See Fred Hechinger, "Adolescent Health: A Generation at Risk," *Carnegie Quarterly* (vol. 37, no. 4, Fall 1992).

• measures primarily intended to reduce the numbers of parenting adults on welfare—and thus reduce benefit costs: Major examples among many are America's Family Support Act (FSA) of 1988, the first major reform of AFDC in nearly twenty years, and Britain's Child Support Act, effective from April 1993.

• too little and too late: See Kelly and Ramsey, "Poverty, Children and Public Policies."

190 • chances that a baby will be born prematurely: See "Preventing Low Birthweight," Infant Mortality Fact Sheet, National Commission to Prevent Infant Mortality, 1990.

• Swedish study: H. Forrsman and I. Thuwe, "One Hundred and Twenty Children Born After Application for Therapeutic Abortions Refused," *Acta Psychiatrica Scandinavica* (1966); "Continued Follow-Up Study of 120 Persons Born After Refusal of Application for Therapeutic Abortion," *Acta Psychiatrica Scandinavica* (1981).

191 • A study of working-class families in London: Michael Rutter, *Changing Youth in a Changing Society* (Cambridge, Mass.: Harvard University Press, 1980).

• Dr. David Rogers: The Robert Wood Johnson Foundation annual report, 1984.

192 • savings of at least three times its magnitude: National Commission to Prevent Infant Mortality, "Preventing Low Birthweight."

A synthesis of the best available information concerning the importance of prenatal care can be found in the report of the Public Health Service Expert Panel on the Content of Prenatal Care, *Caring for Our Future: The Content of Prenatal Care*, U.S. Department of Health and Human Services. (Washington, D.C.: 1989).

• A study by the Urban Institute: F. A. Moore and R. F. Wertheimer, "Teenage Childbearing and Welfare," *Family Planning Perspectives,* 1990.

• The Children's Defense Fund: These and other child health and welfare measures were extensively discussed during a Child Watch Visitation Program to the Boston City Hospital, sponsored by CDF and led by Barry Zuckerman, Professor of Pediatrics.

193 • Homebuilders program: Cost estimates come from the Behavioral Sciences Institute Federal Way (Washington, D.C., 1987). This program, and other successful interventions, are fully described in Schorr and Schorr, *Within Our Reach.*

• Committee for Economic Development: *Children in Need: Investment Strategies for the Educationally Disadvantaged* (1987).

194 • Norway, for example, is the first country to have a Children's Ombudsper-

son: The first holder of this office, Malfrid Grude Flekkoy, has written an interesting account sponsored by UNICEF, *A Voice for Children* (London: Jessica Kingsley Publishers, 1991).

• The role envisaged for a Children's Rights Commissioner: M. Rosenbaum and P. Newell, *Taking Children Seriously: A Proposal for a Children's Rights Commissioner* (London: Calouste Gulbenkian Foundation, 1991).

195 • child impact statements: According to the *Harvard Review* (September–October 1992), 49, John Ramsey of the Boston Foundation, as Co-Chairman of the Coalition of Community Foundations for Youth, funded by the Rockefeller Foundation, has engaged Jay Winsten, who masterminded the "designated driver" campaign, to design a campaign to bring this concept to national consciousness.

• 1990 survey of the European Economic Community: Peter Golding, "Poor Attitudes," in Saul Becker, ed., *Windows of Opportunity* (London: CPAG Ltd., 1991).

• "those people": Dan Quayle is said to have referred to the poor as "those people" in a debate with Senator Lloyd Bensen (quoted by Michael Katz in *The Undeserving Poor*, 236).

196 • "midnight picnic": Personal communication.

198 • Babies-for-gain are a myth: See a report of a cross-national study by Sheila Kamerman and Alfred Kahn, "What Europe Does for Single-Parent Families," *Transatlantic Perspectives* (no. 19, Spring 1989), 9–12.

• French provision: Kamerman and Kahn, "What Europe Does for Single-Parent Families."

• Belgium's family allowance: For details of Belgian arrangements and of a European Survey in 1990, see Hewlett, *Child Neglect in Rich Nations*, 43–45.

199 • A state-by-state comparison: D. T. Ellwood and M. J. Bane, "The Impact of AFDC on Family Structure and Living Arrangements," *Research in Labor Economics* (1984). For further data on birthrate to young single women and rates of benefit, see S. B. Kamerman and A. J. Kahn, "Explaining the Outcomes," in J. Palmer et al., eds., *Changing the Well-Being of Children and the Aged in the U.S.: International and Intertemporal Perspectives* (Washington, D.C.: Urban Institute, 1990).

201 • weigh more heavily in the scales of justice than the needs of those children: See P. Leach, *Stress in Young Children's Lives,* Starting Points Briefing Papers (London: Voluntary Organisations Liaison Council for Under-Fives, 1993).

10. New Approaches to Human Rights for Children

203 • objects of adult concern: "The child is a person not an object of concern" was the opening statement of the *Report of the Inquiry into Child Abuse in Cleveland, 1987* (London: HMSO, 1988). This encapsulation of an important concept has become a watchword of the children's rights movement in the United Kingdom, giving rise, for example, to the slogan "Children are people too," which is the title of Peter Newell's book on physical punishment (*Children Are People Too: The Case Against Physical Punishment* [London: Bedford Square Press, 1989]).

206 • "he's only a baby; he'll soon forget": Personal communication.

206 • "The well-being of children requires political action": The United Nations Convention on the Rights of the Child has a much longer history than most people realize. In 1924, the Save the Children Fund International Union set out, in the Declaration of Geneva, a first attempt at a codification of basic children's rights to welfare and protection and this was endorsed by the League of Nations. In 1948 it was revised and amplified and it then formed the basis of the ten-point Declaration on the Rights of the Child which was adopted by the United Nations General Assembly in 1959.

Declarations are statements of principles; governments accept them without incurring specific obligations. Conventions, on the other hand, are binding, and therefore require states to take an active decision to ratify them. A convention was first proposed by Poland on the eve of the International Year of the Child (1979). A working group was set up by the United Nations Commission on Human Rights, composed of representatives of forty-three of its member states but welcoming participation in the ten-year drafting process by all other member states of the UN and many organizations. The convention was officially opened for signature in January 1990, but signature only commits a state to giving it serious consideration with a view to taking the final step: ratification.

By June 1991, ninety states had ratified the convention and a further forty-nine had signed but not yet ratified it. By September 1993, 147 states had ratified, not including the United States.

The vital importance of the UN Convention on the Rights of the Child is that it is the first binding international instrument to bring together states' obligations to children. What ratification really means, or should mean, is set out in detail with reference to the United Kingdom in P. Newell, *The UN Convention and Children's Rights in the UK* (London: National Children's Bureau, 1991).

207 • Children's Ombudsperson: See note to page 194.

208 • Hillary Rodham Clinton: See "Children's Rights: A Legal Perspective," in P. A. Vardin and I. N. Brody, *Children's Rights: Contemporary Perspectives* (New York: Teachers College Press, 1979). See also Gary Wills, "H. R. Clinton's Case," *The New York Review* (March 5, 1992), 3–5.

209 • complaints received: See note to page 000 regarding Malfrid Flekkoy.

210 • CHILDREN ARE NOT ALLOWED: The rules are quoted in Flekkoy's *A Voice for Children* (see note to page 194).

212 • not intended to be imprisonment: See *One Scandal Too Many: The Case for Comprehensive Protection for Children in All Settings* (report of a working group convened by Peter Newell, Chair of the Council of the Children's Rights Development Unit, for the Calouste Gulbenkian Foundation, London, 1993).

214 • confidential medical help: See, for example, L. S. Zain and S. D. Clark, "Why They Delay," *Family Planning Perspectives* (1981), and E. F. Jones et al., "Teenage Pregnancy in Developed Countries" (New Haven: Yale University Press, 1987).

216 • The United Nations Convention on the Rights of the Child: See P. Newell, *The UN Convention and Children's Rights in the UK*. There are three articles of the convention that are especially relevant to the question of corporal punishment: Article 2 insists that all rights under the convention must be available

to all children without any discrimination whatsoever. Article 19 says that states must "... protect the child from all forms of physical or mental violence, injury or abuse, neglect or negligent treatment, maltreatment or exploitation including sexual abuse, while in the care of parent(s), legal guardian(s) or any other person who has the care of the child." Article 37 states that children must not be subjected to torture or to "other cruel, inhuman or degrading treatment or punishment."

217 • Oprah Winfrey, "Oprah" talk show, September 1992.

220 • Whatever traumas those Scottish children had already suffered: See *Report of the Inquiry into the Removal of Children from Orkney in February 1991* (London: HMSO, 1992). In this particular incident, the cases against all the parents were eventually dropped for lack of evidence. We shall never know whether or not the charges were well founded. For the purposes of this argument that is irrelevant.

• alternative forms of care *and* scandal after scandal: See *One Scandal Too Many.*

221 • If a child does not want to leave her home: See notes to Homebuilders program on page 193.

• independent litigation by children: During the summer of 1992 in Florida, twelve-year-old Gregory Kingsley successfully terminated his legal relationship with his abusive natural parents in order to free himself for adoption by his foster parents. At the time of writing, several similar American cases are said to be forthcoming. The case of a British girl, aged fourteen, who sought and obtained court permission to leave her mother's home and live in a home she had chosen herself (with the parents of her boyfriend) was widely reported as similar to Kingsley. In fact it is crucially different. Under the British Children Act a parent retains parental responsibility forever. The girl did not "divorce her parents," as media suggested—and as Kingsley did. She simply obtained a "residence order," which her mother is legally obliged to abide by.

11. New Approaches to Working and Caring

226 • post-industrial nations have seen their birthrates drop: *Eurostat Demographic Statistics* (1988), tables 6 and 10.

229 • "48 hours": Quoted by Patricia Hewitt in the introduction to *About Time: The Revolution in Work and Family Life* (Concord, Mass: Paul & Co., 1993).

230 • "The problems of employment": Commission on Social Justice, *The Justice Gap* (London: Institute for Public Policy Research, 1993).

231 • a preference for part-time or more flexible working hours: See Catherine Marsh, "Hours of Work of Women and Men in Britain," Equal Opportunities Commission (London: HMSO, 1991); David D. Roediger and Philip S. Foner, *Our Own Time: A History of American Labor and the Working Day* (London: Verso, 1989).

232 • engineering shift workers: "Reorganizing Working Time," Income Data Services, September 1988, 18. "Negotiating Shorter Working Hours in the European Community," *Bulletin of European Shiftwork Topics* (no. 1). See 1989 European Foundation for the Improvement of Living and Working Conditions, 12.

232 • campaign by the Confederation of Shipbuilding and Engineering Unions: Hewitt, *About Time*, 26–29.

• "flexitime, four day weeks": This quote, and extensive research references to support it, come from Hewitt, *About Time*, 5–6.

233 • "telecommuters": American figures from *The New York Times*, Business section, "Working at Home for Better or Worse" (April 18, 1993). U.K. data are from a 1993 report of a study carried out for British Telecom: "Strategic Workstyles 2000."

234 • America's newsrooms: See Barbara Selvin, "Do Newsrooms Value Families?" *CJR* (September/October 1993), 42–45.

• A very high proportion of part-time workers are women: Principal statistical sources for this discussion are, for the United States, *Marital and Family Characteristics of the Labor Force from the March 1993 Current Population Survey*, U.S. Department of Labor, Bureau of Labor Statistics (October 3, 1993); for Europe, *Employment in Europe*, Directorate General Employment, Industrial Relations and Social Affairs (Luxembourg Office for Official Publications of the European Communities, 1993).

236 • "Regardless of the pattern": Quote is from *Made to Measure*, a British government brochure for civil servants (London: HMSO, 1990).

• "The rapid growth": Hewitt, *About Time*, 102.

237 • first-ever city election: Kenneth E. Yeager and Myrah Strober, "Financing Child Care Through Local Taxes," *Journal of Family Issues* (vol. 13, no. 3, September 1992), 279–96.

238 • helping future parents to finance "sabbaticals": "Time pensions" were first proposed by the Norwegian Commission on Working Hours in *Report from the Year 2000* (1987).

• "mommy track": Felice N. Schwartz, "Management, Women and the New Facts of Life," *Harvard Business Review* (January–February 1989).

12. New Approaches to Practical Parenting

247 • "Anyone who is buying": Interview with a police-schools liaison officer. Personal communication.

248 • battle for sick children's right: See James and Joyce Robertson, *Separation and the Very Young* (London: Free Association Books, 1989).

252 • places where children grow up: What effects would centers such as those suggested here have on children's familial relationships? A study of daycare in Denmark, Norway, Finland, Iceland and Sweden by Dion Summer describes and recommends a complementary role for parents and child-care workers and "dual-socialization" for children. Although Nordic daycare centers do not offer the kind or level of parent participation or parent benefit suggested here, the discussion in this paper is highly pertinent. See "A Child's Place in Society: New Challenges for the Family and Day Care," *Children and Society* (vol. 6, no. 4, 1992), 317–35.

253 • program developed in the late sixties: S. Provence and A. Naylor, *Working with Disadvantaged Parents and Their Children* (New Haven: Yale University Press, 1983).

255 • Homebuilders: J. M. Kinney, "Homebuilders: An In-Home Crisis Intervention Program," *Children Today* (1978). This and other initiatives are fully

described by Lisbeth Schorr and Daniel Schorr in *Within Our Reach: Breaking the Cycle of Disadvantage* (New York: Doubleday, 1988).

• That Homebuilders program *has* lasted: See Lisbeth Schorr, "What Works: Applying What We Already Know About Successful Social Policy," *The American Prospect* (no. 13, Spring 1993), 43–54.

257 • Better dentistry for Norwegian children: An account of this project is given by Malfrid Flekkoy in *A Voice for Children* (London: Jessica Kingsley Publishers, 1991).

258 • Parents have less time to spend with their children: See, for example, Victor Fuchs, *Women's Quest for Economic Equality* (Cambridge, Mass.: Harvard University Press, 1988), and William Mattox, "The Family Time Famine," *Family Policy* (vol. 3, no. 1, 1990).

INDEX

Page numbers in *italics* refer to endnotes.